RYAN WHITE
My Own Story

BY

Ryan White
AND
Ann Marie Cunningham

A SIGNET BOOK

SIGNET
Published by the Penguin Group
Penguin Books USA Inc., 375 Hudson Street,
New York, New York 10014, U.S.A.
Penguin Books Ltd, 27 Wrights Lane,
London W8 5TZ, England
Penguin Books Australia Ltd, Ringwood,
Victoria, Australia
Penguin Books Canada Ltd, 10 Alcorn Avenue,
Toronto, Ontario, Canada M4V 3B2
Penguin Books (N.Z.) Ltd, 182–190 Wairau Road,
Auckland 10, New Zealand

Penguin Books Ltd, Registered Offices:
Harmondsworth, Middlesex, England

Published by Signet, an imprint of Dutton Signet,
a division of Penguin Books USA Inc. Previously appeared in a Dial
Books edition.

First Signet Printing, August, 1992
20 19 18 17 16 15 14 13 12 11

Acknowledgments
    Lyrics from "Authority Song" by John Mellencamp on page 64: Copyright © 1983 by Full Keel Music Co. All rights reserved. Reprinted by permission of Full Keel Music Co.
    Lyrics from "My Hometown" by Bruce Springsteen on page 133: Copyright © 1984 by Bruce Springsteen ASCAP.
    "I Guess That's Why They Call It the Blues" by Elton John, Bernie Taupin, and Davey Johnstone on page 219: Copyright © 1983 by Big Pig Music Ltd. Reprinted by permission of Big Pig Music Ltd.
    "Candle in the Wind" words and music by Elton John and Bernie Taupin. Copyright © 1973 by Dick James Music Limited. All rights for the United States and Canada controlled by Songs of PolyGram International, Inc. International copyright secured. All rights reserved. Used by permission.
    "Man in the Mirror" by Siedah Garrett and Glen Ballard. Copyright © 1987 by MCA Music Publishing.

 REGISTERED TRADEMARK—MARCA REGISTRADA

Printed in the United States of America

The following constitutes an extension of this copyright page.

To my teachers
R.W.

CONTENTS

Gonna make a difference
Gonna make it right . . .

from "Man in the Mirror" sung by Michael Jackson

Your candle burned out long before
Your legend ever did.

from "Candle in the Wind" sung by Elton John

PROLOGUE

THERE WERE so many TV lights in my eyes I couldn't see the crowd. But I could hear them. Thousands and thousands of people were clapping and cheering for me. And I hadn't even opened my mouth yet!

I'd had a pretty good year even before this. I had fought for the right to go back to school in my hometown—Kokomo, Indiana—and I'd won. People there had tried to keep me out because I have AIDS. The fact is, AIDS is one disease that's pretty hard to catch. No way you can get it from just being around someone who has it—even if you eat off their plate or drink from the same glass. If you could, my mom and my sister would have picked it up a long time ago.

Still, plenty of people in Kokomo thought I could give other kids AIDS if I kissed them or sneezed on them in school, or if I dripped sweat or tears on them. Fat chance! I mean, that's disgusting! I'd *never* do that. Even if I did, nothing would happen—except that I wouldn't be too popular.

Well, panic spread all over town anyway. Lots of times kids flattened themselves against walls when I walked by. I heard kids telling Ryan White jokes. And grown people passed along lies about how they'd seen me biting people, or spitting on vegetables at the grocery store. I never did and I never would.

When I finally did get back into class, after a judge said the school was wrong, an awful lot of people still wanted me gone. To make the point, someone even put a bullet through our front window. So my mom, my sister, and I moved to a new town—Cicero, Indiana. People here were much friendlier, especially at my new school. Every now and again, a little bit of the old, mean stuff would happen—just enough to keep me going, speaking up.

So here I was in New Orleans, giving a speech to this national convention of 10,000 teachers about having AIDS. I wondered if Mr. Burkhaulter, my math teacher back at my old school, was out there somewhere. I remembered how I couldn't believe it when I'd heard him say on TV that *he* didn't want me in school—my favorite teacher!

Anyway, I started to tell this giant crowd

about what it was like when my school found out I had AIDS. "I was labeled a troublemaker, my mom an unfit mother, and I wasn't welcome anywhere," I told the teachers. "When we went to restaurants, people would get up and leave, so they wouldn't have to sit anywhere near me. Even in church, no one would shake my hand.

"AIDS can destroy a family if you let it," I went on, "but luckily for my sister and me, Mom taught us to keep going. She said, 'Don't give up, be proud of who you are and never feel sorry for yourself.' "

All I ever wanted to do was be one of the kids, because thats what counts in high school. That and graduating. In Cicero, I said, my dream was coming true. Even my sister was easier to get along with now—she could be a roller skating champion again, which is what she really loves.

When I finished my story, I stepped back from the mike. More cheers were coming at me—even bigger ones this time. Those teachers were giving me a standing ovation! I still couldn't see them, so I looked over at my mom. She had tears in her eyes. She usually does when I give a speech. She gets goosebumps too. I grinned at her. For what? the five hundredth time?—I was just amazed that complete strangers understood me and were treating me so much better than people I'd known all my life.

I never wanted to be famous. It's embarrassing to be famous for being sick, especially with a disease like AIDS. I never wanted to be the "AIDS boy" who was always in the news. I just wanted to be like every other kid my age—which is how this story happened.

1

Growing Up Different

SOMETIMES WHEN I give some speech about AIDS, I say things that sound like an actor on TV. Like, "I came face to face with death at age thirteen." Pretty dramatic, huh? To tell you the truth, AIDS didn't seem like such a big deal at first—just another illness. I'd been sick with an incurable disease since the day I was born, and I was used to it.

I was born in Kokomo on December 6, 1971. Right away, the doctors found out I had severe hemophilia. What happened is, they circumcised me. That's a rough enough way to start life, but on top of it, I didn't stop bleeding. This is what having hemophilia means. Normally, when you get a cut, your blood starts to clot in less than twelve minutes, and then pretty soon you have a scab and your cut begins to heal. But *my* blood takes thirty or forty minutes to clot. Which is so slow that if I got cut, I could bleed to death, just waiting for my blood to clot.

That nearly happened to me, only three days after I was born, because no one ever expected me to have hemophilia. It was a big shock to my doctors and my relatives. You can't catch hemophilia from anyone. You have to be born with it, because it runs in families. Women carry the hemophilia gene and pass it on to their babies. But usually only boys actually *get* hemophilia—and just one out of every 10,000. The weird part was no one in my mom or my dad's family had ever had hemophilia, as far back as anyone could remember. So I started out my life as a mystery!

When the doctors couldn't stop my bleeding that first time, they rushed me to a hospital in Indianapolis. They had to give me lots more blood to make up for what I'd lost, and something to make my blood clot. They did it through twenty-one pinholes they made in a pattern all over my head. Babies don't have enough veins anywhere else, so they shaved part of my head and gave me a Mohawk. My mom showed me a photo she took of me in the hospital.

"I look like a punk!" I told her. "At least I started out looking hip." I always like to look good—makes up for being sick. Remember John Travolta in *Saturday Night Fever* yelling at his father for mussing up his hair? "Don't mess with the hair!" That's me.

I was too young to remember anybody making holes in my head, of course. But from ages two to four, I had to go to the hospital two or three times a month. When you're the first hemophiliac in a family, you have a real bad case. So all my life, I've always, always hated hospitals and I've worked as hard as I can to stay out of them.

As far as I'm concerned, the main problem with having hemophilia is grandparents. Every so often my mom would cry and tell me that she felt bad because she gave me hemophilia without knowing it. I would just tell her, "Stop. Don't think about it. *I* don't." Which is true.

Most of the time, though, Mom was pretty cool about the whole thing. Not her parents—my grandparents. I was their first grandchild, and they were very proud. My grandmother carried around some photos of me in a little leather folder with "Grandma's Brag Book" in big letters on the front. Still, I guess my grandparents thought it was their job to worry about me. They're like that; they worried about Mom too. She was their oldest, so they were probably extra cautious. Before Mom married my dad, she had another boyfriend named Wayne— same name as my dad's, actually. The first Wayne was from Georgia, and my grandparents were scared stiff that my mom would marry him and move away from Kokomo. People in Kokomo like it so much that they have trouble imagining how you could get along anyplace else.

Kokomo is pretty much smack in the middle of Indiana, in the middle of the Midwest. Indiana is a big, flat state with quite a few pigs and cornfields. There are some big cities here—Michael Jackson comes from one of them, Gary—but mostly you have small towns and farms. John Cougar Mellencamp is from Indiana, and one way you can tell is that he sings about being born in a small town.

People who live in Indiana talk all the time about how great a state it is. We even have a special name picked out for ourselves—Hoosiers. It comes from "Who's there?" In Indiana, all the license plates say "Hoosier Hospitality." If you're planning to pay a visit and take us up on our hospitality, you should know that there are a few things that everyone in Indiana talks about. Most kids here—girls and boys—are really into sports: They play 'em, they cheerlead 'em, they watch 'em on TV. Especially basketball. Everybody, I mean everybody, knows how well the Indiana University basketball team is doing. Usually they're doing very well—often they're national champions. If you don't want people to think you're ignorant you'd better know who Bobby Knight is. He's the I. U. coach, he recruits all the star players, and he *is* college basketball in Indiana. We also have a professional basketball team, the Indiana Pacers, and a pro-football team, the Indianapolis Colts.

Most every house here has a basketball hoop outside over the driveway—and my house is no exception. My mom's younger sister Janet moved to Birmingham, Alabama, after she got married. Janet loves basketball so much that she gets her younger brother, my uncle Tommy, to tape all the I. U. games and mail them to her so she can watch them in Birmingham, and then she and Tommy dissect the games over the phone for hours.

Besides basketball games, everyone here goes to church. There are over 300 churches just in Howard County, where Kokomo is. If you live in a small town, church and school are the two places you can see all your friends. When we lived in Kokomo, we went to church with my grandparents every Sunday. Kids *and* grown-ups all go to Sunday school. My mom taught Sunday-school classes for ten years. You pray at home with your family—at least, we always do. It's been a big help to me. And if you turn on the car radio on Sundays, you'll probably hear a preacher preaching.

You'll also hear a lot of talk here about cars, especially from me. Basketball is okay, but when you have hemophilia, you can't play sports too well because you might get hurt and start bleeding. So I love cars. When I was really little I collected Matchbox cars. Now I would love to collect real cars! I've had two, and I'd really like an old '65 Mustang or a Saleen—that's a very expensive customized car made in California. Right now all I can do is look at photos, go to car shows in Indianapolis, and dream. I always check out *Mustang Monthly*—that's my magazine. I have all the back issues.

Every year in May we have the Indy 500, the Indianapolis 500 speed race at the track in downtown Indianapolis. When spring's here, my high school has "Skip Day," a special day when you can officially skip classes to drive down to the track, watch the race cars practice, look them over, and meet some of the drivers.

Even though there are some pretty cool things to do in Indiana, I've spent a lot of time bugging my mom to let us move to California to get away from winter. Especially once I got AIDS, I was always cold. And I'd love to go to race-car driver's school out there. But until we moved to Cicero, my mom never wanted to leave Kokomo, much less Indiana. That's how most people in Kokomo feel.

For Indiana, Kokomo's a good-sized town—nearly 50,000 people. When you're driving into Kokomo, you see big signs along the highway that say "Welcome to Kokomo—City of Firsts." People in Kokomo love to tell you about our Firsts—all the things that were invented there. There used to be a McDonald's in Kokomo that had models of all our Firsts up on the walls. Some of them look pretty strange. It's hard to tell what they are, especially when you're eating French fries at the same time. Most of Kokomo's Firsts aren't things you'd think would put a place on the map. Like the first canned tomato juice. The first mechanical corn picker. You get the idea. Actually, most of the Firsts have something to do with cars, so they stick in my head. The first car made in a factory came from Kokomo. So did the first modern rubber tire, the first carburetor, and three different kinds of car radios.

Almost everybody in Kokomo, you see, lives off of cars. Some streets in Kokomo are even named after cars. I used to ride my bike around Cadillac Street, Chevy Street, and Olds Street. All General Motors cars. That's because just about everyone in Kokomo works at Delco, a division of GM that makes electronic parts, mostly for cars. People tell you they work at "the plant," but there are really ten gigantic, gray Delco plants in Kokomo. Each one goes for blocks and blocks. There's a Chrysler plant in Kokomo too, and some other factories, but not so you'd notice. Delco is pretty much where everyone is at. Where the jobs pay good money.

Lots and lots of people in Kokomo finish high school, go to work at Delco, and end up marrying someone they've known most of their lives who works at the plant too. Then their children grow up in Kokomo and do the same thing. That's exactly what happened to my grandparents and my parents. My mom graduated from Kokomo High School, where she hoped I'd end up. Now she's so disgusted with the way the town treated us, she won't go to reunions or to see the Wildcats, the school's basketball team. But when she was in high school, she was the biggest Wildcats fan that ever was.

After high school, Mom became a Delco Dolly—that's how a popular radio show in Kokomo, called "Male Call," refers to women who work at the plant—and then got married and had me and my sister Andrea. My grandparents have some hilarious old home movies of my mom and dad up at a trailer they had at Lake Manitou, about one hundred miles from Kokomo. They look real sixties—my dad has a convertible, and my mom and my grandmother have those big beehive hairdos that look like nests sitting on top of their heads. Whoever was holding the camera even caught some shots of my mom wearing humongous rollers!

I love my mom a lot, and I feel proud when I see some of the pictures of her that my grandma keeps in her old photo albums. My mom—her name was Jeanne Hale—was very pretty. My grandmother loves those old movie stars from the forties. Tyrone Power is her major heartthrob. She's such a big movie fan that she named my aunt Janet after Janet Leigh—my aunt's middle name is actually Leigh—and my mom after Jeanne Crain, because they both had curly hair. Jeanne Crain's hair was flaming red, but it looked dark like Mom's in black and white movies. There's one shot of Mom lounging by a swimming pool, wearing a white bathing suit and a ribbon that says "Miss Kmart of 1964." Sometimes when I want to get her riled, I call her "Miss Kmart."

Usually she just rolls her eyes and ignores me. When I was only two, I was the poster boy for the Howard County Hemophilia Society. I was kind of carrying on a family tradition, I guess.

My dad, well, I wish I could tell you more. We don't have a lot of snaps of him. Mom and Dad divorced when I was seven and we didn't see Dad much at all after that. We do have pictures of my parents' wedding, with them cutting the cake and kissing and looking happy and sipping champagne all at the same time. My dad is smiling away, and I can see that I look just like him. Except that I have dark hair and brown eyes, like my mom. My sister Andrea, who was born when I was two, has my dad's blue eyes.

My dad's name is Wayne White, and he still lives in Kokomo and works at Delco. He and my mom knew each other from grade school. My mom says she couldn't stand him back then. He used to yell, "Hey Hell!" whenever he saw her. He was making fun of her family name, Hale—probably just his way of letting her know he had a crush on her. But she thought he was a smart alec, trying to embarrass her. She said she couldn't wait to get married—just to change her name! Later on, after they'd both finished high school and my dad was out of the service, they were both working at Delco. My mom was dating the other Wayne from Georgia. He was in the Air Force and was stationed at a base north of Kokomo for a while. After he and my mom started to really like each other, wouldn't you know, the Air Force discharged him and sent him home to Georgia.

My grandparents were relieved because they were so worried he'd take my mom back to Georgia. Meanwhile, my dad started asking her out. He didn't seem as bad as he had in grade school, so she started going with him, and after three months they got married, in 1968.

The other Wayne had been trying to reach Mom all along. Finally, my aunt Janet told him how to get in touch with her. So they did talk on the phone. But my mom was already married to Wayne White, so they had to say goodbye.

By 1971 my mom was expecting me. People in Kokomo like to say it's a great place to raise a family. For a lot of families, it is. Once you get away from the plant, the rest of Kokomo is ranch houses and streets with backyards and sidewalks for kids to play on. Dad and Mom had an older brick house with a big front porch. Mom really loves to decorate and fix up any place she lives in. So she made curtains and trimmings for my room out of yellow and orange gingham. Later on she got my dad to outline pictures of Snoopy and his doghouse on the walls, and she painted them in. One day she went to see *Love Story*, and she liked it so much that she decided that if I turned out to be a boy, she'd name me Ryan, after Ryan O'Neal. He was the star—it was his first big movie, although Mom had already been following him on a soap, *Peyton Place*. I've never seen *Love Story*, but it sounds romantic. I guess Mom thought so too. When I was sixteen we actually met Ryan O'Neal at an AIDS benefit in Los Angeles. My mom told him she'd named me after him. Ryan O'Neal said, "I always wondered about that!"

Mom was hoping for a boy so bad, because she wanted him to play basketball for the Kokomo High School Wildcats. I was born long and skinny, and Mom was tickled to death. She thought, I'm going to have my basketball player.

Big mistake! The doctors told her I'd never play any sport and if I were ever in a terrible car accident, I wouldn't live. For a while she was scared to let me ride in a car. Then she thought, Well, at least there's nothing else wrong with him.

When I finally did come home from the hospital, with marks all over my head from the doctors' pinholes, poor Mom had her hands full. If you're looking after a baby with hemophilia, you don't just think, What if he cuts himself? Any time a hemophiliac falls down and knocks his elbow or bumps his knee, he can start bleeding from a broken blood vessel or vein. The blood has nowhere to go, so it swells up in a joint. You don't see any blood, but your knee or elbow gets very swollen and may turn black and blue. It's as though your body tried to pour a quart of milk into a pint-sized container. If you know a hemophiliac, and he comes to school with his arm in a sling, or on crutches with an Ace bandage on his knee, and he tells you, "I got a bleed," that's what's going on. He had an accident, and he's probably hurting, even though he hasn't got any cuts. He's going to be in a lot of pain until clotting plugs his torn vein or blood vessel, and the swelling in his joint goes down.

With little kids who are hemophiliacs, the main thing you have to worry about is, Will they hit their heads? If a hemophiliac starts bleeding inside his brain, he could die. When I was small, I had to go to a hemophilia clinic in Indianapolis sometimes. In the waiting room I used to see two-year-olds running around with helmets on. Their parents made them keep them on every second in case they fell on their heads. Some kids hardly ever go out in the car, either.

My grandparents tried that kind of thing with me. When I was a baby, my grandma made pads for the crib. She was afraid I'd knock myself against the bars. One day my mom heard a loud thump in my room and came rushing in. There I was, out of my crib, sitting up on the floor. No one could figure out how I managed to get there. But I was perfectly okay. Not even bruised. So after that my mom decided to relax and forget about the knee pads Grandma wanted to put on me once I started crawling, and the padding she thought we should have on all the furniture. Mom wanted me to live as normally as possible. I never did have to wear a helmet—except a play helmet when I got my first race car (the plastic kind that hasn't got a motor, only pedals under the hood). And *that* helmet I loved to wear.

I have to say that I feel sorry for parents and grandparents of hemophiliacs, I really do. I wish I had a dime for every time my grandpa said, "That boy has no business doing that!" or "Jeanne has no right letting Ryan do this!" Grandpa carried on like that all the time, especially when I was learning to ride my bike and then my skateboard. The trouble is, just like most hemophiliacs, I'm a real daredevil.

Sometimes I was covered in bruises because hemophiliacs bruise easily. The more Grandpa complained about me, the more bruises I seemed to collect. When I was only three, I started giving my grandparents heart attacks by pedaling my new race car over to visit them all by myself. They were only three blocks away—no big deal. When I got there, I'd try to calm them down. I like arguing, so once I said, "Don't worry about me; I'm smarter than you are, Grandma."

"Maybe," Grandma said, "but you sure don't act it right now."

Then I'd get my grandpa to push me in the swing he'd hung on a tree out back for me. I was never happy until he'd pushed me so high that my feet touched the leaves. If he wouldn't swing me, I'd climb up into the tree and sit in the crook of my favorite branch for hours. Grandpa'd come out and holler at me to get down. Until one day he decided to spray the tree, and sprayed it so much that it died. Now that I think about it, I wonder if it was a total accident.

My mom let me do pretty much anything. She wanted me to play with other kids in the playground at recess and learn to ride a bike. She figured, if I got hurt, I got hurt. A big reason why she was so easygoing was Factor VIII, which came out just before I was born. Factor VIII is a blood product. That means it's made from parts of the blood that thousands of people have donated. Factor VIII is made up of the clotting factor that makes most people's blood clot normally. So when a hemophiliac gets an injection of Factor VIII, he gets a concentrated dose of clotting factor. Then his blood can clot too. And if he's been hurt, he will heal.

Most hemophiliacs look like me—small and skinny with knobby knees and elbows from all the times our joints got swollen from bleeds. Me, I look at myself in the mirror and figure, small but tough. But I guess a lot of people, my grandparents included, think we hemophiliacs don't look like we're built to last. Before Factor VIII, we didn't. Doctors told Mom that a severe hemophiliac like me could only expect to live maybe to age fourteen or fifteen. In between, he'd spend a lot of time being rushed to the emergency room whenever he got a bump or a scrape. When he got there, all the doctors could do would be to give him big transfusions to replace the blood he'd lost. Sooner or later, he'd end up bleeding to death. Before Factor

VIII, quite a few hemophiliacs got so discouraged by living this way that they ended up committing suicide.

I could never see that myself. I mean, I'd certainly rather not have hemophilia. But if you feel sorry for yourself, you'll be so down you won't notice anything in life to enjoy. My mom always says, "That's not how we live in The White House." That's what she likes to call our home. We have a shiny brass plaque by the front door that says so.

All my mom and I knew when I was growing up was that if I got myself in trouble, my Factor would help me out. Until I was five, we had to go to the hospital to get it every time I got hurt—more times than Mom says she can remember. I did manage to have three really scary accidents. The first time, I was still a baby. I was so fond of my Matchbox cars—I had more than fifty!—that I would crawl around with one in my mouth, and take five or six to bed with me. Mom usually sneaked in after I fell asleep and took them all away. But once she missed one. The next morning, I was a true-to-life no-neck monster: My neck had swollen up like a balloon because I'd slept on the car all night. Poor Mom—another trip to the hospital. But the swelling went down once I had some Factor.

Mom had so much practice that she got so she knew more than most doctors about hemophilia and how to treat me. Later on, when I was three, I fell in the bathroom and cut my head open. The hospital gave me six stitches and some Factor, kept me overnight, and then sent me home. Mom said I hadn't had enough Factor and ought to stay five or six days. The doctors said, "Forget it; he's had enough."

That night Mom decided to put me in bed with her. My head was all bandaged up in a turban, and she was worried I might start bleeding again. Sure enough, she woke up in the middle of the night in a puddle of blood. We rushed back to the hospital, where I got a transfusion and more Factor. If I'd been alone in my own bed, I would have bled to death.

My third accident also happened when I was three. Another kid and I were using my parents' bed as a trampoline. I lost my balance, fell off, and banged my elbow against an electric heater. I found my mom in the kitchen and yelled, "I've been electrocuted!" I really thought that's what had happened, because the blow felt like pins and needles were running up and down my arm. Well, I didn't have an electric shock, but I couldn't move my arm because my elbow was broken—in three different places. This time I had to stay in the hospital longer and wear my arm in a sling afterward. The worst part was the way I stood out at day care. Everyone asked me, "What happened?" When I said, "I got a bleed," they asked, "What's that?"—and I had to give a long explanation. It was very boring, talking about hemophilia over and over, and I sincerely wished I could be invisible until my arm healed.

This accident was also a real drag because the hospital kept insisting that I needed physical therapy, or my arm would never be right. Before Factor VIII, if you had too many bleeds in a joint, it could get stiff. Then you'd get arthritis, it would be really painful to straighten out your arm or your leg, and you might end up a cripple on crutches or in a wheelchair. So the doctor and nurses told me that if I didn't keep coming back for therapy, my arm would get stiff. I'd never be able to even lift my arm so I could touch my hand to my shoulder. "No way I'm going to therapy," I told them. "I'll move my arm on my own." I hate the idea of anything that makes me seem sick forever. Maybe I have an incurable disease, but I don't have to be a permanent invalid. Well, after six weeks I could touch my shoulder—without bothering with physical therapy. From then on, I decided I knew a thing or two about my own illness.

I figured out a couple of other things in the hospital too. One was how to handle pain. There's nothing great about having to stay in the hospital, but the worst part is how boring it is. If anything hurts, it's real easy to let the pain take over, because there's not much else to think about. You need as much distraction as possible. Once I started practicing not thinking about pain, I got to be fairly good at picking up a magazine until that didn't work anymore, then trying the TV, and after that setting up my G. I. Joes. The trick is to have a lot of different things to do, because each one can work for only so long. My mom says I have a real talent for ignoring pain. She thinks I'm much better at it than most people, and certainly better than she is. I don't think there's much to it, myself—just practice.

The other thing I learned for sure in the hospital is that hemophilia isn't the worst problem a kid can have. I met plenty of kids in bigger trouble than I was. Hemophilia's not nearly as painful as cancer, where you might need treatments that make you vomit all the time, or make all your hair fall out. I felt for kids who had to have chemotherapy. Being bald at age three would kill me right there! Then there are horrible burns, or having something wrong with your mind, or all kinds of defects and other diseases you might be born with that mean you need operation after operation. I'd already decided that I didn't *have* hemophilia— I was living with it. You *can* feel well no matter what's wrong with you. I think that's the only way to think.

Besides, with Factor VIII, hemophilia didn't seem that bad. As I got bigger and didn't fall over so much, most of the time I stayed well. By the time I was five, the hospital said I could start having regular injections of Factor at home, as a precaution. Once a month, Mom picked up a fresh supply for me from the hospital. We kept it in the refrigerator in big plastic bags. Sometimes we didn't have much food, but we always had plenty of Factor VIII. My pediatricians taught my mom how to tie a tourniquet around my arm, find a vein, and inject the Factor. It's not the easiest thing to do, and it always stung—you know what a blood test feels like—but Mom got to be better at it than a lot of nurses I met in the hospital. We always used a vein in the crook of my right arm. I took to calling it "Old Faithful" because it worked so well. I could shut my eyes, lean back, and relax. Mom gave me injections two or three times a week—unless I had a bleed, then I needed more Factor more often, sometimes every day.

Still, when you have a disease, any disease, sometimes you just plain hurt. Some days I'd wake up stiff and sore for no reason. But I can't stand being babied, so I never said anything. I just did my best. Even when I had a bleed in my knee, I wasn't going to limp and shuffle around like I was ninety years old. If I did, kids would make jokes like, "What's wrong with you *this* time?" But sometimes someone would guess how I was feeling, which I hated.

There's a big park in Kokomo called Highland Park. My mom and her brother and sister played there when they were growing up, and I guess that's partly why my grandparents loved to take Andrea and me there. Sometimes we went with my cousins. The most interesting parts of the park, in my opinion, are the stump and the bull. In a big log building, kind of like an extra-large log cabin with glass windows, you can see a huge stump of a sycamore tree here in Indiana that grew to be 100 feet tall.

When a wind storm finally blew it down, it was 800 years old. Behind the next window is a giant stuffed bull who weighs nearly 5,000 pounds. The sign says, "A Whole Lotta Bull." The biggest bull that ever lived came from Indiana! Maybe that's not so hard to believe.

The park also has some Indian trails that run along a brook. Andrea never wanted to look at the bull and the stump. She was always out on the trails, looking for alligators and snake holes. I knew there weren't any—I thought the trails were pretty stupid—so I practiced jumping off a bridge into the brook, to see if I could splash anyone on the banks. After one jump—yow!—my leg hurt. I went right back up on the bridge to try again. But my grandmother had spotted me, and she said, "Ryan, when you don't want anyone to know you're hurt, you walk straight as a stick."

I think my hemophilia was tough on Andrea. The whole family was always eyeing me and paying more attention to me, whether I wanted them to or not. Most of the time my hemophilia meant that Mom spent more time with me than she did with my sister. Andrea never has come right out and said anything about it. She's the shy, quiet type, especially about private stuff like how she feels about things. But that makes it even harder for her to get people to pay attention to her. When my aunt Janet got married, I was about four, and Andrea was about two. I was the ring bearer in the wedding, and ndrea was the flower girl. I had a new blue suit, to match Janet's husband's tuxedo, and Andrea had a long blue dress. Anyway, I started down the aisle first, and Andrea was supposed to follow me. But she'd barely gotten started when she saw all the guests standing and grinning down at her. Poor Andrea had a shyness attack, and she started to cry. I went back and put my arm around her and whispered, "What's the matter, Sissy?" Then I took her hand and we walked the rest of the way together.

Andrea and I have always been close because we were only two years apart. When we were growing up, Andrea didn't like dolls or frills. She wanted to do what I did. But I guess you can't imagine a sister and brother who are more different than we are. We don't look or act alike at all. When she's with her friends, Andrea talks a mile a minute. But most of the time Andrea is quieter than everyone else. Like when I was in the hospital, Andrea would come to see me and usually sit in a corner. Sometimes a nurse would come by and try to talk to her. It was like Andrea knew only three words: "Yes," "No," and "Fine."

As far as I'm concerned, Andrea's very messy. From my mom I caught the collecting bug. Mom loves to collect dolls and figurines, and Christmas and Easter ornaments. She's always on the lookout, even in June or July, for a Christmas store where she can find something new to hang on our tree. I talked her into buying an egg tree for Easter as well. I started out with miniature cars, and then I moved on to comic books. My grandpa is a major collector. He used to have the original Superman comic! The very first one! It's worth maybe $35,000. Now he says he can't find it; he doesn't know what happened to it; maybe he gave it to a neighbor. Every week he'd take me to a comic-book store in downtown Kokomo so we could hunt for more collectors' items: X-men, Wolverine, Superheroes, Marvel—I had them all. I started going to comic-book club meetings to talk to other collectors. I was usually the youngest. Everyone had a nickname and mine was Ry-man. Then around the same time, I got hooked on collecting G. I. Joe. I had practically all the figures, and even some camouflage pants to wear, and camouflage sheets on my bed.

Now, if you have a collection, you have to take care of it. Even comic books. You can't keep them in a pile under the bed. They have to stay clean and unwrinkled, or you can't sell them to other collectors when you want to. And I liked to see my G. I. Joes in rows on my shelves, so I knew which ones I had. Andrea didn't care about collecting dolls or anything else. Once Mom threw a fit after Andrea gave a Fisher Price doll a haircut that looked like the Statue of Liberty's crown. Andrea certainly didn't care about keeping things neat—hers *or* mine. So we had fights, sometimes just about every day. For a long time, Andrea was a real tomboy, and she's always been a good athlete.

So when we were growing up, she quickly got to be stronger than I am. But when we fought, she never hurt me, even when I hurt her. So I know she loves me quite a lot, because she put up with a lot.

With Mom it was almost as though my hemophilia made things better between us. My mom is very homey, and likes fixing up the house and baking cookies—she would cook anything to help me gain weight when I was sick. She certainly wasn't pleased that I was ill, but I think she liked that I was home a lot. I mean, she had worked hard to put together a nice house, and here was someone who stayed in it! Andrea was always out running around, playing tomboy games with her friends, or she'd find things to do by herself. Mom and I had more in common. We both liked things neat—though my mom would yell when my dogs chewed up an end table or got into the trash.

Mom read to me all the time—books and magazines. That got me started doing well in school, and in learning about what's going on in the world. What we liked to do as a family was fix some Cokes and popcorn and a tray of sandwiches, grab blankets, pile up together on the couch, and watch TV late at night on weekends—especially Johnny Carson, my favorite. We always watched movies and the news, and I liked keeping up with how the world works. That's how I knew, starting in 1982, that a new disease called AIDS had been discovered.

Mom and I also care about looking good. Now that she's a teenager, Andrea cares more too. But not when we were growing up! Mom would laugh when she took us shopping for clothes. I am particular. I want the name brand. I work hard to get Mom to spend more money on everything, but especially on clothes. Andrea never was fussy. If Mom said, "We can't afford that," Andrea would say, "Well, fine. I don't care. You pick something out." Then she'd wander off to the five-and-dime, or to those candy machines in the supermarket where you put in a nickel and get back bubblegum or a whistle or some other tiny toy. The smaller and cheaper it was, the better Andrea liked it. The more she could get for ninety-nine cents, the happier she was.

Especially if it was a magic trick. When I was sixteen, my grandparents moved their trailer to Florida. They'd spend the winter down there, then come back to Kokomo to see us in the summer. Sometimes we'd meet up with them in Florida on spring break. Andrea discovered a magic store down there. After that, she never bought anything except fake baby rattlesnakes— really just two paper clips and a rubber band in an envelope—or plastic noses that had little candies falling out of the nostrils. Flies in ice cubes, squirting pens, whoopie cushions—Andrea had a way to freak out just about everyone.

It was funny to watch Andrea try out her stuff on people, but let's face it—she was buying junk that didn't last or got used up right away. That's not for me. I really love Guess? jeans but you can't find them for boys in Indiana. Once Mom tried to fool me with a girls' pair, but I knew because the label was red, not green. So I would call my aunt Janet and ask her to buy them for me in Birmingham. I figure, that's what being a collector is all about. You get the best, and then you have something.

Andrea and I were alike in one way: We were always bugging Mom to have another baby. Boy or girl, I didn't care. But Mom said she had to be married first. So Andrea and I put a lot of time into matchmaking. Then Mom said the problem was she might have another boy—who could have hemophilia. She felt bad enough about me. But thanks to my cousins, there was always a baby, and I love to hold babies. When I was four, my uncle Tom, who had married my aunt Deb, had a baby girl they named Monica—and then they had three more kids, all boys: Josh, Matt, and Brian. When I was nine, my aunt Janet, who went off to Alabama after she married my uncle Leo, had a girl, Misty, and went on to have two more, Sara and Lisa. Whenever we all went to Highland Park, I'd always be trying to pick up whoever was the baby—and the baby would be wiggling and squirming and trying to get away from me.

Right about the time when we started using Factor at home and I didn't have to rush off to the emergency room constantly, my mom sat Andrea and me down separately, and told us she was asking Dad to move out because she wanted a divorce. I can't say I was real surprised. It already seemed like a long time since any of us had seen Dad. He was always out with his friends. He never seemed to have a couple of hours to stay around and hang out with Mom, Andrea, and me.

After Dad moved out, he didn't call us. When we asked him why, he said, "Well, *you* never call *me*." A few times, he came to pick Andrea and me up to spend the weekend at his new place. But instead of staying with us, he would leave us with his parents, and go off with his friends. Staying with our other grandparents wasn't so bad. They didn't have a dog, like my mom's parents, but Dad's father did have an antique car. Sometimes he'd go to a rally with other old cars, and we'd see him in a whole parade of them, going down the street in Kokomo.

Actually, staying with Dad could be a whole lot worse than when we were left with his parents. Once Andrea and I were sleeping over with Dad at his new place. Dad got us a frozen pizza for dinner, which was fine with us, and put it in the oven to heat up. Meanwhile, he decided to take a short nap on the couch. Well, the pizza heated up, all right—in fact, it was burning up. The living room was filling up with smoke, and we couldn't wake Dad! Remember, Andrea and I were only five and seven—a lot smaller than Dad. Finally, we got him to get up, and we all stumbled out of the house.

After that, we told Mom we didn't want to stay with Dad anymore. Andrea said, "It's boring. He's never there, and there's nothing to do. I don't want to see him." I agreed with Andrea about the boring part, but I did miss Dad. One evening he said he was coming over. I sat out on the front porch waiting for him until about eleven o'clock, when Mom finally made me go to bed.

If my hemophilia was hard on Andrea, maybe it was hard on Dad too. Or maybe there was something else that bothered him. I'd like to ask him about that sometime, just so I know.

I've always been smaller and weighed less than other kids my age. That's why I'm careful about clothes—I try to wear loose jeans and sweatshirts so I don't look so skinny. I'll never play football or basketball or baseball—any of the sports that kids my age play. Once I even asked my doctor for steroids. He explained that they weren't very good for me and he wasn't going to give me any. We live in a place where sports are important, but I'd like to remind Dad that there *are* plenty of other things I can do. And I could tell him that once I got to be famous, and started meeting stars, I found out that most celebrities are short.

The strange part is that Dad didn't dump us completely. You hear about fathers who abandon their kids and never send them any money. We hardly saw my dad, he didn't seem to want to know us at all, but we had enough to live on because he always paid child support. And when I've gotten sick, his insurance has paid my hospital bills. That counts, as far as I'm concerned.

Most of the time I can't be bothered thinking about the past. I figure, if things have been bad, that means you have something to look forward to, right? But sometimes I wonder what would have happened if the other Wayne had gotten through to my mom first, before she married my dad. Maybe I never would have been born, but maybe I could have had another father and a whole different life. In Georgia, or someplace else.

I know my sister wonders too. Maybe five or six years ago, a long time after my parents had gotten divorced, Andrea decided to try to find the first Wayne. Without telling my mom, she called information in the Georgia town he was from. She told the operator all she knew: Wayne's full name, and another clue—his father owned a casket company. But Wayne wasn't listed. Maybe he moved. My mom says he had a bad heart, so he might even be dead by now. He never did call her again, even after we started getting splashed all over the news.

About three months after my dad left, Mom did get re-married—to another man she worked with at the plant. I guess her second husband—his name is Steve Ford—liked her a lot, because she ended up getting a job at Delco that he was supposed to have. Steve is a great big, cheerful guy with a bushy beard. People are always telling him he reminds them of Kenny Rogers—

and he does look just like him. It helps that Steve likes country music and dancing the two-step. He'll drive as far as Louisville, Kentucky, way south of here, to try out a new dance joint he's heard about.

The other thing that Steve likes is Mustangs—mostly because of his name. He's always driven a Mustang, and I never had any trouble talking him into taking me to car shows. He taught Andrea and me to drive, and he even ended up giving Andrea one of his old Mustangs. She has her eye on the one he has now—a convertible!

Steve lived outside of Kokomo in a little country town called Windfall that makes Kokomo look like New York City. So when Mom and Steve got married, we moved there to live with him. Andrea and I played together a lot because there weren't many other kids around.

Indiana's a windy place, especially in the winter. Windfall gets its name from all the tornados that pass through—even more than you usually get in the rest of the state. Since everything around Windfall is flat, and there aren't any tall buildings, you can see the sky in every direction. When a tornado's on the way, you can see its black funnel stretching from the storm clouds on the horizon to the ground below. The tornado's moving all the time, and usually looks like it's coming straight at you! It gets very dark out, and it looks like the whole earth and sky is being sucked into the funnel.

The best thing to do in a tornado is to go

down into your basement or your root cellar. In *The Wizard of Oz* Dorothy didn't do that, and look at all the trouble she got into! Our house in Windfall didn't have a cellar, so we just stayed indoors. One time a tornado struck our house. It roared like a freight train coming through, moving all around and under the house—like we were going to be lifted up into the sky! Mom, Andrea, and I lay on the bathroom floor, but there wasn't room for Steve. He had to stay out in the hall. In the end the tornado pulled the back wall of the house out six inches, and then moved on. We had a pretty close call, I guess. When I was almost sixteen, Andrea, Mom, and I were out in California with my grandparents when there was an earthquake at seven o'clock in the morning. Our hotel swayed for twenty minutes, the power went off, and we could see cracks in the walls of our room! My grandparents wanted to get on the next plane home to Indiana, but I thought the whole thing was pretty exciting. An earthquake that's 6.5 on the Richter scale with twenty-one aftershocks doesn't happen in Kokomo.

I would say that tornado was the most excitement we ever had in Windfall. But Andrea would disagree with me, because while we were living in Windfall, she started roller skating. All thanks to Steve: He liked to skate, and at first he took both of us along with him. I thought skating was okay, but as soon as Andrea laced on her first pair of skates, she was in love. She bugged and bugged Mom for lessons. At first, Mom thought she ought to switch to ice skating, but Andrea said, "There's no ice rink here, and all my friends roller skate." Then the teacher said she wouldn't take Andrea because she was too young—only seven—and she should wait 'til she got better. Andrea just said, "That's why I want lessons." Pretty soon both Mom and Steve were taking turns driving her down to the rink for lessons on weekends and skating practice after school up to four times a week.

I should have mentioned that for many girls in Indiana, roller skating is about the same as the Indianapolis 500. See, you can do just about anything on roller skates that you can on ice skates—all the fancy jumps and spins and fig-ures. The movements even have the same names as in ice skating—the double flip, the lutz, the salchow, the axel, triple mapes. Roller skaters look just as graceful and glamorous as ice skaters. They get to wear glittery costumes and headgear with sequins and feathers. Mom designs Andrea's costumes—sometimes they have to drive all the way to Chicago for the right material and trim—and a friend of Mom's sews them.

Skating's harder on roller skates, because you're on two sets of wheels on a smooth, wooden rink. You don't have blades with edges that cut into the ice. On ice your skate blade turns easily; with rollers, you have to position yourself on the edge of your wheels to turn. And each skate weighs as much as eight

pounds—much more than ice skates! Roller
skating isn't an Olympic sport yet, but lots of
fans are working hard to make it one. In the
meantime there are tons of local and regional
competitions and national championships to go
out for. There are even world championships,
and roller skating is in the Annual Olympic
Sports Festival and the Pan-American Games.

Andrea set out to be a champion. I took some
lessons too, and went out for some figure skating and dance contests. But I couldn't compete
in singles events because skaters fall all the
time. I mean *all* the time. I had enough trouble
with bleeds without taking up roller skating.

But Andrea didn't fall—at least not when it
counted. She kept taking lessons, she kept
practicing, she started to win and she didn't
stop. Soon she had skating ribbons and trophies all over the walls of her room. She wants
to win the national championships—she went
for the first time only a year after she started
skating—and she's been out to the U.S. Olympics
autumn training camp in Colorado Springs. And
she and Mom got to spend more time together:
Most of the time Mom drove Andrea to skating
practice, and then to meets. Andrea loved having Mom there to watch her, and they hung
out with the other skaters and their parents.
My mom says she always knew that one of her
children would be famous. For a long time she
thought there would be just one: Andrea.

I wasn't as lucky in the athletics department
as Andrea. When I was eight, I was all set to

go out for the Windfall Little League. Grandpa had a cow, but Mom paid no attention. The coach put me in the outfield where he thought I couldn't get into very much trouble. He told me, "Don't charge the ball—let it come to you." One day a ball came at me. I waited for it, like the coach had said, but it hit me square in the mouth. I began to bleed. The coach was much more frightened than I was. I did what I always did when I got hurt: I told him to call Mom. She came and picked me up and gave me some Factor in the kitchen at home. I hated having to leave the game, and going to school with a bandage on. What a disaster! As usual, kids kept asking, "Whats wrong with you now?" But I wasn't scared. I had no plans to quit baseball.

Then came another game when I was playing first base. A line drive came right at me, and hit me in the stomach. I fell back like a tree you'd chopped down. I wasn't hurt, but the ball knocked the wind out of me. I couldn't move, but I could see the whole team crowded around, looking down at me, shouting, "You hurt?" The coach ran up with a towel in case I was bleeding. That *was* scary. I quit at the end of the season. I was never going to be an athlete, and I decided I had to learn to live with that.

WE SEEMED pretty well settled in Windfall. My grandparents weren't so close by to worry about me. But in 1982, when I was eleven, Mom and Steve decided to divorce. Like Dad, Steve wasn't home much. But after Steve and Mom separated, and she moved back to Kokomo with Andrea and me, Steve didn't disappear the way Dad had. He called us every week, and he came to see us every Sunday and mowed our lawn. Lots of times he still drove Andrea to skating practice, and he took Andrea and me skating at the rink in Kokomo, though I paid more attention to the pinball machines. After I got AIDS, he always visited me in the hospital when other people were scared to come near me. When my friends asked who he was, Steve would laugh and say he was my unwed stepfather. He has something like twenty or thirty nieces and nephews, so he's used to being the official baby-sitter. He and Mom talked on the phone constantly, about everything, like brother and sister. They were so friendly that people asked Mom why they didn't get back together. Mom said the point was they *were* like brother and sister, not husband and wife.

Even though I couldn't play baseball, and my mom was divorced, I felt like I had a pretty normal childhood. Mom had to be two parents in one, but lots of kids in Kokomo had single mothers. Women could support their families on their jobs at Delco, so they didn't have to stay married if they were in bad situations. Andrea and I never felt out of it at school. We went away on vacation—once my grandparents took us to the NASA Space Center—just like other kids. And you'd never guess I had hemophilia unless I told you. Andrea might tell you not to play rough with me, but I never would. If I got hurt, I called Mom, and she drove home and gave me some Factor in the kitchen. There wasn't anything to worry about. So I couldn't figure out what was going on when Grandpa started fussing about my Factor.

2

How I Got AIDS

In August 1984 I was twelve and a half—looking forward to turning into a typical obnoxious teenager. I was an honors student just about to start junior high at Western Middle School, a few miles outside Kokomo in Russiaville. Kids from Kokomo are bussed to Western along with kids from other towns close by. Indiana has lots of towns named after foreign places—Valparaiso, Vincennes, New Paris. Russiaville is pronounced ROOshaville—just so you won't think you're really in Russia, I guess.

Andrea was eleven, and after four years of practice, she was the ace roller skater she'd always dreamed of becoming. This month she was finally going to the national championships out in Lincoln, Nebraska. She and Mom were very busy. If you want to be a skating champ, you have to practice, and if you're too young to drive to the rink, someone has to take you. So, on weekdays Mom got up at 4:00 A.M. to be at Delco from 6:00 A.M. until 2:30 in the afternoon. She worked on a computer, making sure that three assembly lines in the plant had all the parts they needed. When Mom got home, she and Andrea left for the skating rink, and didn't come back until 8:30 at night. On weekends Mom and Andrea commuted to meets out of town, or to Chicago where Andrea practiced with a boy who would be a great partner when she competed in events for pairs.

Well, we all went to the nationals, and saw Andrea place second in dance, fourth in freestyle, and fifth in pairs. I was really so proud of her! We all figured, next stop—the Olympics.

I couldn't go on all her skating trips, so I stayed home alone a lot. Mom wondered whether I'd be scared, especially after the year before, when the tornado hit our house in Windfall. But I wasn't lonely. I had a girlfriend named Kris who went to Western too, and lived in our neighborhood in Kokomo, so I could walk over to see her when we wanted to do our homework together. If the weather was fine, we sat side by side on her stoop. One day she gave me a needlepoint picture of four hearts surrounding my name. She had stitched it herself and had it framed for me. Wow! I thought. She knows I love presents, so I guess she really likes me.

Then I also had three other good friends who lived right across the street—Chris Sadler, Blair

Brittain, and Heath Bowen, who was a year behind me at Western. Sometimes Grandpa took Heath and me fishing with him. Grandpa feels the same way about his fishing boat as I do about cars. It's a motorboat with high seats so you can see out over the water. He belongs to a bass fishing club in Kokomo, and he's usually number one in the club because he's caught the most and the biggest fish at Lake Manitou. But he says there's always a couple of other guys nipping at his heels, and he has to keep his hand in. I doubt Heath and I were much help with the competition because we usually didn't want to wait around for a bite. We'd try to get Grandpa to rev up his motor pretty quick and race his boat up and down the lake. When we were along, he didn't catch very many fish at all.

When we weren't scaring off Grandpa's bass, my friends and I all biked endlessly around the streets in our neighborhood, racing each other. We rooted for the Dodgers and the Cubs. Grandpa had loved the Dodgers ever since they played in Brooklyn. I know the Cubs always find a way to lose the World Series, but since we live in Indiana, they're the closest we have to a home team.

And we were all into playing army, especially me. I felt like I'd started our fad. I already had a big toy-gun collection. Even Andrea had a few pink and green plastic water pistols. I was big on building models of fighter planes. My bedroom ceiling looked like a squadron flying in formation. My aunt Janet had mailed me some camouflage pants and a real parachute from an army store in Birmingham. Chris and Blair and Heath and I would head for the woods, hunt each other over rocks and through trees, and demolish each other with fire crackers. Sometimes we let my oldest cousin, Monica, come along. But Blair and Heath would try to teach her swear words, and I had to shut them up. Her dad, my uncle Tommy, drove me out to the lake every week to go swimming with Monica and her younger brothers, and I didn't want him getting mad at me.

It's okay going someplace with my boy cousins, or practicing karate with them in the backyard. But I wasn't too happy about them coming over and getting into my Star Wars or car collections, or about my sleeping at their house. I mean, a door has a handle; it works nicely. But you can bet that my cousins will ignore the knob and leave their fingerprints all over the door frame and even the wall. Another thing: My youngest cousin, Brian, likes racing up and down stairs. For no reason. Asking him to stop—or just telling him—doesn't work. Believe me, I've tried.

So most of the time when Mom and Andrea went away, I stayed at my grandparents'. That summer Grandma had broken her leg, so I told her, "I'll take care of *you* for a change." I fetched her sodas, heated up food for her in her microwave oven, and ran errands on my bike. There was only so much worrying she could do when she couldn't follow me around. Every now and again, it was a big relief, I can tell you, to have a relative who was sicker than I was. The pressure was off—my family had someone besides me to fuss over for a change. Besides, I could really help because I knew about broken bones and sicknesses from spending so much time in the hospital. Whenever I was stuck in there, I always asked a lot of questions and made sure I knew what medicine I was getting, how much, and why.

Once, later on, I even figured out that Grandpa was having a heart attack before he did. He was sitting on his sofa complaining about chest pains and having trouble breathing. He was sweating something awful, and he was going kind of gray in the face. He couldn't imagine what was wrong with him. Seemed pretty obvious to me, and it turned out I was right. He got to the hospital, had a big operation on his heart, and he's been okay since.

That summer Mom didn't read the papers or turn on the news much. That was before we were on it all the time! Mom was like everyone else in Kokomo: She chatted about what her friends and relatives and coworkers were up to. But Grandpa and I always read *Time* Magazine. For two years we'd been reading about a new disease called AIDS, which stands for Acquired Immune Deficiency Syndrome. Just that spring, scientists had figured out that AIDS is caused by a virus—the kind of bug that gives you the flu—which gets into your blood. Once it's been there long enough, it knocks out your immune system, which is made up of particular types of cells in your blood that usually help you fight off illnesses and keep you well. Right now there is no vaccine or any other kind of medicine that rids your body of the AIDS virus and repairs your immune system. So once you have AIDS, you start coming down with all kinds of other diseases, and eventually you die from them.

When Grandpa and I first started reading about AIDS, doctors weren't absolutely sure about all the ways the new virus they had discovered was spread around. They did know that you could get it by having sex with someone who had it, or by using a hypodermic needle that was contaminated with the virus. During sex your body absorbs your partner's semen or vaginal discharge, which could carry the virus. A needle with contaminated blood on it is like a four-lane highway to AIDS, because you could inject the virus right into your own bloodstream. A third way the virus can get into your blood is from a transfusion of blood or blood products like Factor VIII that happened to come from someone with AIDS.

Because you can get AIDS from doing certain things, some groups of people were in more danger of catching it. One group was gay men, who passed the virus along through sex. For a while, scientists thought only gay men got AIDS, and many people still think of it as "the gay disease," even though drug addicts get it too. Some addicts who use needles, share them, and they can spread AIDS to others that way. Whenever I had an injection at home or in the hospital, we used a new needle. After all the times I've been stuck and all the medicine I've had to take, I can't imagine anyone actually *wanting* to use needles or drugs. But people do. They should find out what it's like to *have* to take drugs *all* the time!

The last group who could get AIDS were hemophiliacs and other people who needed blood transfusions and injections of blood products. AIDS was kind of lurking around in the background for all families of hemophiliacs, but back then nobody I knew except Grandpa seemed to take it very seriously. Grandpa and I had read everything we could find about it. We heard about older hemophiliacs with severe cases like mine, who had gotten AIDS from the Factor that they needed as much as I did. That upset Grandpa. He started telling Mom not to give me Factor anymore. "I just have a bad feeling it's not going to work out like we hoped," he said.

"Dad!" You could tell Mom was irritated. "It's Factor that's kept Ryan alive all these years. You know I can't stop his shots now. It wouldn't be fair. Without Factor he'd be in the hospital all the time."

"Jeanne, I'm just scared to death Ryan's going to catch AIDS," Grandpa said.

"But Grandpa," I cut in, "we saw in *Time* that less than one percent of hemophiliacs have

AIDS, and they're older guys—not kids. Maybe they're gay too, and got AIDS that way.''

Less than one percent—none of them children. That was practically nobody.

Even so, I hadn't felt very well all summer. Nothing in particular. I didn't look sick—just kind of sluggish. Mom was so worried, she told Andrea to forget about her partner in Chicago. It just didn't seem like a good idea to leave me on my own so much. Andrea wasn't at all pleased—she had finally gotten a partner who was as good as she was—but at least she kept on doing well in her singles events close to home.

I started school okay at the end of August, but by September I was having diarrhea and stomach cramps and even something that hadn't come my way before: night sweats. I'd wake up all of a sudden in the dark with my sheets sopping wet. Sometimes I had even soaked the mattress. Night sweats don't hurt, but they're like throwing up in the middle of the night: You feel out of it and helpless, like you're two years old. I had to shout for my mom to come help me find something dry to wear and change my bedsheets—camouflage ones, of course. All this work is no fun late at night, but if you don't do it, you're very uncomfortable.

After my night sweats started, Mom took me to our regular pediatrician, who wasn't disturbed by anything she told him had happened to me. He had a simple explanation: "There's a bad flu going around." He thought my swollen lymph nodes meant bronchitis. In November we went to the local hemophilia clinic for my regular annual check-up. The staff tested my blood, as they always did, and told Mom it showed that I'd had hepatitis during the past year—a liver infection you can pick up from contaminated Factor. Mom said to me, "Well, that explains how you've been."

On the way home from the clinic, we picked up a new batch of Factor from the hospital, and noticed something on it that we hadn't seen before: a warning about AIDS, like the notice on a pack of cigarettes that says you should know that they're hazardous to your health. I felt funny seeing that—especially since I'd read that Factor was being treated with heat to wipe out the AIDS virus. The sign made Mom uncomfortable too. "I feel like I'm playing Russian roulette with your life, giving you this stuff," she said.

I TURNED thirteen on December 6, and being a teenager was no big improvement. I couldn't seem to stop coughing, and by the time I got off the school bus at the end of the day, I was beat. The day after my birthday, a Friday, was particularly bad. I just about managed to stagger into the house. "Mom, you've got to do something!" I yelled. "I could hardly drag myself off the bus."

I spent the whole weekend sleeping on the couch, barely bothering to hit the bathroom. I was coughing so much I was out of breath. When Mom took my temperature and discovered it was 103 degrees, we took a fast trip to the local hospital. The doctors took some X rays of my chest. Pneumonia in both lungs, they said. After three days, I had to be transferred to James Whitcomb Riley, the special children's hospital in Indianapolis. By that time I needed an oxygen mask to breathe. The doctors and nurses had been pounding my back to make me cough.

"You're not coughing hard enough," they said. I got mad because I was coughing as hard as I could. But my lungs wouldn't clear. I was burning up with fever, and could only bark out quick questions, like "Mom, what's happening? What are they going to do to me?" Mom squeezed my hand tight, but she had no idea.

Mom told me later that as my ambulance took off for Riley, all its sirens wailing at once, all she could think was, *I can't lose Ryan.* She grabbed Andrea and a little Christmas tree she had put beside my bed. All of a sudden Mom remembered the warning on my Factor. She turned to one of my nurses, and asked, "Did my son's doctors say anything about AIDS?"

The nurse looked shocked. "Oh *no*," she said. "That never came up." Mom thought she could relax. She and Andrea followed me down to Indianapolis.

But when we got to Riley, the doctors rushed me into intensive care and told Mom I might have tuberculosis, lung cancer—or AIDS. They ruled out TB almost immediately, so Mom found herself actually praying that my problem might be *just cancer*. Imagine, my own mother! Because I had pneumonia, which is infectious, I was assigned to a new doctor at Riley, a specialist in infectious diseases named Dr. Martin Kleiman. Mom liked him right away. She said he reminded her of the Nutty Professor—probably because he has a beard. Dr. Kleiman always takes care to speak precisely; he never sounds nutty. If he ever does, I suspect it will be because Mom and I drove him nuts. We ended up knowing him for so long! When I met him, Dr. Kleiman was a bachelor. Now he's married and has a son and two daughters. He always wears a button with a photograph of them on his jacket lapel. And he has more gray in his beard than he did when I first knew him.

I had been on medication for twenty-four hours, but I was getting worse and worse. Dr. Kleiman told Mom, "We're going to have to operate on Ryan right away. The surgeons have to cut out a small piece of his lung so that we can test it and find out what's wrong with him. Then I'll know how to treat him. Right now, I don't."

Now, surgery is always something a hemophiliac wants to avoid. You need Factor the whole time so you don't bleed to death. So Mom knew that what Dr. Kleiman wanted would be difficult and dangerous for me. I might die if they operated—and I might if they didn't. Still, she was impressed that a doctor was telling her he didn't know it all. "Go ahead," she said.

I was still feverish and confused about where I was and what was going on. Mom did make it clear that I would be put out and wouldn't feel anything, so I nodded my okay. I didn't want to be in more pain than I had to be.

My operation was long and complicated. It was getting late, but Mom knew she'd never get any sleep until my surgery was over, all my tests had been run, and the doctors could tell her the results. So she and Andrea camped out in the visitors' lounge. Mom tried to doze in a chair, while Andrea curled up in a sleeping bag underneath, holding on to Mom's hand the whole time.

Close to midnight Dr. Kleiman came looking for Mom.

"What's wrong?" she asked. His face said his news wasn't good.

"I'd like to tell you in private," Dr. Kleiman demurred. There were still about a dozen visitors sacked out around the lounge.

Mom gently shook Andrea, and still holding hands, they followed Dr. Kleiman to an empty conference room and sat down, their eyes glued to him.

"We got the test results back," Dr. Kleiman began. "They show that Ryan has pneumocystis pneumonia. It's a very rare type of pneumonia. Jeanne, it means Ryan has AIDS."

Mom started to sob. She cried very easily in those days. Andrea didn't cry and she didn't say a word. She just clutched Mom's hand tighter than ever. Andrea is better at keeping how she feels to herself. An older brother can be a royal pain, but she was thinking, I don't want him to die! He *won't* die!

"How long does Ryan have to live?" Mom managed to ask.

"I can't say because I don't know," Dr. Kleiman said. "He came through surgery okay, and I think we can get him over his pneumonia, but it could come back again. That happens to quite a few AIDS patients."

My fate was as bad as it could be—and Mom felt it could be her fault. She blurted, "Oh, why didn't Ryan die during surgery?" Then she realized what she'd said. "I'm *really* sorry," she told Dr. Kleiman, "I didn't mean that at all."

"I know," he said. "It's all right, Jeanne."

Mom thought a minute before she spoke up again. "How long has Ryan had AIDS?" she asked. She was wondering which batch of Factor in our refrigerator had been the evil one. One batch is good for about a dozen injections, so Mom figured she could have been giving me contaminated Factor for a long time.

"We have no way of knowing," Dr. Kleiman said. "We can't tell. Ryan may have picked up the virus a year or two ago, and it lay dormant until now."

A year—maybe two! Mom felt chilly. Was there any chance that she or Andrea—or any of our relatives—had gotten infected too? She tried desperately to think of everything that had happened to our family in the past two years. Her stomach knotted as she counted up all the bottles of soda the three of us had passed around. Had she ever pricked her finger on a needle when she was giving me Factor? Then there had been that field trip my class took to Chicago last year. Mom had come along on the school bus as chaperone. On our way home the driver slammed on his breaks to avoid a car. I had pitched forward and cut my ear on the seat in front on me. All the way back home to Windfall, Mom had kept her hand pressed tight over my ear to try to staunch the bleeding. Now she wondered, Did I have any cuts on my hand then? Would any of Ryan's blood have gotten into them—and into *my* blood? If it did, then *I* could have AIDS too! And what about our plates and sheets and towels and the toilet and even toothpaste? Mom didn't know. She was scared for me, for herself, for Andrea, for our whole family.

She asked Dr. Kleiman to run all my tests again, to make absolutely sure I had what he thought I had. And she asked him to test her and Andrea for AIDS as well.

"Of course," Dr. Kleiman said. "But you don't have to worry. Nobody who lives with an AIDS patient has ever gotten the virus. You can't catch it from casual contact with Ryan, and neither can Andrea."

"I can kiss Ryan, can't I?" Mom asked.

"Yes, Jeanne," Dr. Kleiman said, "you can kiss him."

*　　*　　*

So Mom went to intensive care to kiss me. When she looked in, I was still unconscious after my surgery, and I was a pitiful picture. I had drainage tubes running out of the incision the surgeons had made in my chest. To get medicine and nutrients into me while I was out, they had put intravenous tubes, or IVs, in my feet because I had gotten so thin from having diarrhea that they couldn't find any veins in my arms. I was glad I was asleep when they did *that*.

But worst of all, according to Mom, I had tubes up my nose and a plastic mask over my mouth that was hooked up to a scary-looking machine called a respirator or ventilator, which gives you oxygen and breathes for you when your lungs are weak. The machine chugs away like a steam engine, filling your lungs with oxygen and then taking it out, so that your lungs fill and deflate just as they would if you were breathing on your own. Even if I had been awake, I couldn't have spoken to Mom. My eyes were bandaged, so that when I came to, I wouldn't see myself and panic.

My room was dark, except for the blinking lights on the ventilator's controls, and my guardian angel, a little night-light that had been a present from one of Mom's friends at church. Mom always put it in my room whenever I was in the hospital. If I woke up late at night, there was my angel, glowing in the dark.

Mom couldn't stand to see me looking so sick and pathetic. She started to cry again, and hurried out of my room. She'd vowed she was never going to cry in front of me, because she figured that if I knew how scared she was, I might give up. She was still hoping that my tests might be wrong, because she didn't think she could face telling me I was dying.

She called my grandparents in Kokomo, who were waiting by their phone for news about me. Grandpa was devastated. He'd read that AIDS patients usually live only three to six months.

"Well," Mom answered, "Dr. Kleiman didn't say that. He said that AIDS is so new, we should take this whole thing one day at a time."

Poor Grandpa wasn't really listening. All he knew was that his worst fear was real now: His first grandson had a deadly disease with no cure. He began to cry and had to get off the phone. Grandma told me later it was the first time in forty years of marriage that she had seen tears in his eyes.

Grandma was more mad than sad right then. "It's homosexuals that started this disease," she declared. Now, that's a myth that a lot of people all over the country believe. Especially in Kokomo, it doesn't make sense because ninety-five percent of the people are just like everyone else, and the other five percent lie pretty low. Mom had told me she had a sense that one or two people she knew at work were homosexuals, but they were extremely discreet. Grandma probably thought AIDS was gays' fault because she's very, very religious, and according to her religion, being homosexual is a sin.

"Listen to me," Mom said to Grandma, very slowly and calmly. "Ryan has AIDS because of his hemophilia. I gave him the bad gene that passed hemophilia on to him. I gave him the Factor that infected him with AIDS. So if you want to blame this on anyone, blame it on me."

Even though my grandparents were so very, very upset, it never occurred to them to stay away from me or from Mom—then or ever. They wanted to lend Mom a hand, or at least a couple of shoulders to cry on. They were ready to start for the hospital right away, that night. But Mom told them to wait until the next day. She had asked Dr. Kleiman if she could be the one to tell me what was wrong with me, and she didn't want to do it right away.

"If you come so soon, he might guess," she explained. "I want to wait until the day after Christmas. You know how he always loves Christmas and all his presents. Let's let him enjoy this one—it might be his last."

Next Mom felt she had to call Dad.

"Why bother?" Andrea snapped. "He won't care."

Andrea had a point, but even though my parents had been divorced for seven years and hardly spoke, he was still supporting my sister and me. Mom believed that Dad had a right to know what happened to us. The few times that Mom had called him, he usually answered with a nasty, "What is it *now*?" This conversation was no exception. Mom gave Dad the news. He seemed to have nothing to say about me, so she hung up. That was that.

Eventually, Dad did show up at the hospital, but right away he and Mom got into an argument because he wanted to tell me I had AIDS *now*. Otherwise I might hear about it from someone in the hospital, he said. Mom told him off good: "Don't you *dare!* My son has been through plenty of pain and misery ever since he was born. I'm not going to ruin his Christmas!"

Next, Mom called Steve, who worked nights at Delco. He drove straight down to Riley as soon as he got off his shift, so she told him about me in person. He was much more upset than Dad had been, and he told Mom she was doing the right thing by holding back her news until after Christmas. Mom also wanted to wait until I was stronger. Once I was off the respirator, she knew I'd realize I was getting better, and wouldn't be tempted to give up after I heard the truth.

I was awake by now, but I was still in intensive care. I didn't feel so hot. My operation hadn't been nearly as bad as this tube I had stuck down into my chest. A chest tube is painful even when you're feeling great. But because I still had pneumonia, every cough and every breath made the tube hurt more. The more I moved, the more the tube rubbed against my throat, and the more I felt like coughing. The tube made it almost impossible to get into a comfortable position and lie still, even though I was taking painkillers.

Not a great situation. Besides, you can never get any sleep in a hospital. Someone is always shining a flashlight in your face to wake you up so they can take your blood pressure or something. I couldn't relax, but I had to, because I was still on the ventilator. You can't fight the machine; you have to lay back and let it do its work. I had to tell Grandpa to do that, when he was on a ventilator after his heart attack. If you get tensed up, it's even harder to breathe. And you must make sure that the nurses clean out your mask regularly—otherwise your saliva collects in it, clogs it up, and makes you cough more. I couldn't talk, so I scrawled notes. I had to write the nurses a good many notes about that.

That's what I was up to the first time Mom and Andrea and Steve came in to see me. They were all wearing surgical masks and hospital smocks, but I barely noticed. Mom and Andrea seemed fairly subdued. Steve chatted about how the weather was turning colder and there was a good chance we'd have a white Christmas. That December was very mild, and my room was very hot—close to ninety degrees! Soon time was up, and as my family filed out, Mom kissed me on the forehead—the only part she could reach—and handed me my guardian angel.

Christmas was still a week away—a week that Mom had to wait out, behaving as normally as possible. She and Andrea got a room across the street from Riley at the Ronald McDonald House, a place where relatives of kids who have to stay in the hospital can sleep over—not that Mom got much rest. My mother and sister spent all day, every day, in the visitors' lounge. Andrea could only see me once a day, but every forty minutes, Mom would dry her eyes, take a deep breath, push open the swinging doors into the intensive care unit, and visit me for twenty minutes. Our conversations were still one-sided, though I wrote her notes like "Rub my neck gently," or "Thanks for coming to see me," or "Itch the top of my head." (I'm better at math than at English.) I had a rash because I turned out to be allergic to some of my medicine. Last thing we did every night was pray together. Mom and I would clasp our hands together, and she would say, "Thank you, Lord, for another day. Lord make everything come out okay, in Thy precious name, Amen." I would chime in silently, and then she'd kiss me good night.

Once my intensive-care nurse, Laura Kreich, came in to see me while Mom was still visiting. Laura was only twenty-two, just out of nursing school. She was pretty, she came from a big family, and she was practically a kid herself. She was always dropping by to talk to me, even though I could only nod or shake my head. We'd do stuff where I didn't have to talk, like playing cards or watching movies on the VCR Mom had rented and brought in. When I first went into the hospital, Mom had given Andrea and me two of our Christmas presents early: a jam-box for Andrea and a radio/cassette player for me. Laura never left my room without first changing my tapes for me. If I was asleep when she arrived, she'd leave me a little note on a paper towel, telling me when she'd be back. This time she had work to do: She was there to hook me up to a new IV.

"What are you giving him?" Mom asked, thinking I might be on new medication.

"It's Factor VIII," Laura said. "It'll help him heal."

Mom couldn't say a word, but she wanted to yank Laura's needle out of my arm and dash the bag of Factor on the floor. She knew I needed it to recover from my surgery, but she was furious that what had been keeping me well had given me AIDS, drop by drop.

I waved at Laura. I had a note ready for her: "How will they take out my chest tube?"

Laura knew me well enough to realize that I was worried about being hurt. "They'll just slip it out," she said soothingly. "It won't be painful."

As soon as Mom had left me, she always started crying again immediately. Andrea was waiting for her, and sometimes Steve or my grandparents, and Mom would cry along with them. There was even another mother who was practically living in the visitors' lounge. Her daughter Julie had a brain tumor. She and Mom cried together all the time—but one day the other woman disappeared. Mom wondered what had happened to her, and to Julie.

That night, walking back to the Ronald McDonald House, Mom turned to Andrea. "If anything happens to Ryan," she said, "I don't want to go on without him. You and I should go out to the garage, close the doors, sit in the car, and let the motor run."

Andrea didn't think Mom was one hundred percent set on a suicide pact, but she sensed it wasn't a good time to say so. Andrea has a lot of sense. She put her arm around Mom, hoping silently that Mom would start getting some sleep. Probably then she'd change her mind.

But Mom certainly fooled me. I never suspected what she knew or how awful she felt, and I truly believed I was getting well. It helped that Dr. Kleiman treated me like I was a grownup. When you're in a children's hospital, lots of people speak to you in baby talk. I hated that. But Dr. Kleiman seemed to realize that as far as I was concerned, being sick was a way of life. He understood that if I was in the hospital, his job was to get me home, and keep me there. He knew I had some smarts and wanted to be told what was going on; I didn't like medical types trying to put anything over on me. I let him know how much I hated having blood samples and IVs—they make your arm ache and the bandage pulls your skin. Dr. Kleiman promised to keep me informed about what he was doing and why. He said he'd always tell me the truth, and he'd never do anything to me that he wouldn't do to his own kids if he thought it was absolutely necessary to help keep them well. And he gave me his home phone number. I could call him anytime to check if I wasn't sure about some treatment the hospital wanted to give me. All right!

I did call him, maybe three or four times. When you're in a big hospital like Riley, lots of doctors and even medical students come through your room all the time and ask you questions. Most of the time they're asking as part of their training, but sometimes they think you're an unusual case and they're just curious. (No one knew all that much about AIDS yet, especially pediatric AIDS. Every single patient could be a little different.) Sometimes these doctors—and nurses too—haven't read your chart, where your regular doctor writes down everything he knows about your case and all the medications you've had or are supposed to get. So they bop on in, take a look at you, and try something they think is right. The trouble is, it may not be necessary at all, but they'll make you suffer through it.

For instance, one time a pair of nurses appeared by my bed with a new needle. "Dr. Kleiman wants you to have another IV," they told me.

"Dr. Kleiman didn't tell *me*," I protested. Why should I get stuck again so they could have some practice? "I'm going to call him to make sure."

"Dr. Kleiman's gone home," one of the nurses said. "You can't call him."

"Oh yeah?" I said to her. "Watch me!"—and I grabbed the phone.

It turned out that Dr. Kleiman *had* ordered that IV, but had forgotten to tell me. So I had to have it. At least I had stood up for myself and gotten the straight scoop.

On Christmas Eve day Dr. Kleiman took me off the ventilator. What a great present—my throat was still very sore, but now I could almost talk to Laura! When she was around, I felt like I had a big sister with me at Riley. She made being in the hospital almost bearable. Laura didn't feel too old to look at my G.I. Joe collection, or to sing along to my John Cougar Mellencamp tapes. I was big on John Cougar. To say "so long" to the ventilator, we'd go,

> When I fight authority
> Authority always wins
> Well, I've been doing it since
> I was a young kid
> And I come out grinning!

I couldn't wait for Christmas. Dr. Kleiman also had a present for Mom—some good news. Starting the day after Christmas he was putting me on a new drug called pentamidine that he didn't think would make me itch. At first I had to have pentamidine shots in my thigh—yech!—but later I could get it intravenously. When Mom heard this, she began to believe that I'd live longer than the three to six months Grandpa had predicted. She asked my grandparents to take poor worn-out Andrea home with them so she could sleep in a bed for once instead of under a hospital lounge chair. That night Mom slept well herself for the first time since I'd gone into the hospital.

The next day was her favorite of the entire year—Christmas. Mom starts planning for Christmas well before Halloween. She begins decorating our house at Thanksgiving, and sometimes leaves all the trimmings up until March, just because she hates taking everything down. "The house looks so blah," she complains. We always have at least two trees: a big one covered with all kind of ornaments that Mom has collected, and a little one hung with framed photographs of everyone in the family. Even Dad is on our family portrait tree—and certainly Steve.

As for our big tree, Mom's been known to set the whole thing up, lights and all—and then decide she doesn't like the way it looks, tear everything down, and start all over again. She crochets snowflakes, and she clips real candles in tin holders onto the tree's branches. She makes popcorn chains for the tree that she puts in the freezer after Christmas so they'll keep until the next year. She bakes her special stained-glass cookies, made with melted Life-Savers inside. They're so pretty that they make perfect ornaments, but she can never save them; someone always eats them long before Christmas!

When Mom said good night to me at Riley she left the winking lights on my little tree, along with my guardian angel. We had lots of cards to decorate my room—word had gotten around my neighborhood and church. Some kids at Western, my school, had sent me cards too—even some kids I didn't know. They said they thought I was brave, and they hoped I was feeling better. My school also sent a giant computer banner. The computer had printed out "Get Well Soon" in huge letters. We hung it over my window and made a wreath of cards around it.

Every year Mom makes sure that Andrea and I find tons of presents under our tree. She gets a kick out of picking out things she knows we want. "If I don't have anything to show at Christmas after all my years at Delco," she always says, "I'm in bad shape." That year she'd worked a lot of overtime in October and had done all her shopping by the time I got so sick. She had plenty of presents for both of us in her closet, including a computer for me. She asked my grandparents to bring our gifts on Christmas Day so Andrea and I could open them at the hospital.

On Christmas morning—it *was* a white Christmas—Mom was eating breakfast in the hospital cafeteria when she was paged. My grandma was on the line, frantic.

"Jeanne, this is terrible! I dropped by your

house to get your gifts—and you've been robbed. Christmas is gone. They took all your presents and your VCR and your videotapes of Andrea skating at the nationals.''

Mom felt numb. She'd worked hard to make this Christmas as perfect as possible—and now she didn't even have any presents for us. The culprits must have been some neighbors whom she suspected were into drugs.

"I'll just have to try to explain things to the kids," she sighed to Grandma. In Mom's bedroom Grandma had uncovered some stocking stuffers that the burglars had overlooked. At least Andrea and I would have a few small presents.

Poor Andrea was devastated. No presents was bad enough, but her skating tapes couldn't be replaced. Now she would never be able to show anyone what she'd done to win at the nationals.

Mom found me listening to tapes on my new cassette player. When she told me what had happened, my stomach dropped. The thought of Christmas had kept me going. Without the tons of presents we always got from Mom, today wouldn't be like Christmas at all. I didn't want to talk about who might have robbed us or why or what the cops could do—it was too depressing to wonder who had my computer now. All I said to Mom was, "Let's forget about it." I tried to think of our burglary as that book, *How the Grinch Stole Christmas*, come to life.

The story of what had happened to us got

around the hospital. My neighbor in the next room was a five-year-old girl named Jennifer. Jennifer had Reye's Syndrome, a disease that makes your brain cells swell so there's terrible pressure inside your skull. She was one of the other children who helped me remember that I could be in much worse shape. Most of the other kids had been allowed to go home for Christmas, but Jennifer and I were stuck.

My grandparents arrived with Uncle Tommy and Aunt Deb and my cousin Monica and her brothers. Tommy and Deb and their kids were like Grandma and Grandpa: They stood by us no matter what. Everyone jammed into my room with Mom and Andrea, and sat on my bed and even the windowsill, handing out cards and presents. With all the packages my relatives had brought, I hardly noticed that anything was missing—though a computer certainly would have been nice. I liked math and science, and really wanted to learn to use a computer. It would be a big help with homework.

Even Dad dropped by with some Izod shirts for me. Mom had put them in layaway and had asked Dad to pick them up for her. I appreciated that present: I always liked to wear my own shirts in the hospital, and now I had some new ones to put on when I left for home.

All of a sudden Jennifer's relatives walked in carrying several big brown grocery bags. They'd found a drugstore that was open on Christmas, and they'd bought Andrea and me a bunch of little presents: a metal model car that ran on remote control, Care Bears, comic books (yay!), a miniature basketball game, a set of oil paints. Nothing was wrapped, but who cared? Even Andrea began to cheer up. She and Mom and I even got little extras from the hospital staff. It was a pretty great Christmas, after all.

We never did get any of our presents back, even though we found footprints in the snow leading from our house to the druggy neighbors', and Andrea saw their little girl wearing my jeans and carrying a Cabbage Patch doll Mom had bought me! You know those dolls are only one of a kind, so there was no mistake. Still, the police claimed they couldn't arrest anyone. The worst part was the robbers knew I was in the hospital with AIDS. Word was racing around our neighborhood and our Methodist church in Kokomo.

The day after Christmas Mom arrived with Andrea and a surprise visitor, our minister. Mom had been struggling to get her courage up all week. She could see I looked pretty good— nothing like a few presents to perk me up—so she decided the time had come.

"Ryan, you know you've been real sick," she started out. She was surprised at how calm she sounded.

"Uh huh," I said. "What's the matter?"

"They've done a lot of tests on you," Mom went on.

"Yeah," I said. "So?" What *was* all this?

"Ryan," Mom said, still very calm, "you have AIDS."

I stared at her. Everything, everyone seemed frozen still. All I could think was, Laura. What about Laura? Did she know she'd been looking after someone with AIDS? Would she stay away from me now?

"Does Laura know?" I asked. I didn't realize Laura was listening in on the nurses' intercom and trying not to cry.

"Yes," Mom assured me. "Laura knows."

Whew. If she'd known all along, she'd probably stick around. I *would* get to see her again.

The other giant worry I had was whether having AIDS meant I'd have to spend the rest of my life flat on my back in a hospital bed.

"Am I going to get out of here?" I wanted to know.

"As soon as Dr. Kleiman says so, you can come home," Mom said. "You're getting over your pneumonia."

That left only one question. I took a deep breath.

"Am I going to die?" My voice came out steady, not squeaky. That was some relief.

"We're all going to die someday," Mom answered, just as steadily. "We just don't know when."

I thought a minute. So what was the big deal about AIDS? I was a hemophiliac, so I already had my limits. But I'd been having an okay time, anyway. I certainly wasn't about to die yet. Why not just get back to being a normal kid?

"Tell you what, Mom," I said. "Let's just pretend I don't have AIDS."

"Ryan, we can't," Mom protested. "We're going to have to take precautions, make sure you don't get any sicker."

"Mom, you don't understand!" Andrea came to my rescue. "You don't see what Ryan means."

"I just don't want everybody feeling sorry for me and thinking 'Poor little Ryan, he's dying.' I just want to make believe I don't have AIDS and do what I want to do. Like, I want a dog."

"Dr. Kleiman says we shouldn't have any animals," Mom said.

No way I was going to give away Herbie, my hamster. Herbie lived in my room at home, and I missed him every day.

"I want my own dog, Mom. I don't care if he takes six months off my life. I want that dog to like only me. Nobody else feeds him—nobody else has anything to do with him. I just want him to come to me."

I think our minister was afraid Mom and I were getting into a fight. "Ryan, can we all say a prayer together?" he broke in.

"Sure," I said. I listened to the others with half an ear, adding my own prayer for a pup. And just the way I always did, I said thank you to God for another day of life, and asked for one more. Lord, please let me live—go back to school, see my friends again.

THE DAYS dragged on by, the way the days after Christmas tend to do, especially when you're in the hospital. I began to find out what having

AIDS and a weakened immune system really means. Some people are HIV positive. When they are tested to see if they are infected with the AIDS virus, they test positive. But they have no symptoms yet. Some people have mild symptoms. Sometimes doctors say they have ARC, or AIDS-related complex. But some people have many symptoms. They have full-blown AIDS. I was one of them.

When you have full-blown AIDS, you don't pick up every cold and flu that other people have. AIDS doesn't seem to work that way. It's as though your immune system is going up and down. When it's weak, you can catch certain odd illnesses that don't bother most other folks. For instance, I still had chronic diarrhea—ever since the summer. Dr. Kleiman said I got it from a parasite that your digestive tract usually kills off for you—unless you have AIDS. Same with my pneumonia—it was a very unusual kind that mostly hits AIDS patients. If you come down with pneumocystis pneumonia, it's a very big clue that you have AIDS too.

Just as my pneumonia was beginning to clear up, I got thrush. It means you have a yeast infection—that's the kind of organism that makes bread rise. But inside your body, yeast is not so pleasant. I developed funny-tasting white patches inside my mouth and had to rinse with some truly vile liquid medication to prevent it from spreading. I was supposed to swallow the stuff, but I also had herpes in my throat, which made it incredibly sore—far worse than any normal sore throat. I didn't want to swallow a thing.

Anyhow, AIDS takes away your appetite. It does weird things to your sense of taste and smell. Even your favorite foods smell repulsive—or your first mouthful will taste fine, and then your next one is like eating paste. Mostly I lived on sodas.

I've always been a real picky eater—long before AIDS. Don't come near me with a lukewarm Coke, or one that's been sitting open in the refrigerator for half a day. Because Riley treats only kids, they're used to hard cases like me—or even worse. They'll literally try anything to get a sick kid to eat. They'll let you cook your own food, or if you won't touch anything but Frosted Flakes or hot dogs, you can get them, three times a day.

I wasn't that extreme, but still, there were days when my mouth and throat were simply too sore, or when I just didn't feel like eating. Sometimes I couldn't sit up, so I'd use that as an excuse. Then Laura would tell me, "You act like a kid—I'm going to treat you like a kid. Choo, choo—here comes the train!"—and she'd zoom a spoonful of vegetables into my mouth. Sometimes I'd manage to duck in time—and then there'd be peas all over my bed.

Laura never talked to me about dying. She figured Dr. Kleiman's job was to keep me up-to-date about life-and-death medical matters. Hers was mainly to give me as good a time as possible. She always volunteered to be assigned to me, and after word got around the hospital about what was wrong with me, that was important. AIDS was so new that even some people who worked in medicine were nervous. Some nurses found excuses to avoid caring for me: They said they had colds and didn't want to infect me. Some just asked for other assignments. But others weren't so subtle. Mom overheard one nurse telling a doctor, "I don't want to go near him, and I don't see why I have to."

Much as I hated having my finger stuck for a blood sample, I always tried to help the nurses by sitting very still, breathing deep and slow to stay calm. I'd ask them to say, "One, two, three—stick!" so I could get ready. Sometimes you can be so afraid of being stuck that all the veins in your arm disappear completely! When that happens, the nurse's job is much harder and the whole awful process takes ten times longer. The nurse or technician would tell me, "I don't want to hurt you."

Since I knew perfectly well they were going to, I just said, "Don't worry about it."

I wondered if they were really saying that they were worried about getting hurt themselves. Much later I found out that one nurse who had been drawing my blood had stuck herself with the same needle right afterward. She was just about to get married, so she asked her fiancé if he wanted to call off the wedding. He didn't; she got tested for AIDS, and her test was negative. If you've been infected, you'll test positive within three months, though you may not show any symptoms for up to eight years.

Once I asked Laura why *she* wasn't scared of me.

"About the only precaution I have to take with an AIDS patient is to wear rubber gloves when I might touch your blood," Laura told me. "That's in case I have any cuts on my hands. Besides, I think my job is to treat *every* patient like they're an AIDS patient. If I do my job like I'm supposed to—wear gloves when I should, scrub down, and wash up well—then I don't have to be scared. If I'm not scared, then my hands won't shake when I draw your blood. That's how things can go wrong and you could stab yourself with an infected needle."

Sometimes the hospital staff wanted to stay away from me—not because of AIDS, but because I was ornery. When you're really sick, you often don't realize you're being crabby. My uncle Tommy found out about this when he had bad cancer for a while. One day my aunt Janet called him from Birmingham and started chatting about how the last I. U. basketball game had gone. Uncle Tommy, who's unbelievably patient—you know he has to be because he lives with my cousins—just about took her head off over the phone.

"You're being *ridiculous*," he insisted to Janet. "The game wasn't like that *at all*."

Janet was taken aback. Tommy's always so mild-mannered. "Well, Tommy," she said finally, "if I'd known you felt so strongly, I wouldn't have said anything."

Then Tommy could hear how he'd sounded to her, and he apologized. After that he always knew that lots of times I couldn't hear how I talked to people, either. Laura understood that too, but she never let me get away with bad behavior.

Sometimes I was scared and upset, and it came out in tears. I never cried in front of anyone at Riley—not even Dr. Kleiman or Laura—only when I was with Mom. Other times I didn't cry; I got mad. Once Laura happened to walk in while I was being really mean to Mom, who was visiting with Andrea.

"Ryan," Laura said firmly, "we don't cuss in here. You're not going to talk to your mom like that in front of me."

"I'm sorry, Mom," I said. "I love you." Whenever we had a fight, I told her that right afterward and kissed her. "I'm sorry, Laura. I didn't mean it."

Just then I felt a wriggling under my blanket. I remembered I might be in *real* trouble with Laura. Herbie, my hamster, poked his head out and then the rest of him. He started climbing up and down my legs and all over my bed. Good old Andrea had smuggled him into the hospital in a doll's suitcase. He seemed just as excited to see me as I was to see him.

Laura looked at Herbie for a minute, and then started smiling up one side of her face. "You better not let Dr. Kleiman see him," she told me. "I'm not getting into trouble on this one."

Still, she must have gotten a kick out of Herbie's visit, because she told all the other nurses about him. Several of them dropped by and asked to be introduced. I wasn't expelled from Riley after all.

Mom didn't say much when I had my outbursts. She knew what was really bothering me. Sometimes I got so I just told her flat out, "Mom, I'm scared."

"I know," Mom said. "I'm scared too, but we can't dwell on it."

When I was diagnosed, the hospital had suggested family counseling, but Mom and I figured we had each other to talk to. Andrea was like me: She didn't think I was really going to die. Besides, I didn't want to *talk* about AIDS; I just wanted to get on with the rest of my life.

This may sound hard to believe, but after a while, things changed and I really, truly wasn't scared of dying. A big reason was that one night in the hospital, when I was off the respirator but still very sick, I had an amazing dream. I thought I was making my way through blackness. The devil was all around, trying to pull me into his house of hell. But I just kept straining and reaching and pulling away from him—when suddenly I saw a blaze of the brightest light you can imagine. God was there. He spoke to me. He said I had nothing to worry about. He was going to take care of me.

The next day when Mom came to see me, I

told her about it. She said she'd heard other sick people say that they'd had a dream like mine. Suddenly I knew what I'd dreamt about.

"Mom," I said, "I've seen heaven. I'm not afraid now."

"What did God look like?" Mom asked me.

I thought for a moment. "Well," I said slowly, "He sure didn't look like that person in the picture I have on my bedroom wall." I meant Jesus with long hair and a beard.

THERE WAS another reason I wasn't afraid: I *was* getting better. Hemophilia had taught me I was always going to have to go for it—to concentrate on all the things I wanted to do. Mom had taught me to look for the happy parts of life, and to look away from the bad parts. If I had started dwelling on all the bad stuff connected with hemophilia, I'd never have left the hospital at all. I didn't want to *have* AIDS. I wanted to *fight* it. I wasn't going to be an AIDS *victim*. No one was going to make any kind of victim out of me.

When I got to high school, I learned in psychology class about voodoo, how if you believe in it, it will work on you and for you. If you think zombies and hexes and spirits are dumb, voodoo won't work. I didn't know about this when I was lying in the hospital, hearing for the first time that I had AIDS, but somehow I figured out that if you believe you're going to get better, you will. If you sit around moping and thinking, "I'm not going to make it," then you won't.

So I had made up my mind. I'd been told I'd never ride a bike. Now I rode a bike *and* roller skates. When I broke my elbow, I was told I'd never be able to reach my shoulder again. A month after my cast was taken off, I could do that. I'd fallen out of my crib—and once I even went through a plate glass window at Grandma's, hands first—and I didn't bleed at all.

I had plans, and I wasn't about to drop them. I wanted to go to high school with all my friends. I wanted to graduate and go to Indiana University. Even though I didn't know what my major was going to be yet, I meant to make something of myself. Besides that, being a teenager was supposed to be fun, and I meant to have some. I certainly intended to learn to drive.

"Sure you can lead a normal life," Dr. Kleiman told me. "There are a few things I want you to stay away from, like cigarettes and bird droppings and animals. Don't swim in rivers or lakes."

I didn't say anything. I wasn't about to give up my plan to get my own dog. Part of being a teenager was trying cigarettes. Well, I thought, I'll stay away from *other people's* cigarettes. There were some things Dr. Kleiman just couldn't know.

"How long do you think I have?" I asked.

"I don't know, Ryan," he said. "Besides, if I told you something like, 'Until April,' and then you were still alive in April, you'd never believe another word I said, would you?"

I had to say, "No, I guess not." Then I thought of something. "Dr. Kleiman, they're working hard to find a cure for AIDS, aren't they?"

"Yes, they certainly are," Dr. Kleiman answered.

"Well," I said, "I'd like to tell them to hurry up." Grandpa and I had read that people with AIDS were lucky to live two years after their diagnosis. I wanted to be the one they found the cure for in time.

"I bet if I live five years," I went on, "I can beat this thing." I grinned at my doctor. "Or I'll die trying."

3

How I Tried to Go Back to School

FEBRUARY HAD almost arrived when Dr. Kleiman finally let me go home again. Mom had left up our two Christmas trees and all our other decorations. I was pretty feeble, too weak to go out in the cold or do much besides watch TV. I still had thrush, and my diarrhea and my coughing didn't seem like they'd ever go away. All I could do was let time go by until I felt stronger.

"We will get through this," Mom would tell me. "We're not going to live in misery. Every day is going to be the best."

But it was beginning to dawn on me that AIDS was going to be harder to live with than hemophilia. Sometimes I felt scared, just the way I had in the hospital. Most often I was afraid I'd never feel well again. Then I'd just sit with Mom. She'd put her arm around me or rub my head, and we'd talk.

Mom claimed I looked like a concentration camp inmate: just skin and bone. I'd dropped almost twenty pounds, and I'm not chubby normally. But I did have all my hair, thank you very much. Dr. Kleiman had told Mom that whatever she could get me to eat was okay with him. Mom and Andrea prefer salads and cottage cheese and light food that keeps weight off you. But I might go all day without feeling hungry, and then start craving pork chops, French fries, hot chocolate, and anything else in sight. Grandma started working nights so she could cook for me during the day while Mom was at the plant. She and Mom would drop whatever they were doing and cook whatever I wanted whenever I was willing to eat. Some days I wanted four or five small meals, a couple of them late at night.

Once a month, Mom had to take me back to the hospital in Kokomo for gamma globulin therapy. That's a dose of concentrated antibodies that helps kids with AIDS resist infection. And I had to go see Dr. Kleiman to snort pentamidine in an aerosol spray.

"Why can't I do this at home?" I asked him.

"Because then I'll never get you in here," Dr. Kleiman answered.

Andrea helped out by making Mom and me posters with fancy lettering that said "Number One Brother" or "Love You Mom." She also got chores done after Mom asked her to do them only once—something you can almost never say about her. My grandparents and some of Andrea's skating friends took her to practice while Mom stayed with me. Mom said the worst part of my being sick still was that she had to look after Herbie for me. But I never let up telling her how much I wanted a dog of my own. Just in case she ever forgot.

Having AIDS is very expensive. Drugs for AIDS cost so much that if someone in your family has it, you can lose your house and everything you own, trying to pay for treatment. Mom's coworkers at Delco had collected some money for us, which was really kind of them, but we still had huge medical bills. Especially when Mom wasn't able to work because I was in the hospital. Nobody in Indiana seemed to know anyone else with AIDS. Even some congressmen Mom called couldn't give her much advice. She decided her best shot was to sue the company that made my contaminated Factor, to try to have them pay my expenses. This didn't work, but when Mom's lawyer, Mr. Vaughan, filed the suit, we found out that this company got blood for making Factor from big cities like New York, San Francisco, Chicago, and Los Angeles. In one of those cities they had collected some blood given by someone who had already been infected with AIDS. Even though you need blood from thousands of people to make Factor, just one infected person can contaminate a whole batch.

I thought about that person, whoever he was. More and more, women and babies are getting AIDS, but back then I figured it had to be a man. Probably a drug user who needed money to buy a fix. I certainly was mad that he'd given infected blood that made me ill too. But maybe he hadn't known he had the AIDS virus. I wondered what his story was—where he was, how he was doing, whether his family cared about him. Some AIDS patients end up abandoned by their families because they find it's too tough to look after someone who's deathly ill, or else they're ashamed to have a relative with AIDS. I knew I had been pretty lucky that way, and I wondered about him. By this time he probably was a good deal sicker than I was. Perhaps he was dead. We shared the same blood and the same problem. He had changed my life forever, but we would never exchange a word. I thought maybe now I knew a little bit about how adopted kids feel when they discover they've never met their real parents.

Because of our suit, a reporter from the local paper, the *Kokomo Tribune*, called Mom and asked her a bunch of questions. So there it was in newsprint: Ryan White, 3506 South Webster Street, has AIDS. Now everyone in Kokomo knew.

Plenty of out-of-towners heard too. I told you that churches and preachers are a big part of life in Indiana. Once we had been in the *Tribune*, all those preachers seemed to be trying to move in with us. We got phone calls and visits from healers as far away as Tennessee and Florida. One man was from Poland, and brought a translator with him! They all claimed—we must have heard from fifty or sixty of them—that they had been sent by Jesus, special delivery, to cure me. I'm religious, but I couldn't believe that Jesus had sent *all* of them. Mom wanted me healed so bad, she was ready to try anything that might make me well. She said, "What if one of them *is* Jesus—and I turned my back?"

So she let a lot of them come by and take a shot at curing me. Every night one or two showed up and they all had to stay at least four hours. They took over my life—I had no privacy left at all! First, each one had to sit on our sofa for a couple of hours and tell us how holy he was, how many people he'd already healed, and how he'd gotten his call from Jesus to cure me. I wanted to ask, "How did Jesus get your phone number?" but I didn't dare in front of Mom.

Then each healer had to lay their hands on me, which is how they heal. This usually meant I had to sit or lie on my stomach while he adjusted the vertebrae in my back and neck and realigned my spine. During some of these treatments my bones would make a loud crack, and I'd feel like I'd had an electric charge pass through me. I didn't think any of this could make much difference if you had AIDS, but I often felt fine afterward for a little while. Maybe nothing else about me was well adjusted, but at least my backbones were!

Then each preacher wanted to pray with us

for another hour or so. Even after they'd left, we couldn't get rid of them. They'd all call back to see if their treatment had worked. Was I healed yet? Mom would take all their calls. I'd mouth, "Get rid of him!" to her, but she felt obliged to be polite. You can't be rude to someone who might be Jesus. Things got so bad that if the three of us were sitting around in the evening watching TV and the phone rang, we'd look at each other and go, "Uh oh!" Finally I got Mom to start saying I was too weak and worn out to see anybody.

There was no way, though, to stop the "cures" that arrived by mail. When you're too sick to go out, trust me—the mail is the high point of your day. I'd be tickled when I saw the brown UPS truck pull up to our house and deliver—oh boy!—a package for me. Andrea would get jealous and want to know, "Where's mine?" I couldn't wait to open my parcel, but when I did I'd find . . . seaweed. Ginseng, specially grown in Wisconsin. Homemade herbal solutions. Nerve medicine for Mom. We got so many free samples of vitamins and nutrients and pills and formulas and supplements from nutritionists that soon our garage was crammed to the ceiling with cartons and cases and bottles and jars full of stuff we didn't want. We couldn't fit the car in anymore! We had enough to open a nutrition store. Mom did take the Wisconsin ginseng to work to give her friends a little extra boost.

These nutritionists also sent me plenty of free

advice. Mail is mail—I read all of it. One morning my first letter said, "Whatever you do, don't touch salt or fried food or pork—it puts worms in your system and it's deadly to AIDS patients." These people must have been peeking in Mom's kitchen window, watching me gobble pork chops and French fries after I'd poured salt on everything! One doctor advised, "If you want to get well, eat five walnuts a day for twenty-one days." Often the next letter I read contradicted the previous one, and sure enough, my third letter said, "Medicine is poison! Don't go near anything doctors give you. Fasting is the only road to health." I was supposed to starve myself to get well.

The next time we saw Dr. Kleiman he asked, "Got any more cures?" Mom told him about the walnut idea. Dr. Kleiman raised an eyebrow at me. "Well, Ryan, do you like walnuts?" he asked with a straight face. That was as close as Dr. Kleiman ever came to the Nutty Professor.

One man who said he was a scientist brought us his personal miracle cure himself. He'd driven all the way from Arizona in a beat-up pickup truck to see us and someone in Russiaville who had lupus, another incurable disease. He handed us a foggy baby shampoo bottle that looked about fifty years old. I hate to tell you what the stuff in it looked like. It was the color of pee and it had brown balls floating in it—rotting leaves and buds, I think. I didn't really want to get close enough to investigate it thoroughly. I said to myself, "This stuff is going to mean the slow and painful death of Ryan White."

The man from Arizona insisted that I had to take a teaspoonful a day. He was determined. I had to start right now and take it in front of him immediately. He said he'd take a dose first, if I wanted, to show me it was safe—and he did! But he still wouldn't tell us what was in it. Furthermore we had to swear that we wouldn't tell anyone else about his medicine, or have it analyzed. I guess he was worried that we were going to swipe his top-secret formula, make some more of our own, and sell it to every drugstore we could find.

Since Mom didn't want either one of us to expire in front of her right then and there, she persuaded the so-called scientist that I'd take my teaspoon later. Much later. We got him on the road to Russiaville. Naturally, he called back that night, wanting to know if I'd taken his medicine. Mom can't tell a lie, so she told him no. He got really mad, and said he wanted his shampoo bottle back. He showed up the next day to reclaim it and then stormed off toward Arizona. I guess we seemed ungrateful and unappreciative of all he could have done for us.

So Andrea didn't have to envy me about most of my mail. But I admit I did get some nice letters and presents. Some girls enclosed their pictures in scented pink or lavendar envelopes. "Well, hello!" I said, when I opened these. "A date for the movies!" I even got some good letters from other teenage hemophiliacs with AIDS. They didn't always come right out and say they had AIDS, but somehow you could tell it was there, between the lines. One boy wrote me, "How old's your sister? Mine is three years and a *pest*."

Many entertainers and sports stars and other celebrities make a point of writing to sick kids to cheer them up. I got autographed baseballs from the Cubs and the Dodgers, an autographed football from the Chicago Bears, and autographed photos from Ronnie Milsap, the country singer, and David Hasselhoff, the star of the television show, *Knight Rider*. He even came to see me. Mom and Grandma were thrilled that I'd heard from stars, and their photos looked great on my bedroom walls. I was more excited when one of my buddies from the neighborhood or from school dropped by in between the preachers.

Mom finally decided that since so much else had gone wrong, she couldn't deny me my own dog, even if Dr. Kleiman yelled at her. On Valentine's Day Mom's friend Mike from the plant came over with—you guessed it—a litter of five puppies. They were mutts—"Heinz 57 Varieties," Mom called them—but who cared? They were all adorable and affectionate. I was so happy Mom had changed her mind that I gave her a giant hug. Then I hugged each pup. They wiggled and bounced all over me, licking and scratching. I had trouble choosing, but finally I settled on a brown one with a pug nose and uneven black and white patches. Since I was watching so much TV, I had a name all picked out for him: Barney, after Barney Fife on *The Andy Griffith Show*. And just like I'd hoped, my Barney wouldn't let anyone but me feed him or walk him. Best of all, if other people tried to pet him, including Mom and Andrea, he growled at them.

Mom was certainly my main Valentine, but I wanted to surprise Laura too. Mom took me by the hospital and I presented Laura with a red plastic rose on a long stem that had a light inside the petals. If you put it in a vase, like you would a real flower, it made a reddish glow on the wall and looked real romantic. Laura was very happy to see me well enough to be up and out. I invited her to come by and meet Barney, and to watch Andrea skate, and she said she'd be there.

Over Andrea's spring break, Mom took the two of us south to visit Aunt Janet. I'd finally gotten over my thrush, and I was coughing less in the warm weather. While we were in Birmingham, my diarrhea stopped too. My whole family celebrated! I was a medical miracle!

My cousins showed us a new playground in Birmingham where you could swing yourself on a long rope out over what looked like a gaping ravine. Mom took some home movies, and my grandparents were so pleased to see me back in action that they almost forgot to fuss.

By the time we came home, I was feeling the best I'd been in two years. Some nights Steve took all of us to the rink together, and Mom was able to start driving Andrea to skating practice again. One day they stopped on the way at a drive-in restaurant to pick up Cokes. While they were sitting in the car waiting for their order, Mom remembered something. She turned to Andrea and said, "You know my plan? The one I had in the hospital? To shut ourselves in the garage with the car motor running? Just forget I ever said it."

Andrea replied, "What plan, Mom? I don't know what you're talking about." They grinned at each other.

"Thanks, hon," Mom said.

I WAS well enough to get a paper route, and to play with my friends across the street once they got home from school. Some idiot asked Blair if he was scared to hang out with me. Blair knew he was not supposed to touch me now if I started bleeding, but that had never happened, even before I had AIDS. He had a snappy comeback.

"Ry-man?" Blair said. "It's not like he has a green aura around him."

Back then I assumed the kid Blair had talked to was the exception. I was sure that my friends at school wouldn't act like that. I really missed them. Most of the day I was home on my own. Now that I felt well, Mom had gone back to work. I was very, very bored. All I did was watch reruns—*Andy Griffith, Lucy*, whatever was on. I wanted to be able to get up every morning and pick out what I was going to wear to school. I wanted to pack my books in my backpack and study math and history and science again. I began to bug Mom to call school and find out when I could go back, or at least visit and have pizza with my buddies in the cafeteria. I took up the art of note writing again: "Mom, call school. Want to go back. LOVE (capitalized, circled, and underlined), Ryan." Sometimes I'd sneak these notes into Mom's pockets, and she'd find them later at work.

One day she found a note from me at the bottom of her handbag and showed it to a friend on the job. "Jeanne," her friend said, slowly, "you don't *really* think they'll let him go back, do you?"

Mom didn't know what to say. This was a good friend talking. Mom had expected everyone to treat me the way she had. This was the first time she realized we were in for a lot of trouble.

Soon it started happening in the oddest places. Our church has always been real important to Grandma. She goes to services regularly, and she tries to do as much church work as she can. The first time Mom and Andrea and I started going to Sunday service again with my grandparents, once the weather warmed up and I was strong enough to be outdoors, a good old friend of Mom's, someone she's known since grade school who sings in our church choir, was sitting in the front pew. Alice saw us walk in together, and she came all the way down the aisle with a beautiful smile on her face to greet us. She gave Mom a long hug. "Alice looked like an angel to me right then!" Mom told me afterward.

But as the service got started, we could tell that the rest of the congregation wasn't quite so glad to see us. Every time I coughed—I never did stop coughing, ever—people turned around to see how close I was to them. During the sermon I had to go to the bathroom, and I could feel dozens of pairs of eyes following me. All the parishioners seemed to be whispering to each other, "Did you see where he went? What's he going to do now? Better watch him!" No one would use the bathroom after me. On the way out of church, people shooed their kids away from us. The next Sunday we were asked to sit either in the very first pew or the last one, so everyone would know where we were at all times.

It's hard to say your prayers when everyone else in church seems to be watching you out of the corner of their eye. But Grandma liked having us go to Sunday service with her and Grandpa; she thought I needed church. "They'll get used to you," she said. "Just give them a little time."

The next weird event was that before school was let out for the summer, my friend Chris Sadler got in big trouble over me. Some kid had come up to Chris in the hall and said, "Hey, have you heard this one? What kind of bread do fags eat? Ryan White bread." Chris hauled off and slugged the kid. The principal expelled Chris for three days. But his mother told Mom, "That kid deserved what he got. He knew Chris was Ryan's friend. I'm kind of proud of Chris."

I couldn't believe that these people at church and school considered themselves intelligent. Dr. Kleiman and a lot of other experts had said you couldn't catch AIDS from being around someone who has it. You can't get it from a doorknob or a toilet seat. If you could, how come Andrea and Mom had tested negative and were still well? And how could anyone who was paying attention decide that I had AIDS because I was gay? There were other hemophiliacs in Kokomo, and some of them must have gotten AIDS the same way I had. Didn't people in Kokomo have any common sense?

One day in late July Mom arrived home from work and told me that she'd talked to Western. "They don't want you back, Ryan," she said. "Even for a visit. They're afraid you'll infect the other kids."

"But that's impossible, Mom!" I shouted. It was bad enough that I had to start seventh grade all over again. Now I was being expelled for no reason.

"I know," Mom said. "But they're scared. Remember last fall when you had a nosebleed because your locker door flew open and bumped your nose? Mr. Colby, the principal, and the school nurse looked after you. They were so scared they both got tested for AIDS. They say they need guidelines from the State Board of Health for handling kids with AIDS in case something like your nosebleed happens again. They don't have any."

"They're dumber than a box of rocks," I yelled. "This is crazy! I can ride my bike, I can do my paper route, I can go to the movies. I can do everything! I *like* being at school. I don't want to stay home alone—I want to be with my friends, just like everybody else."

"I'm not sure I know how to fight this, Ryan," Mom said. "I'm afraid I couldn't handle it. I never know what to say in public."

"We *have* to fight, Mom," I said. "If we don't, we won't be allowed to go anywhere or do anything. What they want to do isn't right. We can't let it happen to anybody else."

A couple of days later, while Mom was still trying to figure out what to do next, something we never, ever expected happened. A local station, which had been working on a story about me as an example of an AIDS patient who was doing well, found out that Western didn't want me back. When Mom got home from work that night, there was a TV truck parked in front of the house, and a bunch of reporters at our front door.

So I ended up on the national news the next morning, the first kid with AIDS to protest publicly about being barred from school. It felt good to get the word out. "I understand why the school is scared," I told everyone out there, "but they should just listen to the facts." Some of the reporters wanted me to talk a whole lot longer, but I said no. Mom's insurance had replaced my computer that was stolen at Christmas and I was busy trying to get it to talk to Blair's computer across the street.

Since I wouldn't say much, the reporters interviewed Blair and Heath and Chris too. Chris told me that his family taped the TV report he was on. "I've watched it maybe two hundred times," he told me.

Not me. Mom tapes me every time I'm on TV, but I can't stand to watch myself. I put my hands over my eyes or my fingers in my ears. I think I look and sound like an even bigger jerk than I am, and it gives me the creeps. The one time I was happy about being on television was when we noticed afterward that I had been wearing a T-shirt that said, "Don't Die Wondering." I don't know about the TV station, but *we* thought that was hilarious.

At least life wasn't quite so boring. In fact it got hectic, very hectic, and stayed that way. The next day Indiana's health commissioner, Dr. Myers, called Western and said if I wasn't sick, I belonged in school. Then he asked Mom and me to come with him to a press conference where he was going to announce guidelines for schools that had students with AIDS. At a press conference you have to stand at a microphone in front of a big crowd of reporters and they get to ask you questions. Usually the press conference doesn't last very long. This is just as well. If there are TV cameras there, you really want the whole thing over with fast. The lights shining in your eyes can give you a bad headache inside of two minutes.

This time most of the reporters wanted to bother Dr. Myers. But a couple of them asked me, "How do you feel about not being allowed back in school?" Press people always want to know how you feel. "I'm pretty upset about it," I told them. "I'll miss my friends, mostly."

You'd think I had declared war. The new state guidelines didn't stop the Western school board from voting the very next day to keep me out. Then about fifty teachers came back from vacation early to take a special vote to refuse to teach me. One mother, Mitzi Johnson, whose older daughter was only in the first grade, not even in junior high with me, started going around with a petition, collecting signatures from parents who supported the school's stand. "We have to protect our children," she was saying.

Mom wasn't sure it would be good for me at all to go back to school. She was already worried I'd be exposed to some illness, and now everyone was being so unfriendly. I told her I didn't care; I could ignore them. I had my own friends. So she called Mr. Vaughan, and he filed another suit for us to get the school board to readmit me. Mom and I went to court with Mr. Vaughan, and listened while he told the judge that Western was discriminating against a handicapped child, meaning me. But the judge wouldn't discuss whether I was healthy enough to go to school. He said that he couldn't make a decision because we hadn't done things right. We had to present proof that the school was discriminating against me before he would allow us to come back to court.

"But, Your Honor," Mr. Vaughan shot back, "Western has already decided they don't want my client. A hearing will take up valuable time. Time is running out for this young man." I knew he didn't just mean that school was about to start. He was talking about the fact that I might die.

Rules are rules, the judge said. We had to present our case at a hearing on November 1 before we could sue. "This judge is a wimp," Mom said to Mr. Vaughan as we left court.

Meanwhile Mrs. Johnson and over a hundred other parents pledged to sue too, if Western backed down and let me come to school. One way or the other, the school board was going to be in court. I was turning into some kind of strange new First for Kokomo.

Heath thought the whole dumb thing was pretty ironic. "You're unAmerican, Ry-man," he said. "Suing to go to school. You don't know how lucky you are. You can stay home legally."

"You're not home all the time, the way I am," I replied. "I can't have fun unless I have something to do." I needed school. Besides, as my cousin Monica said, "If you don't go to school, you will grow up dumb."

By then it was the end of August, almost the first day of school. Western had promised to send me a tutor for free, but no one wanted the job. One woman told the school that she'd checked with her father, a doctor, and he'd said, "Stay away." Mom called Mr. Colby, who claimed he'd solved our problem. Western was going to give me something no other seventh grader had: a two-way phone hookup between our house and my classroom. (A lot of people thought I had a computer system and screen so I could see the class—but I didn't.)

"Western still doesn't get it," I complained. "I don't want to be treated worse than other kids, but I don't want to be treated better either. I just want to be the same."

But Mom said, "If the school is willing to do this, we have to try it."

On the first day of school, all the reporters came back to watch me try out my new speaker phone, which was set up in my bedroom, next to my computer. Some of them were surprised to see our Christmas tree was still in our living room. Mom had left it up all year, just in case I got sick again. Mrs. Samsel, my science teacher, had to test the phone hookup several times before we got it going right. Even so, sometimes I could hear her and my other teachers, sometimes I couldn't—especially if they moved around the classroom. I never caught what my classmates were saying at all. It was very frustrating. I couldn't see the work on the blackboard, and what was I going to do when the class had to watch a film?

When class broke for lunch, I slammed down the phone. A reporter from a local station asked me what I thought of the hookup.

"It stinks," I said. I wanted to say, "It sucks," but this was television.

Andrea's first day back was no fun either. First she found out that a kid I liked a lot, who had come to see me in the hospital, had started going around making fun of me. Then a couple of other kids came up to her at the lockers, smirking. "We know how your brother *really* got AIDS," they sneered at her. Andrea is strong and has a lot of muscles from skating. She doesn't talk much, but when she says something, she means it. "Want me to deck you?" she asked them. The kids slunked off— but first they tossed a few more insults over their shoulders. They even said Heath was a fag too, because he hung out with me.

"We can all survive this," Mom said. "Just keep your heads held high."

In the next few days I discovered one great big advantage to being on the speaker phone. If the teacher paused during class for kids to read or write something, I could usually finish ahead of them. Everyone else was stuck in class, but I was free to do as I pleased with the extra time. I made a few trips to the refrigerator, and then realized I could turn on the TV and watch cartoons until the teacher started again.

But once I made a fatal mistake and turned the volume up too high. Suddenly, through the speaker phone at school, everyone heard "Ya-ba-da-ba-DOO!" The entire seventh grade cracked up. Andrea or a friend always picked up my homework for me. That afternoon Andrea brought home along with it a stern note from Mr. Colby. "Ryan is not to watch television during classroom hours," he wrote Mom.

After my main distraction was forbidden, I took to crossing off on the calendar each day I had to spend hanging on the speaker phone.

One afternoon I went to see my girlfriend Kris. I thought we could do our homework together. When I rang her bell, she came out on the stoop, but she didn't seem happy to see me.

"What's wrong?" I asked her. She looked at the step, at her house, at the sky—anywhere but at me.

"My parents don't think we ought to hang out together anymore," she mumbled.

I didn't have to ask her why. There was no point talking about it. There was nothing I could change even if I wanted to, so I decided, Let's not waste time. I hadn't got any to waste.

"Okay," I said. I heaved myself up off Kris's steps and walked away.

"Ryan, I'm sorry," she called after me. Kris's parents were divorced, and she lived with her mother and stepfather. About a year later she wrote me that they had sent her away from Kokomo, to Detroit, to live with her father. I couldn't help wondering if I was the reason, but I didn't write back to ask.

In early September I got a change I liked even less. I had to go back to the hospital twice because I was coughing and vomiting all the time, I was running very high fevers, and I always felt cold and tired. When you have AIDS, any fever can be the start of big trouble. Everyone waits and watches you and worries about whether you'll get worse. Dr. Kleiman thought that I might be getting pneumocystis pneumonia again. I was so sick, my hair got very thin. Every morning Mom would find my pillow covered with straight brown hairs. She didn't tell me about this; she knew it would really upset me. So long as I had my looks, I could handle AIDS semi-okay.

While I was in the hospital, I had two seizures. I don't remember anything about them, but Mom does. It's very frightening to see someone having a seizure. Because I had been vomiting so much, my body wasn't absorbing sugar fast enough. My blood sugar dropped way too low, and when that happens—well, in the old days, people used to think a seizure meant you were being possessed by the devil. Mom was terrified.

The first seizure happened around 3:30 in the morning. I woke up, and felt like drinking something for once, so Mom had given me a Coke, which can taste good when you're feeling sick to your stomach. I could only drink about half of it. That's all I remember, but Mom says that the next thing I did was tell her, "Put this Coke in the refrigerator so it'll be cold tomorrow."

Mom was surprised, because I never will drink old Coke. "I'll get you a new one," she said, and went down the hall to the soda machine.

When she walked back into my room, I was sitting up in bed, stiff like a mummy. "I can't see you," I said. Mom was confused: Was I playing some game with her?

Then all of a sudden Mom saw my eyes bulge and roll up in my head until only the whites were visible. My entire body began to shake and jerk uncontrollably in every possible way. Some people howl like a dog or a wolf during a seizure. I made low, growling, guttural noises.

Mom was the most frightened for me that she's ever been. She ran out in the hospital corridor and started screaming for help. The nurses were having a party, so no one came right away.

I had another scary seizure about five o'clock in the morning. But after that my vomiting stopped, and I began to improve. I managed to keep up my schoolwork, and I even got good marks in almost every course. I also must have gotten around five thousand letters while I was in the hospital—from all over the country and the world, even Russia. I got more T-shirts than I would ever end up wearing. Someone who'd heard about my collecting comics even sent me a rare, old one worth sixty dollars.

"Sixty dollars?" Mom said. *"That* is crazy! Do you know what I could do with sixty dollars?"

Some people tried to help us with our bills. Alex Tiensivu, a really nice songwriter from New Jersey, wrote a song about me called "A Little Boy's Dream." He came to see me in the hospital and brought me a tape of the special song he had dedicated to me. He even wrote a sequel called "Quite a Sensation." He was going to try to sell copies to raise money for me, but I don't think he did very well. A high school in upstate New York put on a variety show called "Tryin' for Ryan." They raised a thousand dollars for us and sent us the check along with a videotape of their show. To keep up with my thank you's, Mom helped me write a form letter. "Thank you very much for writing," we started out. "It feels good to know other people are thinking of me . . ." I mentioned my dog and some of the things I liked, like pork chops and comics. Even though we had the letter printed up, with a picture of a dog on the bottom, I signed every one myself. My signature got fancier and fancier. Occasionally I made it diagonal, and the "R" grew to two inches.

Other people tried to help me get well. Because many gay men get AIDS, some of them had organized groups in New York and San Francisco that kept track of new drugs that were just being tested, and weren't available yet. Or they found out about treatments that seemed to work that many doctors weren't aware of. Some people from these groups started calling Mom to give her free advice and information, and suggest questions to ask Dr. Kleiman.

Dr. Kleiman seemed to be keeping me alive, though. When we could, we tried to pass the help we got along. I got a few calls from another teenage hemophiliac with AIDS. His name was Mark, he was thirteen like me, and he lived in Swansea, Massachusetts. Mom talked to his mom too, and told her about my gamma globulin therapy, which she hadn't heard about.

Mark and I compared our collections. He had some G. I. Joe figures, but mainly he was into baseball cards. He had every one that had come out since 1979. I was amazed that before Mark had been diagnosed with AIDS the summer before, he had been a star Little League player— a shortstop and a pitcher, no less. For a hemophiliac to play those two positions, where you might get hit by a ball at any time, is a big achievement.

"Man, you must really know how to play ball," I told him. What's more, Mark's school had let him come back in September without any fuss. They had even kept his last name a secret, so no one could bother him.

"Sounds like your school doesn't want to be another Western," I said. But all his life Mark had wanted to be famous. He wished he could go on TV and give interviews, the way I had.

"Are you nuts?" I exclaimed. "You don't

know how lucky you are. If you're famous, how do you know whether people like you for yourself? Besides, once they know your name, you never get left alone."

I told Mark about one photographer who kept calling and calling our house, saying, "You don't understand! This is for the cover of *Newsweek*!"

I told him, "I understand, and I don't care!" So he tried showing up at our house unannounced, knocking on our door, looking in our windows, trying to take me by surprise. I would run across the street to Blair's house and hide in the garage. His mom had to tell me when the coast was clear, and I could run home again.

Mark seemed even more impressed that this obnoxious photographer had been after me. Just goes to show you—the grass is always greener. I began to notice that the farther away from us people lived, the more they thought we were great and supported what we were doing. Closer to home, it was another story.

On one trip to the hospital Mom and I stopped off at a diner in Indianapolis. The owner recognized us. We asked for glasses of water. He wouldn't let us have any; he gave us cans of Coke instead. As soon as we had finished eating, he had our waitress throw away all our glasses and dishes. "Let's come back every week," I suggested. "Pretty soon they won't have *any* dishes left."

While I was in Riley again, Mom brought in

my favorite posters for my room. I had to have the one of Alyssa Milano! Mom and I watched TV together and kept up with the news. You know what people used to say in the sixties— "The whole world is watching." The whole world was sure watching Kokomo then. Some parents in Queens, New York, were keeping Kokomo company by marching up and down outside a school because their board had let a kid with AIDS in, but wouldn't say who it was. The protestors had some pretty silly signs, like "Enter at Your Own Risk" and "Good Grades, Not AIDS."

Mom said that when she thought about that bus trip back from Chicago, and how she'd worried that my blood might have gotten into a cut on her hand, she could feel for the parents in Queens and Kokomo.

Next we watched a meeting of parents in Kokomo, asking a doctor questions about me and AIDS. One father stood up and demanded, "Can you give me an absolute guarantee that my daughter is safe with this boy in school?"

Just like Dr. Kleiman, the doctor wasn't about to guarantee anything. Doctors and scientists never will. He did talk about two new studies, one of people looking after AIDS patients, the other of families living with AIDS patients. No one in these studies had been infected.

"There just aren't any one hundred percent guarantees in life," Mom said. "Think of all the children who die in car wrecks."

Just then someone familiar showed up on the

tube. Mr. Burkhaulter, my math teacher, was saying he didn't want me back in school.

"I can't believe it!" I exclaimed. "He was my favorite teacher!"

Next the reporter talked to the school nurse, who had always been really nice to me. She thought I should stay home too.

As for the students, the reporter only found one girl, God bless her, who wouldn't mind being in school with me.

"All these people are so two-faced," I complained. "I take that back: I mean three-faced. Four—if you count their butts."

Another thing I couldn't believe was all the rumors going around about me. One night when I was still home, a kid I didn't know too well called up and asked to speak to me. He said he needed the math homework.

But when I picked up the phone, he asked me, "Why do you spit on vegetables in the supermarket?"

"I never did!" I said. I was really shocked. How could anyone think I'd do anything so gross?

"Yes, you did," the kid insisted. "My cousin saw you, and my cousin doesn't lie. He says you sneeze on them too."

I hung up on him, and after that, Mom or Andrea screened all my calls.

But the next Friday night that Andrea and I were down at the roller rink, another kid, only about five or six years old, skated up to me and asked, "Ryan, is it true that you spit on people when you're mad?"

I said to him, "Who told you that?" And then he pointed to a group laughing in the corner. I just said, "No," and skated away.

Sometimes we did get the last word. Once Grandma took me shopping. We stopped at a big drugstore, and I went roaming through the aisles, looking for the comic-book stand. Some older teenage boys spotted me and started whispering and snickering to each other. I always figured the best strategy with mean kids was to act like they're invisible, pretend they weren't there. Grandma did things differently. Before the bunch could start after me, she marched right up to them—all taller than she was.

"That young boy doesn't have long to live," she told them loudly, so other people in the store could hear. "When he's dead, wouldn't you rather remember that you had said something nice to him?"

You could tell the boys knew they looked foolish. They shifted their weight from one foot to another, and then kind of melted away into the stationery section.

I DIDN'T get home from the hospital until the day after the hearings, so Mom and Mr. Vaughan went without me. Both sides had to present their case to the hearing officer, another lawyer. The school board had found a law that Indiana

had passed way back in 1949, long before anyone with AIDS was around Kokomo, that re-
quired any child with an infectious disease to
get a health certificate before he or she could
come to class. Since I didn't have this piece of
paper, the school board said they would be
breaking the law if they took me back.

Mr. Vaughan brought along three doctors:
my pediatrician in Kokomo, the Howard County
health official, and an infectious-disease expert
from the Indiana State Board of Health, Dr.
Myers' agency. All of them said I was no threat
to other kids. I belonged in school.

The hearing officer wasn't planning to make
up her mind for nearly a month.

"They're trying to drag this out as long as
possible," I said to Mom. "They're hoping I'll
die, and the problem will go away, right?"

Mom said nothing.

"They better not hold their breath," I said.

Since I was sick again, Andrea had taken
over my paper route. One afternoon she was
folding the papers she was going to deliver,
when Heath dropped by. He and Andrea started
fooling around with a tube of fake blood that
she had bought at her favorite magic store.

When Mom came home, she found an angry
neighbor who was on Andrea's route, shaking
a copy of the *Tribune* at her. At least he was
shaking it as well as he could: He had stuffed
it in a plastic bag, and he was holding a corner
of the bag between his thumb and forefinger.
He held the paper out for Mom to inspect.

"Who bled on my paper?" he cried. "What's going to happen to me now?" He threw the bag down and took off.

Mom picked it up and saw what certainly looked like blood on his paper. She went after Andrea.

Andrea looked at the paper sheepishly. "Heath and I were playing vampires," she explained.

"How could you?" Mom wailed. "When you know how everyone feels? This is all we need." The only thing I could do to calm down our neighbor was to give up my paper route, so I did.

The rumors were pretty hard on the rest of my family too. My aunt Deb is a nurse. She was working in a doctor's office with four other nurses. One wouldn't touch her or go anywhere near her, and she didn't want Deb around her own kids. Meanwhile my cousin Josh, Monica's second brother, was coming home from school every day in tears. Uncle Tommy and Aunt Deb couldn't figure out what was wrong. Finally Josh fessed up. A kid at school had said to him, "If Ryan White's your cousin, you're going to catch AIDS and die too."

But Mom caught it the worst—I don't know why. She had four loyal friends at work, but when she walked into the cafeteria, no one else said anything to her—they just stared, like she was from Mars. If she dropped into Scotty's or McDonald's, the same thing happened. People would get up and walk to the other side of the restaurant to get an unobstructed view. She certainly had no dates. When Mom ran out to pick up some milk at a convenience store, the clerk didn't want to hand her the change. She dropped the coins into Mom's palm from about a foot and a half in the air.

There's an institution in Kokomo called "Male Call." It's a radio call-in show that's on the air five days a week. The two hosts, Dick and Charlie, know most everyone in town. Their friends call them up, and they let them rattle on and on over the airwaves. At Delco everyone on the assembly line listens to Dick and Charlie over the public address system. Lately they'd been getting a lot of calls about me and Mom.

One woman who called in must have been in the convenience store when Mom came by for milk. "She bought groceries!" the woman was saying, over and over. From the tone in her voice, you'd think Mom had held up the cash register. "I thought we collected money so Jeanne White could pay doctors!" Mom doesn't smoke or drink; she hadn't blown any contributions on six-packs. How dare Mom spend money on food!

Other callers repeated all the rumors, and came up with some new ones. For instance, they had unusual theories about how I got AIDS. Mom hadn't fed me properly. She didn't clean. She was a trashy housekeeper. What's more, she was lying: She knew perfectly well

AIDS was infectious. Hadn't she sent her own daughter away last summer?

Mom is even neater than I am—and that's saying a lot. And for as long as I can remember, Andrea has gone to what I call "skaters' camp" in the summer. She lives with her coach or another pro for several weeks, and practices all day long. The autumn after she placed in the nationals, she went to the Olympics training camp in Colorado.

One day I was home from the hospital with nothing better to do, and I made the mistake of tuning in to Dick and Charlie. Some of the calls could be good for laughs. But then they started in on how Mom was taking her sick son to the cleaners, trotting me out on television so she could get money and publicity. "She obviously doesn't care about her boy," someone said. Enough was enough—I was furious. I reached for the phone.

"You got no right to talk about my mother!" I screamed at whoever was on the other end. "She's a great person, and she *does* care about me!" Then I hung up fast. I didn't want to talk to those guys; I just wanted Mom to hear me at work. She didn't, but she was glad to hear about it.

Dick and Charlie really got to Grandma too. She hated knowing that people in Kokomo, where she'd lived all her life, were bad-mouthing us. As far as she was concerned, Mom was the best mother in the world—Grandma was right about this, of course—and she was furious that anyone would criticize her.

"Just don't listen to Dick and Charlie, Mom," my mother told her. "Then you won't know what people are saying. You won't even know they're talking about us." Mom never called the radio show because she had decided that she didn't want to say anything she might regret. It didn't work to say anything thoughtful or logical to Dick and Charlie anyway.

But Grandma wanted to beat them up. One day she heard the mayor of Kokomo call Dick and Charlie, and claim that the police had never caught our Christmas burglar because Mom hadn't reported the robbery. Grandma got right on the line.

"This is Gloria Hale, Jeanne White's mother," she told the mayor and anyone else who was listening. "I want you to know I discovered the theft. I called the police and reported the theft myself."

One day the paper ran a letter that criticized Mom *and* the other side. A woman in Indianapolis thought that "some parents, including Ryan's mother, have climbed aboard a bandwagon that just keeps rolling them along into the limelight." Along with the letter, the paper ran a photo of me on a bad day. The writer thought I looked "so alone and confused most of the time." Thanks a lot. It didn't seem to occur to the people who criticized Mom that she was only doing this because it was what *I* wanted.

You'd think they'd agree with me that that made her an even better mom.

People at work wanted to make sure Mom didn't miss any letters in the paper about her. She found many, including this one helpfully stapled to her time card, with the "bandwagon" part underlined and an anonymous note scribbled on it: "Get a look at this!! In the news again!"

Grandma decided it was time to take on Kokomo in writing too. She sent off her own letter to the editor: "Jeanne White is a compassionate and loving mother. The medical experts have told her that Ryan is not a threat to other children or adults. If she had the slightest doubt that Ryan could transmit this disease to other children, she would not be trying to get him back in school. I'm proud of my daughter. She has a daughter living in the same house that she loves just as much as you love your child. Do you think if Andrea could get AIDS from Ryan, Jeanne would let Andrea live there? No way. Andrea would be living with us."

Mom was getting some anonymous hate mail at home, signed "An interested citizen" or whatever, all with Kokomo postmarks. Some people wrote us all the time—we could tell by their handwriting. Mom didn't want to open any of these letters; they were starting to upset her. She wanted to throw them away as soon as they arrived. But I always opened them and read them aloud for laughs.

"Listen to how silly these people are," I

would tell her. One of these letters opened with, "Mrs. White, I can't believe you are such a puke! We all in Kokomo are so sick of seeing your face in the *Tribune* and on TV!" It cracked us both up. For a month or so after that, every time I thought Mom sounded down, I'd say, "Hi puke!"—and we'd both start laughing again.

Mom got particularly confused by letters from ministers. Some of the healers said that the reason I wasn't cured was that we weren't good Christians. If we joined *their* religion, I wouldn't have AIDS. The Reverend Jerry Falwell, who's on the radio a lot, said that AIDS was homosexuals' punishment for their sins. Mom heard he'd said she was using me to give AIDS a good name.

"A minister saying these things!" Mom said. "It doesn't sound very Christian. God wouldn't give anyone AIDS, especially a child."

She started to cry. "Ryan, forgive me, honey. All this trouble we're in is my fault. I gave you hemophilia."

"Mom, please don't," I said. "It's not your fault."

"I gave you AIDS," she went on.

"You gave me *life*," I said, hugging her.

I had to write a theme for English class, so I tried to cheer Mom up by writing about her. "My mother is the greatest person in the world," I began. "We've been through a lot together, and she has stuck behind me all the way." I mentioned how much Mom loves to decorate the house for holidays, and how she doesn't like messiness. "She stayed home from work when I was in the hospital for so long. When I got out, she helped me gain my weight back. That's my mother," I ended up, "and I love her."

I got an A on my theme, and even more to the point, Mom was very happy.

THE NEXT DAY I was watching TV when Heath came running into the house.

"Ryan, Barney's been hit!" he shouted.

My heart did a flip-flop in my chest. Barney had gotten out of the house and run into the middle of our busy street. A policeman, of all people, had hit him—and then driven away.

"Barney tried to drag himself out of the traffic," Heath panted. I wished so badly I could have helped him. Mom, Andrea, and I rushed Barney to the vet, who told us he would be okay—he was probably in shock.

The next day the vet called. Barney had died during the night, he said. But I was suspicious. People in Kokomo were acting so crazy, this could be a trick. And I guess I was like Mom who wanted all my AIDS tests done over—I just couldn't believe that news this bad could be true.

"I want to go to the vet's and see for myself," I told Mom.

"Let's let the vet take care of Barney," Mom suggested. "Seeing him will be so hard on us."

"I *have* to see Barney," I insisted. Andrea said

she'd go into the vet's with me. Mom could stay in the car.

When Andrea and I found Barney, he was sealed in a plastic bag. I patted his head through its wrapping.

" 'Bye, Barney," I said. "I'll see you in heaven." As we drove home, we all cried.

Mom called Grandma. "Mom," she said, "what else can happen?"

Just then in the bottom of the ninth, with our team trailing way, way behind, we hit a home run with the bases loaded. The hearing officer ruled that Western couldn't use the law to bar me from class. The school was planning to appeal, but for now we were ahead.

Mom called Grandma back. "Oh shoot," she said, "it's kind of nice to have something go right for a change."

I was almost fourteen, and I had the birthday present I wanted most—though I definitely did want another dog too. I planned on being a real Kokomo First: the first kid with AIDS to speak out, fight back—and win.

4

How I Got Back in School— But Had to Leave Town

AFTER BARNEY died, I waited about a week. Mom hadn't said anything about another dog. Maybe she thought I felt there was no substitute for Barney. Probably there wasn't, but I wanted a companion anyway. So I started lobbying her again: "Mom, can we get a new dog? How soon?"

Now, not everyone in Kokomo hates us. Every week or so, some family in town would send us a card or a letter saying, "Hang in there." After the story about poor Barney spread around, several neighbors offered us puppies. But I decided I wanted a dog that would have been put to sleep if we hadn't taken him.

So Mom drove Andrea and me down to the pound, and I picked out a full-grown dog who looked like Barney—same soulful brown eyes, same questionable pedigree. But when it came to naming him, I was stuck. This dog had a goofy personality—he wasn't as sharp and intelligent as Barney. When anyone except me called Barney, he wouldn't budge. My new dog thought he belonged to the whole family. He was a reliable watchdog with impressive muscles. I thought of calling him Wally, but I wasn't sold. One of the TV newsmen who kept coming around had an idea. "Your dog needs a last name," he told me. "Why don't you call him Wally Waldondo?"

I looked at Wally and repeated the name a few times, sort of rolling the sound around. Wally looked at me expectantly and started wagging his tail. "Okay," I told him, "this is who you are now." I put on his leash, took him out on the sidewalk, and started training him to pull me along behind him on my skateboard. That Christmas, Mom gave Andrea a beautiful fluffy black-and-white cat. I came up with her name, Chi Chi, after my favorite Mexican restaurant. Later on, a friend of Mom's gave me a funny-looking little Pekinese named Gizmo— Gizzy for short. So when you came over to our house, animals followed you everywhere. And if a pet wasn't trailing you, a reporter was.

By that time, we had been in the news so much that reporters were practically part of the family. They came from all over the place, even Japan. I felt like I was growing up with some of them. They followed us into the bathroom to see if we were telling the truth when we said we shared toothpaste and glasses. They stood by the kitchen sink and asked Mom if she was doing dishes by hand so she could use bleach on mine.

"The dishwasher has been on the fritz forever," Mom explained. "Tell the whole world I wash all my dishes the same way everybody else does."

Grandpa had found out that something like seventy percent of all the hemophiliacs in America had gotten infected by their Factor. We knew that there were at least a dozen other hemophiliacs in Howard County, and we found out that I was the second one to be diagnosed with AIDS. But no one else was speaking up about going to school. The others just faded away like ghosts. Maybe they moved out of town. I didn't like the lonely feeling I got when I thought about them.

We talked to some reporters more often than we visited with our friends and relatives. One of these reporters was Chris MacNeil, who wrote about us all the time for the *Kokomo Tribune*. Seemed like he was always perched on a chair in our kitchen. Chris got nearly as many nasty letters and phone calls as we did—so many that he ended up moving away and getting out of journalism. One television reporter, Carrie Jackson Van Dyke, was like Dr. Kleiman—when we met first met her, she had no children, but while she was covering our school fight, she had a daughter she named Lindsay. I used to bug Carrie to bring me pictures of her new baby. Looking at them was the next best thing to actually holding Lindsay.

Andrea hated reporters calling up and coming around. Usually she disappeared into her room until the interviewer had gone. I let Mom do the talking to the press most of the time. They took up hours and hours, and I had a life to live. I didn't have time for everybody. But I liked Carrie. One day I said to her, "I just can't believe the way complete strangers like you treat me so nicely. People in Kokomo, people I've known all my life, treat me like dirt." It was true: Sometimes we felt like reporters were the only company we had. They helped us make new friends too. Like the time Italian TV called. They had read about us in their newspapers and they wanted to fly all three of us to Rome after Christmas to be on a very popular interview and call-in show called *Italia Sera*.

Normally I can't stand long trips in airplanes. My ears hurt, and I get nauseous. Plus I hate being closed up in a small space for hours and hours—I guess it comes from doing so much time in hospital rooms. Besides, nine times out of ten, there's some delay, and you don't get home when you thought you would. I *really* hate that.

But Mom told me, "*I'm* never going to take you to Rome, working at Delco. Let's go."

I remembered that Italy has race cars that you could say were okay. So we flew to Rome for five days. We felt timid because we'd never been to Europe, and there had been a lot of terrorist attacks recently. When we landed, the airport was full of soldiers with machine guns, on the lookout for terrorists and hijackers. For a minute we thought we were going to be attacked!

While we were being interviewed on the show, it didn't matter that none of us could speak Italian. We all had special earphones so we could hear what callers were saying translated into English. Then when I spoke into my mike, what I said was translated back into Italian. Everyone who called in said, "Stay the course" in Italian. Someone even offered to lend us a house in Switzerland. At the end of the show, the hostess kissed me on the air.

Off the set we still got treated like stars. Some people from CNN and NBC took us sightseeing. Andrea collected postcards, stamps, and Italian money for a scrapbook on Italy that she was putting together for school. She wrote in it that we saw "a lot of old buildings, famous fountains, beautiful scenes"—and we did. There seemed to be statues everywhere, even in the middle of the street. I snapped a load of pigeons, some pretty great cars, and some terrible drivers. Italians park anywhere they feel like, even on the sidewalk!

The rest of the time, no one paid any attention to us, except to be friendly. We walked and walked, trying to ask directions in sign language. Once we stopped in a pizzeria, and some American servicemen recognized me and came over to say hello. And an Italian lady spotted us on the sidewalk and hugged us, crying, *"Italia Sera! Italia Sera!"* She knew us from the program. No one in Rome seemed to be afraid of us.

"In Kokomo we've lost practically all our friends, and we get funny looks everywhere we go," Mom sighed. "Rome is so different." We'd almost forgotten what it was like to stroll around a place like anybody else.

Our two trips to New York were even better. The first time, we were on the CBS *Morning News.* Andrea even got to bring a skating friend along. The second time was to be on *The Today Show.* New York! I'd wanted to go there ever since I was little and saw *Miracle on 34th Street* for the first time. It was still my favorite Christmas movie. I watched it every year. On the other hand the flight to New York was pretty long.

"I'll go if I can get to Macy's," I told Mom. Macy's is a huge department store in New York on West 34th Street; it's where most of the movie takes place. "And see if we can go to that comic-book store I heard about." My collection was up to 400 comics, but I was looking for the issue of Batman where Robin dies. That's the one every collector wants.

Mom called *The Today Show* back. "The comic-book store is in a basement in a bad neighborhood," she told me. "But they'll drive us there in a limo and the driver will go in with you."

"Tell them we're on our way," I said.

Mom had to call Mr. Vaughan to let him

know we were going away. "Ryan is going to be on *The Today Show*?" Mr. Vaughan said. "Ryan is going to meet Jane Pauley?"—She's a big deal around here because she grew up in Indianapolis—"And all Ryan's talking about is comics?" For once, Mr. Vaughan couldn't think of anything more to say.

While we were in New York, we went to a hospital so I could have some blood tests to see if I might be eligible for an experimental drug. We sat in the clinic waiting room, and I opened a comic to pass the time.

A man who had been sitting on the opposite side of the waiting room got up, walked over to me and said, "Aren't you Ryan White?"

I looked up and said, "Yeah." I was a little startled. The man was very thin. He must have been at the clinic for the same reason I was.

The thin man said, "I'm really happy to meet you. I'm gay. My whole community is torn up over this disease. And here *you* are, reading a comic book. I just think that's so great."

I never thought much about gay people until I got AIDS. Now I had a lot of respect for them. So many of them were fighting AIDS, but they'd given *me* tons of support—not to mention the latest medical information. In fact, I was at the clinic because we'd heard about it from a gay group.

After he walked away I turned to Mom and said, "I really know how he and his friends must feel. We're fighting the same disease." I figured I had to keep my priorities straight. Being famous can get in your way.

The trouble with being on television is that wherever you go, everyone knows what you look like, and you can't get away with anything. Like the day I met Heath after school, and he gave me a cigarette.

When I got home, Mom told me right away, "You're grounded. You can't go roller skating on Friday night."

"What?" I blurted. "How come?"

"You know how come," Mom said. "I can't believe what you did. I must have gotten four phone calls from people who saw you. Smoking's bad enough, Ryan, with your lungs the way they are—but you had to go do it in front of Mitzi Johnson's house."

"How'd anyone know it was me?" I demanded.

Mom rolled her eyes and threw her hands up in the air like she'd really had it. *"Ryan,"* she said. "You walk outside, and the whole neighborhood is looking out their window to see what you do, where you go, who you're with."

"Every time I see Mitzi Johnson on TV, *she's* smoking," I retorted. "I think I'll go ask her if she wants a puff on mine." But I couldn't; I was grounded. I guess I had to be grateful no one had spotted Heath and me the night we mooned cars and went skinny-dipping in his family's pool.

Still, sometimes it was neat to be recognized. When Mom and I walked off the set when we were on *The Today Show*, there was Tom Cruise in the green room. That's where you wait for your turn to go on the air. Tom Cruise was going on after us.

He stood to shake my hand as soon as I came around the corner. I looked at him. I couldn't believe he was real. I'm really very shy, so I just stared. Very sophisticated.

Lucky for me, he spoke first. "I know you," he said. "You're Ryan White."

"I know *you*," I countered. "You're Tom Cruise."

"Yeah," Tom Cruise said loudly, "but you're *Ryan White*."

Then all three of us cracked up. It was funny and nice at the same time—even better than the surf shirts Mom bought me at Macy's or the comic-book store, which did have the Batman I was hunting for. In New York you can find everything you've been wanting.

But it wasn't the same as going to school with my friends. The yearbook said it all: My photo was set off on a page by itself. "Ryan White, Homebound Instruction." I missed racing for the bus with the other kids. I was bummed when Mrs. Samsel dissected a grasshopper I couldn't see. It was good to meet up with Heath in the afternoons, but I missed eating lunch every day with him. January dragged by.

Western had appealed to the State Department of Education to ask them to ignore the hearing officer and keep me out of school. But the wind didn't seem to be blowing their way.

Mom and I had a good laugh when we read in the paper that the Western school board was having trouble finding a doctor who would side with them. Just about the only one who was willing to speak for them was personal doctor to Lyndon LaRouche, a right-winger who was a big fan of conspiracy theories and once fingered Queen Elizabeth II as a drug kingpin. I don't see how a queen can be a kingpin, but maybe I lack imagination.

Mr. Colby could see the handwriting on the wall. He and the school nurse talked to Dr. Kleiman, and then started prepping everybody at Western. Kids in junior high got a class on AIDS, and first aid kits for their classrooms. Plus every night the whole school was going to be disinfected. The rate they were going, I'd be surprised if anybody caught so much as a cold the whole school year.

Mom thought Western wouldn't be so petrified if we agreed that we'd go along with some extra precautions that Mr. Colby had thought up. They went farther than the state guidelines.

"They're ridiculous," I complained. "I'm not going to infect anyone anyway."

"I think we should make the effort," Mom said. "If they're going to let you go back, let's meet them halfway."

So I agreed to skip gym. I really wasn't supposed to go at all, because of my hemophilia, but I never admitted that. I said that in the cafeteria I'd use paper plates and trays and plastic spoons and forks that could be thrown out when I was done. Mr. Colby thought I should use a separate water fountain, and a private toilet, so I went along with that too.

One of Mitzi Johnson's favorite fears was that I'd chew on a pencil—and then some kid would chew on it after me. Just another way you can't catch AIDS. So I told Mom, "I dare Western to think up anything else."

In early February the state threw out Western's appeal and said I could go back to school. But first, because of that old law, I had to get a medical certificate from Dr. Adler, the county health officer, to prove that I was healthy enough, physically and emotionally, to go to school.

When I went to see Dr. Adler, he threw in some free advice as well. "You'll be watched all the time," he told me. "You'll have to behave yourself." So much for smoking, I thought.

I got the okay from Dr. Adler the day before Valentine's Day, but the school wanted me to hold off for a week. Mr. Colby thought I should start on a Friday and come for just half a day. That way, everyone would have the weekend to adjust. I spent the week debating what to wear on my first day back, and bouncing off the four walls of my room. Finally it was Friday, February 21, the day I was due at school.

We knew there'd be a media mob, so Andrea was going to take the school bus, like it was just another day. Steve said he'd drive me. On Friday morning I woke up at six o'clock. It had snowed in the night, so I began to worry that school would be closed. Not enough snow, said the radio.

So when Steve arrived, we gingerly picked our way out to his car. Steve had on a leather jacket and looked like my bodyguard. Those reporters were waiting. Everywhere I turned, there was a camera or a microphone in my way. Whenever that happens, I'm always tempted to make a face or an impolite noise. But I stayed cool.

Someone was asking me, "How does it feel, Ryan?"

There you go again! Actually, I felt wonderful. "I'm real happy—real happy I'm going back," I said.

As we started out for Western, a bus driver yelled out his window, "Good morning, Ryan!" It did seem like a pretty good day. But my heart sank as Steve pulled up to Western. There must have been a hundred reporters out front. Mr. Colby had said he would be prepared for us at the front door but I had Steve whip the car around to the side entrance so that I could sneak inside. Right away the press people realized they'd been duped, and came stampeding around the building, cameras and all. I could hear kids snickering as reporters racing each other for an exclusive started slipping and sliding around in the snow. Well, if they couldn't see me, they could grab a few shots of the demonstrators. Some kids were marching up and down outside with big picket signs that said, "Students Against AIDS."

Since we hadn't moved back to Kokomo all that long ago, I was pretty much the new face in school. A lot of kids only knew me from TV. I tried hard to fit right in and act no different from everyone else. If a kid came up to me and said, "I saw you on the news last night," I answered, "Really?"—like it was nothing to get worked up about. Some kids stared at me. Still, no one was unfriendly to my face.

But Andrea overheard a kid say that I was a murderer, because now that I was back, other students were going to die. With all the reporters around, I barely noticed that almost half the school was missing. Their parents had kept them out. I guess they agreed with the kid who called me a killer. It turned out that all the extra precautions Mom and I had said I'd take at school had backfired. Some parents were asking, "Why would he have to do that if he's not contagious?"

Before I knew it, I was out of school too. Only my first day, and already I had to go to the principal's office. I got pulled out of class and told to see Mr. Colby. He said I had to leave Western right away and go back to court. Mitzi Johnson and some other parents who called themselves the Concerned Citizens and Parents of Children Attending Western School Corporation were carrying out their threat— they were suing my family, Dr. Adler, and the school for taking me back, in the names of three students I barely knew, two boys and a girl.

The Concerned Citizens even tried to have

our county's welfare director declare Mom an unfit mother, take me away from her, and make me a ward of the court. Then, they figured, the court would keep me out of school. They said that by letting me go to school, Mom was allowing me to kill other kids—and even to be killed myself if I picked up some illness from them! But the welfare director squelched the parents' plan. He said they had no evidence Mom was unfit.

So Mom came and got me, and we found ourselves sitting with Mr. Vaughan in front of another judge. The courtroom was packed with Concerned Citizens. I wondered if I was having a recurring nightmare. The parents claimed all over again that they were worried about their children's safety. The doctors on our side answered all over again that I was no threat. But the judge decided I had to stay home. "I hereby authorize a restraining order," he said.

I was too stunned to say anything. For a few seconds so was everyone else. Then all the Western parents started clapping and cheering, like they'd hit the ball right out of the stadium.

I felt like *I* was being hit. I struggled not to cry. I turned to Mom, who was already weeping. "They've ruined *everything*," I managed to whisper.

We hustled out the back door of the courthouse, and rushed home. I went straight to my room and slammed the door. If I was going to cry, I wanted to do it in private. Am I ever going to win at anything? I thought. Tom

Cruise and regular people in New York and Rome could look me in the eye and not be afraid, but my whole town seemed to think AIDS was God's pest control. I put on my favorite Springsteen album.

> *Son take a good look around*
> *This is your hometown*
> *This is your hometown*

Bruce wasn't a big help. I switched over to Huey Lewis. Later that night, Kris, my old girlfriend, called. Even though her parents didn't want her near me, she could still hang around with Andrea.

"Hey, Ryan," she said. "Sorry I missed your first day back."

"Yeah, what happened?" I muttered. "I wondered where you were."

There was a pause. "My parents made me stay home," Kris said sheepishly.

I threw the phone against the wall.

Rumors about me even appeared in the paper. The *Kokomo Tribune* ran editorials supporting me, but the other side made up for them by writing letters to the editor. Someone who signed off as "A 1983 graduate of Western High School"—in other words, a teenager like me!—wrote in, "Would you want your little brother, sister, cousins, or friends' siblings to be with a young man who constantly threatens to bite, scratch, or spit on children if things aren't done 'his way'? How about eating food from a local store where his family was asked to leave because he was spitting on the fresh produce? Or using a restroom where he urinated on the walls?''

I guess the writer was talking about my private toilet at Western. The day that letter was published, Mom called Mr. Colby at Western to make sure he hadn't fallen for it.

"Mrs. White," he assured her, "I know Ryan has always behaved well. I've never had any complaints about him." So let me come back to school!

Then came Easter Sunday. Normally, at our church, the whole congregation says "Happy Easter!" to each other this way: Our minister steps forward to the front pew, shakes a few parishioners' hands, and says "Peace be with you." Then those people turn to their neighbors and shake *their* hands, and so on, all the way to the back of the church, where we were sitting.

The family in the pew in front of me turned around. I held my hand out—to empty air. Other people's hands were moving every which way, in all directions away from me. No one in the whole church wanted to shake my hand and wish me peace on Easter.

My family and I filed out of church in silence. "Maybe I should run after a few people and grab their hands, just to shake them up," I said to Mom. You could tell nothing was going to make Grandma feel better. She looked devastated, like she was going to burst into tears any minute. Grandpa said grimly, "I'm never going back." And he didn't.

It wasn't over yet. As Mom, Andrea, and I turned out of the church parking lot, our transmission died on us in the middle of the traffic lane. Grandpa and Grandma had already gone, so Mom tried to flag down some other cars leaving church. But no one would stop. A half hour or so went by, and then finally a man in a truck pulled away from the auto-parts store across the street, nosed up behind us, and pushed our car over to the side of the road.

Our rescuer climbed out of his truck and asked Mom, "Need a lift home?"

Mom took a deep breath and said, "First I better tell you who we are," and she did.

The truck driver shrugged. "Well, it doesn't matter," he said. He drove us home. A couple of months later he stopped by and invited me hang gliding.

GRANDMA COULDN'T get over the way I had been shunned at church. She went back and forth between wanting to kill half of Kokomo, and crying nonstop.

Mom got a call from Aunt Janet down in Birmingham.

"Look, Jeanne, I'm really afraid for Mom, Janet said. "I'm scared she's going to have a nervous breakdown."

"I know," Mom said. "She worries about Ryan, and she worries about me too. She thinks she has to change everybody's minds all by herself."

"Please, Jeanne," Janet said, "please stop fighting. Give up your case."

"I can't," Mom said.

"Stop for Mom's sake," Janet said. "This is so hard on the family. Let Ryan go to school at home."

"He's my son," Mom said. "It's his life. I have to fight for him. It's what he wants."

Then the next Sunday something truly awful happened. We still went to church, because it helped us to pray as a family. In church I thought about how much hope I had for the future. We're all going to die of something, and I was so much healthier than some AIDS patients I'd met in the hospital. I felt that God had a reason for that. I had a purpose in life, to keep up my fight.

When we got home, there was a bullet hole in our front window.

Andrea had been having nightmares ever since all our Christmas presents had been stolen while I was in the hospital. "Mom," she said, "I don't want to live here anymore. What if we'd been home?"

"It only happened because we weren't home," Mom said. "They're trying to scare us. We won't let them."

But Mom had problems of her own. Some joker let all the air out of her back tires in the Delco parking lot. Kids biked or drove by our house practically every day and threw beer cans, whiskey bottles, and garbage on our lawn, or egged our windows or our car. They'd yell "Bitch! Bitch!" or "Ryan White's a fag!" Blair Brittain told me his family could hear them in their living room, across the street. Once Mom, Andrea, and I were walking back to the car at a mall. A kid on a bike whizzed right between us, laughing and shouting, "Ryan White's a faggot!"

Mom was telling Andrea and me all the time to keep going, to never feel sorry for ourselves, to remember that we were doing something important—helping people by educating them. But so many people were against her, and there was only Andrea, Steve, and me to help her keep her own spirits up. She wasn't bitter, but she was exhausted.

I tried to make Mom laugh. "Mitzi Johnson doesn't care what you think of her," I said. "Why should you care what she thinks about you?"

Mom winced.

On Monday we went to see Mr. Vaughan about what to do next. Mr. Vaughan had been working on a new strategy. He had gone back to court to force the Concerned Citizens to post a $12,000 bond to show good faith. They had been setting out glass jars at all their meetings to collect money for their legal fees. So we thought that $12,000 would really set them back. But in three nights they raised $19,000! They held an auction in the school gym—kind of a giant yard-sale, with just about everyone in town donating something valuable. TVs, furniture, china ornaments, auto parts, an extra-strong session at a tanning parlor—you name it. The auctioneer was none other than Dick, of Dick and Charlie on "Male Call." He promised to hold an auction for us as well, if we'd just give up.

Mr. Vaughan wasn't about to quit—just the opposite, in fact. Our next move, he said, was to take our fight to state court. But Mom was flat broke. If she stayed home because I was sick or because we had to be in court, she didn't get paid.

She said, "I'm worn down. I want to stop. All the pressure on our family—I just can't take it anymore."

Mr. Vaughan looked at me. "How about you, Ryan?" he asked. "Do you want to quit?"

"No!" I said impatiently. "We're right. They're wrong. We can win."

Mr. Vaughan turned back to Mom. "Well, Jeanne," he said, *"Ryan's my client now."*

I smiled. I liked Mr. Vaughan. The worse things were, the more fired up he got. I was thinking about becoming a lawyer myself. Besides Mr. Vaughan, I admired the lawyer in *Miracle on 34th Street* who says law is the most fun when you're helping people who are being pushed around. Taking on the big guys, just like we were doing now. And Grandma was always telling me I was good at arguing—though I think sometimes she didn't mean it as a compliment.

Mr. Vaughan had decided that because of all the publicity, we'd never get a fair hearing in Kokomo. So he got our next date in court switched to another town, Frankfort, west of Kokomo in the next county. But we had to wait some more—until early April. I was back home and bored again. Sometimes I would write very formal notes to Mom on my computer: Dear Mom, I love you very much. Give me a call from work later. I LOVE YOU, Ryan White, your son." I'd doodle little pictures, including one of myself saying, "Why me?"

One day a reporter stopped by the house to talk to me. He mentioned that most AIDS patients had gotten their disease from sex or drug use. I'm not a typical AIDS patient. The reporter asked me, "How do you think people around here would have reacted if you'd been five years older and homosexual?"

I certainly knew the answer to that one. I held up my thumb and forefinger in the shape of a gun and fired into the air.

"Pow," I said.

I had plenty of time back then to think about why people were being mean. Of course it was because they were scared, but why were they so scared? Maybe it was because I *wasn't* that different from everyone else. I wasn't gay; I wasn't into drugs; I was just another kid from Kokomo. I've been a twig all my life—if you ruffled up my hair, a bird would probably nest in it. But other than that, I didn't even look sick. Maybe that made me even more of a goblin to some people.

You aren't supposed to stand out in Kokomo. If you're sick, you're supposed to stay home quietly and be nursed. But I wouldn't play that game. When I started speaking up, people from out of state sided with me, and some of them wrote the newspaper to say so. So people in Kokomo got even more upset with me. They didn't want outsiders telling them what to do.

Sometimes it was actually harder when people tried to be nice about my having AIDS. Like now and again someone would say, "I don't know how you do it. *I* couldn't do it." I wondered if they were *really* saying, "Thank God I don't have to." Well, if you have no choice, you will. That's why I tried not to think about it. Sometimes I'd forget I had it—except that people kept reminding me. All I wanted to do was go to school, because I didn't know what was going to happen to me with AIDS.

April 10, our court date, finally rolled around and we drove out to the courthouse in Frankfort. The change of scene did us good. Truck drivers drove by honking and shouting, "Good luck, Ryan!" A friend of Mom's from the plant had ordered a bunch of buttons that read "Friend of Ryan White," and quite a few people besides my family were wearing them.

This judge got right to the point. In about half a minute, he overturned the lower court's decision. "This restraining order is dissolved," he announced. Effective immediately I could go back to school.

I jumped up and hugged Mom. It was the Concerned Citizens' turn to cry. We drove straight to Western, and an hour later, I was back in class again.

Mr. Vaughan said we had set a precedent for kids with AIDS. We'd told them, "Yes, you can lead a normal life."

A few parents wouldn't give in. Twenty-two of them came right over to Western and yanked their kids out of junior high. One girl got taken out because she was supposed to have been my science lab partner. A couple of weeks later the parents opened their own school, the Russiaville Home Study School. For the last six weeks of school, their kids went to class in an old American Legion hall. I'd seen TV documentaries about white parents setting up separate schools when public schools in the South were being integrated. Kokomo had thought up another First—a new kind of segregation school!

But the way it turned out, being back at school was almost as lonely as being home. Heath was still my buddy, but he wasn't in my grade. Other kids backed up against their lockers when they saw me coming, or they threw themselves against the hallway walls, shouting, "Watch out! Watch out! There he is!" Maybe some were putting me on. I think most of them were acting like that just to get to me, to make me mad mainly. I worked hard at pretending I didn't see the kids who were making fun of me.

But it hurt that no one wanted to get close to me. "It's okay for him to come to school, just as long as I don't sit by him," one boy said. Some kids were so afraid they wouldn't walk in the same hall with me. I wasn't even five feet and I weighed seventy-six pounds—quite chunky for me actually. But you'd think I was some big bruiser, the way kids ran when they saw me coming. When we had to team up in class, no one wanted to be my partner. One girl complained, "If people with measles and chicken pox can't come to school, why should Ryan?" I called Mom every day at lunchtime, just to have someone to talk to.

A few days after I went back to school though, Mom, Andrea, and I had a nice break. We got another chance to go to New York, this time for five whole days. A big AIDS organization, the American Foundation for AIDS Research, known as AmFAR, was having a benefit party in New York with a bunch of celebrities. One was Elizabeth Taylor, who often helps AmFAR. AmFAR wanted me to pose in an ad for them with a whole crowd of stars, including Elizabeth Taylor and Marlo Thomas. It was going to be the first time I'd ever been around a lot of celebrities. Mom had to rent me a tuxedo. Of course, I wanted to wear it with my high-tops but Mom said, "No way."

I told her, "Elton would." I liked Elton John—he wasn't afraid to be different.

Later, when we got to New York one of the first things we did was go on *Good Morning America* to talk about the AmFAR party. David Hartman asked me, "Which celebrity do you want to meet most tonight?"

I said, "Elton John, definitely." I hoped Elizabeth Taylor wouldn't be too upset with me.

One of the actors I posed with in the AmFAR ad was in the cast of *Cats*, the musical. Next time we came to New York, he said, we could see *Cats* and visit him backstage. I also went to see the headquarters where Marvel Comics are put together. I saw how all the drawings get made into one comic.

The AmFAR people made their party a lot of fun for Andrea and me. They made up special T-shirts for us to wear. Mine was black with a white and silver outline of the New York skyline, and it said, "Watch Out New York!" And they gave us sunglasses and moussed my bangs so I looked like I had a buzz cut. I decided that as soon as I got home, I was going to get a real buzz cut right away. Everyone at the AmFAR party was really nice to us, but Elton wasn't there.

The next morning we had to catch a plane back to Indiana. AmFAR sent a limo to take us out to the airport. The limo had a phone in it, and we got a call. Mom answered.

"Hello, Jeanne, this is Elton John," said a British accent.

Elton wanted to tell us that he'd been watching *Good Morning America*, and he'd heard what

I'd told David Hartman. He wanted to apologize because he hadn't been able to make the AmFAR party. But he was inviting all of us to his next concert, in Texas.

"Well, okay!" I said. I wanted to sound enthusiastic, because he was being so nice. But it was such a surprise, I hardly knew what to say, so I just talked as normally as possible. The plane ride home was less of a drag than usual, and I didn't care what happened in school. I really had something to look forward to! I had a feeling my bad luck was going to change.

BUT THINGS didn't improve much over the summer. I was barred from swimming in several pools in town. One day I fell out of a tree. I wasn't hurt—I didn't bleed—but the fall did knock the breath out of me. So I just lay on the ground for a few minutes. A neighbor leaned over the fence and called to me, "Are you hurt?" I could tell he didn't want to come over and touch me.

Another time I spent the whole day out in the sun, and that night I found great big red spots all over me. I told Mom, "I'm really scared." She was too, but by morning, the spots had disappeared. Whew. It turned out that I had had some sort of allergic reaction to sunlight. Mom was trying to live day to day, watching me for a runny nose or a bad cough or a dragged-out look—any sign I might be getting sick again. I was having night sweats again, and ran high fevers for no reason. That can mean really bad news when you have AIDS, but most of the time, my fever vanished the next day.

"This is like being on a roller coaster," Mom said. "You never know what's next."

In July we got word that Chad had died.

Chad was another hemophiliac, a couple of years older than I was, who lived in Fort Wayne. I had met him when we were both poster boys for the Hemophilia Society. Then I saw him again the last time I was in the hospital, when I was vomiting so much. Chad had gotten AIDS from his Factor, just like me.

At that point, after I'd had those two seizures, Dr. Kleiman was worried about me because I was losing so much weight from throwing up. He wanted me to have a central line, a kind of feeding tube. He explained that if I got one, I wouldn't have to try to keep food down. The central line would put nutrients into me anyway. But I fought him on it because I can't stand anything that shows I'm seriously, seriously sick, or that prevents me from moving around much—that's one reason why I don't care for IVs. You have to sit or lie still while you're being fed through a feeding tube.

Some of the nurses wanted me to talk to Chad, who already had one. Chad moved very slowly, like an old man. He fell asleep constantly. He didn't think he'd ever get better.

As far as I was concerned, he had the wrong attitude.

Chad really liked his tube. "This way I don't have to eat, and I never throw up," he told me.

"No way," I retorted. "No pain, no gain."

Dr. Kleiman won, but in the end my vomiting stopped, and I didn't have to bother with the tube for very long. Chad had had a brain scan, a test that can show whether the AIDS virus has affected your brain. After I had those seizures, Dr. Kleiman wanted me to have one too. I fought him hard on that one too, even though he just wanted to make sure the seizures hadn't caused any bleeding in my brain. (They hadn't.) I didn't want anyone to think I was like Chad.

What has always scared me most about AIDS is that when you have it really badly, it *can* affect your brain. I'd read that it first starts with your not being able to remember things. Then you begin to say things that make no sense. Sometimes you don't recognize your family, and you even fight them off. I never wanted to treat Mom like that. When the AIDS virus attacks your brain this way, you sound senile or demented, because you have dementia. You don't get over dementia. You never improve. Usually it happens just before you die. I definitely did not want to end up like that.

It turned out the AIDS virus *had* affected Chad's brain. That was why he walked and talked like he was eighty years old. He never was well enough to go back to school. His mother told Mom he started going to sleep on his phone hookup. Then he got so he didn't know his mother. When he died, it was less than a year since he'd been diagnosed.

Chad made me feel really lucky. I'm convinced that if you think about dying, you're going to die. If you think about living, you're going to live. I wasn't looking forward to the harassment I'd probably get back at school, but at least I'd be showing up. Like me, Chad had had a girlfriend who wanted to be "just friends" after he was diagnosed. But I figured sooner or later, so long as I wasn't stuck in a hospital, there'd be another girl for me.

I started high school in late August. Most of the kids who had been in the school their parents had set up were back at Western. The parents had been able to borrow the old American Legion hall for six weeks last spring, but they couldn't find a free building for a whole year.

Then in early September I had to go back into Riley Hospital for some tests for my liver and my lung trouble. A couple of months later, in November, I started coughing more than usual. The coughing wouldn't let up. One morning in the bathroom, my mouth tasted strange, and I spat into the sink.

My spit was bright red.

Mom was scared to death. We raced back down to the hospital, with me in the backseat, hanging over a bucket.

I was really sick, so sick I had to spend another birthday in the hospital when I turned fifteen. Mom asked Dr. Kleiman whether it would help to put me in a bubble so I'd be protected from diseases, but he said it only worked for newborns, who hadn't been exposed to diseases yet.

In the meantime we heard that Mark, the baseball player with AIDS who used to call me, had died. The news said he'd been buried like a hero in Swansea. His high school was naming a scholarship after him. I hoped Mr. Vaughan had been right. After me, maybe other kids with AIDS wouldn't have so much trouble.

We had to miss Elton's concert in Texas because I was still in the hospital. Elton had called Mom at work to try to make plans. The operator told Mom, "Jeanne, we only put legitimate calls through, but I think this really *is* Elton John." People crowded around while she was on the phone with him, trying to catch a word or two. He told Mom, "Don't worry—tell Ryan we'll catch up with each other in L.A."

Whenever I was in the hospital, I had a room in the school-age unit, with seven- and eight-year-olds. That way I had more privacy. If any reporters came around, they looked for me in the teen unit. But one day, believe it or not, a reporter disguised herself as a nurse, sneaked into the school-age unit, ran into Mom in the corridor, and started asking her questions. Mom yelled for the real nurses, who came and chased the reporter out. But after that, I was really nervous about being stuck in the hospital. I was afraid that the next invader might be someone who hated people with AIDS coming to put poison in my IV. That idea was much worse than any old tornado. So Mom hardly ever left me. She slept in my room in a lounge chair that turned into a bed.

After that I told Mom, "I don't want to die in Kokomo. And I don't want to be buried there, either." In Indiana, you can see graveyards really easily. They're right alongside the roads. There was one I'd seen near a little church on a hill, along the highway south of Kokomo. We passed it whenever we drove Andrea to skating practice. I told Mom I'd picked out that cemetery for myself.

I wasn't scared of dying, so long as I wasn't in Kokomo. I liked thinking about my cemetery. It looked really peaceful. Maybe I'd put a joke on my tombstone. Something like, "I told you I was sick."

I wasn't in the intensive care unit, so Laura wasn't my regular nurse. Usually I had Connie or Laurie. They were both really nice to me, but I tried to get Laura to hang out with me as often as she could, for as long as she could. I never actually said, "Don't leave me alone" out loud, but I'd bug her to play another game or another tape with me. I tried to trick her with puzzles. Here's one: I drew "IX" on a piece of paper, and asked her, "With one line, can you make this a six?"

Well, I kept her around a long time with that one. The answer is to draw an "S" in front of the "IX," but Laura never did guess right.

Other times I'd quiz her about her boy-friend—she ended up marrying him—and about her car.

"What kind do you have?" I asked her.

"A black Fury," Laura told me.

"Will you take me for a ride?" I asked her.

"You bet!" Laura grinned. Right then, Laura was the closest I had to a girlfriend. I was beginning to see that the big question when you have AIDS is, "Will anyone ever come close enough to fall in love with me?" I was ready to think about dating. I knew I could get a car, but I wondered whether any girl would ever ride in it with me.

But I pushed those thoughts away. I don't care who you are or how bad off you are, there's always somebody out there who's in worse shape than you are. Like Chad. Like Mark. Like the other kids in the hospital with me. I could have been hooked up to a kidney machine all the time. I could have been paralyzed. I could have had cystic fibrosis. When you have it bad, you can't breathe, you can't eat, you can't run around. You spend more time in the hospital than kids with cancer.

Even though I was sick, at least I got a lot of attention. Andrea was left out a lot, though she'd never let out a peep about it. It's always tough for you if your brother or sister is sick all the time. Your parents have to spend so much time with the patient instead of with you. If you sulk, you look bad. Everyone feels sorry for the sick one, and tells you to act more grown-up. In the hospital, one of the nurses told me about two boys, five-year-old twins. One had AIDS; the other didn't. Their parents were working incredibly hard to give both of them enough attention. But the nurse said you could tell the healthy twin was upset anyway.

When Mom had to come to the hospital to be with me, Andrea was always with her, just the way she had been when I was diagnosed. Andrea would sit with Mom and hold her hand. Every now and again, she'd say, "Mom, how's Ryan doing?" or "Mom, do you want me to get you anything?" But Andrea never complained. Steve really loves Andrea, and he always calls her "a day-in, day-out girl." Andrea's very loyal. She doesn't gossip about people, and she'll always put in a good word for someone when you start getting catty. She got mad at Mom if she started worrying about me. "Everyone thinks Ryan's going to die," Andrea would say. "He's going to make it."

But the more I was in the hospital, the more skating practices Andrea had to miss. Skating's expensive. The skates cost a lot, and you have to keep them repaired. You have to pay for lessons, plus rinks charge you for practice time. When you go to meets, you need money for gas and credit cards to stay in motels. When Mom wasn't working, we had to count out pennies from our jar in the kitchen to go for milk.

One day Andrea announced in a flat voice, "I'm giving up skating."

Mom and I looked at her.

"Girls I beat last year place ahead of me now," Andrea said. "I'm not practicing enough. You don't have the time to take me, Mom. You don't have the money."

"You're right about that," Mom said. "I'm sorry, Andrea."

Before I got AIDS, Andrea had been the famous one in our family. She was a national roller skating champion. Her picture was on the wall at the roller rink, and she'd been covered by newspapers and television. Skating was Andrea's whole life. Now she'd just be Ryan White's sister. I'd like to think it's a treat to be my sister, but right now it wasn't, especially at school. One time, driving home from a meet, we had laughed about a rink we passed that had a sign out front saying, "Christian Roller Skating."

"You're a Christian roller skater, Andrea," I said. "You'll fall—and rise again. You'll make a comeback." I had decided to switch from law to advertising. It looked like fun. I spent a lot of time thinking up slogans and rhymes.

But I felt for Andrea. As far as she was concerned, our family's whole life right now was Ryan White, Ryan White, Ryan White. There wasn't much room left over for her.

WHILE I WAS in the hospital, Dr. Kleiman tried to get me on AZT, a new drug that seemed to slow down AIDS. It was an experimental drug then, and not every patient could get it. It's especially hard for children to get an experimental drug. No doctor wants to mess up with them. Now most patients can have AZT. It isn't a cure for AIDS, and it can have serious side effects. We had some hassles getting it, because it can affect your liver, and I'd already had hepatitis.

But I did get better. I went back home, and studied with a tutor. "They're calling you the miracle kid," Mom said with relief. "You always come back. How many parents get their sick children back?"

School didn't improve much though. On Valentine's Day the computer department set up a computer dating service. They fed the names of every student into a computer, and gave you the names of your perfect matches. Someone bugged the computer so that I was matched only with boys, and Andrea only with girls.

Then my very worst day at school arrived. Someone broke into my locker and stole a mirror that Mom had bought for me in New York. I had left a bunch of folders in my lockers. Now they had "Faggot" and "Queer" scrawled all over them. Someone had spray-painted "Why don't you get butt-fucked?" inside the locker too. I'd never even seen that word before.

I was shaken up. What would show up next, a dead cat? I called Mom and told her what had happened.

"You go straight to the principal," Mom said. "Tell him that if your locker isn't cleaned up right now, I'm going to call some reporters and get them to come see it."

Half an hour later my locker looked like new.

Mom was really worried now. She was afraid that if someone else at school came down with AIDS, I'd be blamed. It would be easier than admitting you were gay, or had used needles to take drugs. She'd thought she'd always live in Kokomo, close to Grandma and Grandpa and Tommy and Deb. She'd bought season tickets to the Wildcats' basketball games for years. But she knew I was desperate to get away.

There were just two problems with moving: We had no money, and no one wanted to buy our house. In Kokomo it was known as "the AIDS house." But I had been right that our luck was about to change. A company in Los Angeles wanted to make a TV movie about us and about what had happened in Kokomo. Mom had to take a loss on our old house, but the movie people gave us enough money up front for a down payment on a new house in a very quiet little town called Cicero, about a half hour south of Kokomo.

Andrea didn't think Kokomo should be allowed to forget all about us after we were gone. So we got some bee-bees, and we hammered our names into our stoop: JEANNE RYAN ANDREA. As we left for Cicero, we passed a road sign that said, "Leaving Kokomo, City of Firsts."

"Right," I said. "I'm never coming back "

5

I Come Up Grinning: How Life Changed

IN THE END I did go back to Kokomo a few times, but only to see my relatives. I was much happier when they came to see us. If I ever had to mention Kokomo, I talked about "where I lived before."

Cicero was something different—just a little lake community, maybe 4500 people. More come on vacation in the summer. There's one central street, and not a lot to do except drive around, visit your friends, and hang out at the Dairy Queen. That was fine with me. All I wanted, I thought, was peace and quiet.

As you come into Cicero, you drive past farmers' fields and the town cemetery, and then cross a lake with several docks to get to the main street, which has old-fashioned gas lanterns all along it. Our house was a brand-new Cape Codder, right on the lake. The first

time we saw our future home, it was only half-
built. Andrea and I could pick which of the
three bedrooms we wanted. The ones we ended
up with were joined by a door, but each room
had a separate staircase. So we could walk back
and forth and visit each other easily, but feel
like we had our own apartments. There was a
deck that looked out over the boats on the lake,
and from the kitchen window you could see
birds and chipmunks and squirrels in the
woods out back. When we moved to Cicero in
May, I finally had all the shelf space I needed
for Herbie's cage and my G.I. Joe figures and
my comics—just as I was beginning to get
hooked on other things. Like skateboarding.

I had another year to go before I could get a
learner's permit, so skateboarding was the next
best thing to driving. Whenever Mom and I
drove into Indianapolis to see Dr. Kleiman—
just about once a week right then—we passed
through Castleton, a part of the city where all
the malls are. It's the best place around to see
movies and shop. One day in Castleton I discovered Maui Surf and Sport, a skateboard
shop that carried surfer T-shirts and shorts—
the kind I liked from California that you couldn't
find anywhere else around us. John Riser, the
owner, was a young, athletic guy who let me
grill him about the best wheels and boards.
Since I was just starting to skate, he gave me
some videotapes to inspire me.

I bought plenty of clothes. When I finally got
to California, I wanted to look like I belonged.

I also picked up a board, several pairs of Oakleys—mirrored sunglasses in wild colors like orange—and copies of the skateboarding magazines John carried. I read every page of *Skateboarding, Poweredge,* and my favorite, *Thrasher,* which is the best for skateboarders. At least I could study tricks, even if a wall ride was way beyond me. I began to think all I wanted in life was to work for John when I turned sixteen, so I could learn how to be in business for myself. A long time ago in Kokomo I'd started a little company called Odd Jobs, Inc. I was president, and a girl who lived down the street was vice-president. We mowed lawns and cleaned out garages. Now I wanted to see how to really work on my own—and skate around in the mall parking lot during my lunch hour.

I didn't ride a skateboard much at first. Not because Dr. Kleiman wasn't happy about a hemophiliac doing that. Not because my best move wasn't a curb grind or an ollie. The fact is, I was having a bad summer. My lungs put me back in the hospital for a short while, though I turned out not to have pneumonia. That was a big relief. Mom knew the drill by now: She brought me my Alyssa Milano poster for my room, and my own surf shirts and shorts so I wouldn't have to wear hospital gowns. She sent me a card that said, "Ryan, get well so the mail will slow down." Moving hadn't cut back my cards and letters. Some reached me even though they were addressed just "To the Boy With AIDS, Indiana."

But it's creepy to be famous because you're sick. Now and again my mail reminded me about that. Some letters I got made the hair on the back of my neck stand up on end. Like the lists of strange questions I'd get from a man in Oregon. Mostly he wanted to know, "When will my friend Ryan write to me?" Never, buddy! Then there was the man who had seen my picture in *People* and had decided he was my father. This man even hitchhiked to Cicero and called us. He said he was on his way over to live with me and look after me. We let the police station handle that one. I didn't want to mess with it!

Besides, all the fame in the world wasn't making me well. I seemed to be tired all the time, even if I slept twenty hours a day. I'm not exaggerating. Laura would come down from intensive care and leave me notes like, "I stopped by twice and you were asleep both times. Don't you ever do anything else?"

I certainly was cold—constantly. If I was outside, I buttoned my jacket up to my chin no matter how warm it was. Once I got home, I always wore jeans and sweaters and furry Big Foot slippers with claws. If I was sitting still, I wrapped myself up in a blanket as well and got Wally and Gizzy to nap on my feet. A friend of Mom's bought me a portable hand-heater that I carried around with me. Now and then I had to turn Mom's electric stove all the way up and hold my blue fingers over the hot coil to warm them. Sometimes I burnt them first, and collected a scar or two.

We went to Daytona with my grandparents at spring break, but I had to take my heater along. We stayed in a condo with a balcony looking out over the beach. The weather wasn't great, so Andrea and I spent hours on the balcony feeding the sea gulls. Someone had written "INDIANA" in huge letters along the sand, like they knew we were coming. Actually, they were celebrating because I.U. had won the National Collegiate Basketball Championship again.

When I breathed, I rattled. Sometimes I ran out of breath completely. In the middle of a conversation, I'd have to stop talking, rest my head on my hands, and take some short pants. My voice sounded thin and squeaky, like I had permanent bronchitis. My nose ran, and my chest felt tight. My hearing had gotten peculiar. Sometimes it was so sensitive that when Mom cooked bacon, the hissing sound hurt my ears. Other times, I could barely hear what someone was saying to me.

I hardly ever went out. Now and again we had to go see Dr. Kleiman, or I went along on Mom's errands, or we'd go for Mexican food in Noblesville, the next town. Sometimes people stared, but only because they recognized us— not because they didn't want us around. At least we were just another family here. But I couldn't be far from a bathroom because I was throwing up a lot, or I might need to warm my hands under the hot-air dryer.

Even though I was having trouble keeping food down, you could still tell I was a teenager—I always wanted to eat. Whenever we ordered dinner, I'd ask for nachos to start, and then French fries, steak, and cheesecake. After a few bites, though, I was usually too worn out to finish. Long before dessert, I'd start bugging Mom and Andrea to take me home again. Once we got there, the first thing I'd do was turn off the air conditioning. They probably weren't pleased—Indiana summers can be up in the nineties and sticky—but they never complained. My whole family was very worried about me, except for Andrea, who always told everyone, "Nothing is ever going to happen to Ryan. He'll pull through." The press had started to say that I was dying.

My personal philosophy on that subject was no complaints, baby, no surrender. I wasn't quitting. I could get better, so I would. I liked the Cicero cemetery fine. It looked green and peaceful. But I wasn't about to be carried out there yet.

I watched TV 'til I thought I was going to disappear inside the set. Nothing had changed—the Cubs were underdogs again. Every week I saw some outfielder trying to dig a ball out of the ivy on the wall of Wrigley Field. You'd have thought the Cubs would be world champs now that they had a player named Ryne—Sandberg that is, the star second baseman. I was glad I was called "Ry-man" instead of "Ryno," the fans' name for Sandberg. I decided

I liked Vanna White on *Wheel of Fortune,* though not as much as Alyssa Milano. When *Playboy* published some photographs of Vanna, I kept after Mom to buy the issue for me. Mom said she was embarrassed, but one day she came home with the magazine inside a grocery bag. "From now on, you're not getting *everything* you want," she scolded me.

I tried to keep my mind on stuff I wanted, good stuff. In spite of all the grief we got in Kokomo, we'd been able to see and do a lot. Like the times Greg Louganis, the diving champion who won four gold medals at the Olympics, had visited with us in Indianapolis. He turned out to be not all that tall, but *there* was someone with muscles! Dr. Kleiman wouldn't give me steroids, but maybe there was another way I could look more like Greg. The first time he called us up, we were still living in Kokomo. He'd heard about us on CNN, and he was coming to Indianapolis for the U.S. Diving Championships. Lots of famous athletes show up sooner or later in Indianapolis because of all the great sports facilities that have been built there for events.

Greg invited all three of us to come watch him compete a couple of times. The first time, he gave me the medal he won, the 38th National Title Medal. While he was talking to some reporters, he let me climb up to the ten-meter platform. The platform was tiny, and it was a *long* way down to that pool. I held on tight to the railing the whole time.

Once both my feet were flat on the ground again, I told Greg, "Man, you gotta be nuts to *dive* off that thing!"

Greg laughed. I guess he's heard that from lots of people besides me. He told me he knew how it felt to have other kids in school give you a hard time. All the way through school, he had a lot of trouble doing his work. His classmates called him "stupid" and most of his teachers decided he was retarded. He didn't find out what was really wrong until he was eighteen. It turned out that he has dyslexia, which means you see letters in the wrong order when you read. It must be really tough to have everyone tell you you're stupid, know you're really not, but not be able to get them to believe you.

Later on, Greg invited the three of us plus my grandparents to come see him again at a theater in Indianapolis. He was making his debut as a professional dancer. I liked that—he was already a big deal diver, but he wanted to plunge into something new. Greg was really excited when he found out that my sister was a champion too. Andrea had been invited to roller skate in the opening ceremonies for the 1987 Pan-American Games which were going to be held in Indianapolis. It was a giant step forward for her—and for roller skating. Greg was competing in the Games, and gave Andrea some exercises and tips so she wouldn't get leg cramps. And he gave me one of the two gold medals he won at the Pan-American Games. He said, "I'd give you both, but I'm afraid my mother will kill me. She'll want one of them."

Next time we were in L.A., Greg said we could come visit him at his house in Malibu. He thought I would love his new pool and his view of the Pacific surf. I couldn't wait to try surfing. I remembered the party Elton had thrown for me at Disneyland the fall before. Ever since then I'd wanted to go back to California really, really badly. When I had finally gotten out of the hospital, Elton had flown all three of us out to L.A. I couldn't believe we were actually there until we walked out of the airport. There in front of us was a row of palm trees. And I was finally warm enough!

Before we had left Indiana, Mom reminded me that when I was first trying to go back to school, we'd heard that Rock Hudson had AIDS. "Everyone is running scared now," Mom said. "So please don't do anything like sharing sodas or lollipops—that might upset people."

But we didn't have to worry. Elton passed cans of Coke back and forth with me, and hugged and kissed and joked around with all of us. Elton's always like that, the whole time you're with him.

From L.A., Elton flew us in his private jet to two of his concerts, one in Oakland and one in San Diego. Andrea and I got special sweatshirts and scarves and sunglasses to wear at the concerts. Elton even gave me the beanie he wore on stage.

When we got back to L.A., Elton had arranged a tour of Universal Studios and a party at Disneyland for us. To get us there, he had two limos, and a bus for his band and their families. Elton rode in one limo, which had a sunroof, and we followed in the other. Every now and again, Elton's limo would pull over and he'd stand up and wave at us and anyone else around! It was pretty funny.

At Universal, we got to see Marty McFly's high school and the soda shop from *Back to the Future!* I was still pretty weak from being in the hospital for so long, but there was no way I wanted to miss a minute of this. So at Disneyland, Elton got me a wheelchair and pushed me around himself.

Elton didn't forget about us afterward. When Andrea's birthday rolled around in October, he sent her red roses. He called us now and again from wherever he was touring, to see how we were getting along. We got handwritten letters from him, postmarked all over the world.

I LOOKED over our Disneyland photos, of Elton and me in wild sunglasses. At least I wasn't quite as skinny now as I had been last fall. I could use a few extra pounds though. Maybe I could talk Mom into taking up Mexican cooking.

Something else I thought about was where I'd go from here. After all, the fighting was over, and we'd won. I *was* back in school, though I wasn't sure what my new one, Hamilton Heights, was going to be like—assuming I could keep awake long enough to go. Mom and I had gone to see Mr. Cook and Mr. Dillon, the principal and the assistant principal, about my registering. It turned out that they were expecting us. One parent who was a real estate agent had already called to tell them that we had bought a house in the school district. Hamilton Heights was happy to have me, Mr. Cook said, if I was really serious about school.

I said what I always said. "I like school. I want to be with other kids."

Mr. Cook smiled. "Let's go register," he said, and he led us to the cafeteria to line up at the registration tables with everybody else.

I was pleased, but I've never liked starting a new school. Especially not this time—I had no idea what to expect. I'd managed to open a few doors for myself, but that could mean that I'd find more of them slammed shut in my face than ever. For starters, I wasn't sure I'd feel well enough to start school at all. If I did, things were going to be a little awkward because I was going to be a freshman when I should be a sophomore. And there was something else I wasn't sure of: I'd meet plenty of kids who had only seen me on television. They didn't know the first thing about the real me, and they might not bother to find out.

Around this time a reporter asked me, "Who's your best friend?"

I had to tell the truth. "I don't have one," I replied.

Now that we were in Cicero, I wanted more

than a quiet life. I wanted friends my age. We'd left everyone we knew behind in Kokomo. In one way, that was good. I really wanted to put the past behind me so I wouldn't be bitter. But now there was no one except my relatives who would know what I meant when I said, "Remember back *before* I was in the news so much?"

Maybe everyone I met at Hamilton Heights would think, He's friends with Elton John—he doesn't need us. That was one thing I'd noticed: Fame can isolate you just as much as AIDS. Or maybe kids would try to get close to me only because I was famous, not because they liked me.

Well, I wasn't going to find out by sitting home in front of the TV. I had to move ahead, or else things would start gaining on me. I had to believe that I had a purpose. I must be good for something. The winter before, when I was still feeling pretty well, Dr. Woodrow Myers, the state health commissioner, invited Mom and me to speak at a state conference on AIDS. Dr. Myers asked me to give the crowd some advice.

"Whatever you do, please don't isolate us," I said.

Guess I had to take my own advice right now. I certainly knew I had to keep on getting myself out of the house, just to educate people. They kept imagining that AIDS was a dirty word, a slimy disease. If they saw me walking around, shopping, looking normal, I figured they might have more compassion for people like me.

In Kokomo, fear had gotten the better of everybody. I understood that. No one was really against me; they were against my disease. Parents were worried about their own kids. When I first heard I had AIDS, I was just like everybody else in Kokomo: I was scared, and so was my family.

But the more I thought about what had happened, the more it seemed to me that fear had taken control of adults in Kokomo. Once that happened, they believed whatever they wanted to believe about me and AIDS. Many kids who called me names were only repeating what they'd heard grown-ups say. Kids in Kokomo were just doing what kids do—listening to their parents.

So when I thought about what I'd do next, I decided that if adults ignored the medical facts, I ought to concentrate on talking to kids. Most adults are pretty set in their ways, but kids are still learning. If I hung out with kids, talked to them, maybe they'd go home and change their parents' minds.

I wasn't the only one who had this idea. I mentioned that we were able to move because we got some money from a movie company, plus Elton lent us enough extra to make a down payment on our house in Cicero. Actually, we had had several movie offers, but we picked the Landsburg Company. I had seen a couple of TV movies they'd already made about real people, and I really liked them. One called *Adam* was about a kid, younger than I was, who was kidnapped from a parking lot. Another movie, named *Bill*, was about a retarded man, and a filmmaker who starts to make a documentary about him. The filmmaker winds up making friends with Bill, helping him find a job and learn to look after himself. The real Bill even ended up visiting the White House (the *real* White House). These movies were grim in places, but they kind of gave you hope at the same time. I liked that.

Something else I liked was that Linda Otto, the producer from Landsburg, came out to Indiana from Los Angeles to meet us. No one else did. We sat with Linda around our kitchen table, talking about what our movie might be like. I liked knowing that Mom and Andrea would get some money because of me—I'm a practical person. But I was fairly amazed that a movie producer was sitting right there in front of me, much less interested in me.

"We want to show what you *really* went through in Kokomo, not just the court hearings," Linda explained. "We'll tell the story from your point of view."

That sounded like a neat idea, but I had to ask, "Why would anyone want to make a movie about *me*, anyway? You really think people will watch it?"

Linda told me she thought it was very important to stand up for children's rights. She said she'd picked filmmaking as the way to do it, because you could reach so many people. She tried to make movies that would help kids. When *Adam* was shown on TV, there was a roll call of missing kids at the end, and an 800 number you could call if you had seen any of them. Linda said that over a hundred missing children were found after that—even though poor Adam had ended up dead.

Lots of times, though, producers in Hollywood want to make a certain movie, but it never works out. They just can't find a script that's good enough, or hire the actors they want. Or they do make the film, but they can't make a deal with a network to show it on television. Linda said to me, "I promise you, Ryan. I'll get this movie done."

I hoped it would happen, but I tried not to get too excited. Meanwhile, I had another visitor—totally unexpected this time. One afternoon Mom called down to me. I was in our basement family room, watching TV, as usual. I saw *Who's the Boss?* as often as it was on. It was a chance to catch Alyssa Milano, and besides, Linda Otto was hoping that Judith Light would play Mom in our movie. "Ryan," she said, "there's a girl here to see you."

A girl? I thought Mom must mean a reporter. I climbed the stairs halfheartedly. I wasn't thrilled about talking to some other magazine or newspaper who'd probably end up claiming I was dying. Whoever they were, I planned on giving them five minutes—no more. Instead, there was a girl with long blonde hair standing in our living room with Mom, smiling at me. She was about my height and my age—too young to be a reporter.

"Hi, Ryan," she said. She had a nice smile and a small, sweet voice. "I'm Jill Stewart. I live two doors down from you."

A new neighbor dropping in! It seemed like years and years since *that* had happened. I'd spent so much time by myself, watching other people talk on TV, I was rusty when it came to conversations with anyone who wasn't family. My mouth almost creaked when I spoke, and I squeaked, as usual.

"Hi," I managed to say.

"I'm president of the student body at Hamilton Heights High," Jill added. That meant she must be one of the most popular kids there. Jill was a senior, but she was only a year older than I was. She explained, "I wanted to invite you to our school. Now you'll know someone when you come your first day."

Jill said that Hamilton Heights had already stepped up their AIDS education program in case I enrolled. "No one is planning on treating you badly," she told me. "We just want to be normal."

"I'll second that," I said.

Jill came back again with her father and mother, a nurse. A few days later, Wendy Baker, a friend of Jill's from Hamilton Heights, knocked on our door too. They made a good pair—Jill had fair hair and Wendy's was dark. Wendy was a junior and my age. She lived over on the other side of the lake. Later, after we got to be close friends and visited each other a lot, Wendy told me that she had been really nervous when we first met.

"Why?" I asked her.

Sometimes I make people nervous because I look so young. I stopped growing when I was twelve, thanks to AIDS. Luckily the hoarse rasp in my voice makes me *sound* my age, at least. When I see that someone who's just been introduced is jumpy around me, I stay calm and wait for them to settle down too.

"Well," Wendy said, "I thought you might want to be left alone. And besides," she added, "you were better looking than on TV."

I laughed. That second part was certainly good to hear.

"The last thing I need is people running away from me," I said. "I was really glad you stopped by."

Wendy and Jill brought me photos of all the teachers at Hamilton Heights, so I'd recognize them when I got to classes. The girls called me every week just to say hi, and brought some of their other friends over to meet me and tell me about what would go on at school. By the time school started, I would know about fifteen of the six hundred and fifty kids there.

"What those girls have done!" Mom exclaimed. She was getting to be very good friends with the Stewarts and the Bakers. "These kids are *glad* they'll be going to school with you. They think you're a hero!"

With all this encouragement, I wasn't surprised that I did begin to get better, just as I thought I would, plus I finally started on AZT. I was definitely looking forward to school. Mr. Cook and Mr. Dillon asked me to come two weeks late. "We want to make sure everyone at school is educated and prepared," Jill explained to me. "So we're dropping everything for a crash course on AIDS."

Hamilton Heights had called the State Board of Health, Dr. Myers' office, and asked them to send some experts on AIDS who could talk to teachers and students about how you can and can't catch it. In the beginning everyone was at least a little bit afraid, deep down inside. So there were lectures, tapes, and films for teachers first, and then for students. And in any class, students and teachers could have spontaneous discussions. Someone might mention that I was coming, and pretty soon everyone would jump in and bring up whatever they weren't sure about. A student might ask something like, "Well, what *is* AIDS, anyway?" There was no such thing as a stupid question. Nobody ever replied, "I can't believe you don't know! How dumb can you get?" Instead, people who did know passed it on.

After all this, students who were still confused or frightened could ask for a private appointment with Mr. Cook or a guidance counselor to get the straight scoop. If they were too sheepish to sit down and talk face to face, they could still ask questions by stuffing anony-

The White family, 1974. Left to right: Jeanne, Andrea, Wayne, and Ryan.

The family relaxes at home with cat Chi Chi and dog Wally, 1986. *(Courtesy of Seth Rossman.)*

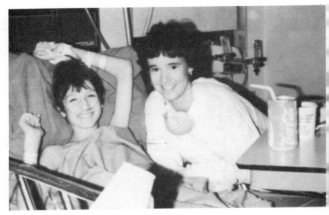

Ryan and his favorite nurse, Laura Kreich, December 1984, at James Whitcomb Riley Hospital.

Ryan, age 13, and Andrea, age 11.

Ryan's first day back at Western Middle School. Behind him is his stepfather, Steve Ford. *(Courtesy of Chuck Robinson.)*

Ryan, age 13, and Jeanne as Ryan follows his science class via telephone hookup. *(Courtesy of AP/Wide World Photos.)*

Heather McNew and Ryan in New York City, 1988.

Ryan and his prom date, Dee Louks, spring 1989.

Michael Jackson and Ryan, 1989.

Elton John and
Ryan, 1988.

Ryan and Lukas Haas sitting on their director's chairs during filming of "The Ryan White Story," 1988.

Ryan in his room decorated with his "Max Headroom" poster, 1988. *(Courtesy of Taro Yamasaki, People.)*

Elton John Sings "Skyline Pigeon" at Ryan's funeral.
(*Courtesy of Taro Yamasaki,* People.)

Ryan's grave in the cemetery in Cicero, Indiana, 1990, with gifts left by young visitors.

Ryan's 1990 yearbook picture that Jeanne placed beside his bed during his final illness and that stood on Elton John's piano during the funeral. *(Courtesy of Dennis Gates, Inter-State Studio of Indiana, Inc.)*

mous notes into a special locker. The experts posted the answers on a separate bulletin board. Jill told me that by the second week, many of the unsigned questions read, "How can we help Ryan?"

Once the kids and teachers were in gear, the school took its AIDS education campaign out into the community. They told the press what they were doing and they sent speakers to church meetings. The school board held a meeting that was open to the public, and one of the state's AIDS experts answered parents' questions.

A few parents told the school board, "I don't know whether I want my children in this school now. I may not let them go." But the school's idea of starting with the students worked. Kids told their parents they understood AIDS wasn't contagious, they weren't scared of me, and they wanted to be in school. One family asked their kid to stay home, and the kid said no!

My first day of school finally rolled around, and I rose to the challenge. Mom drove me to Hamilton Heights, which is in the next little town, Arcadia, about fifteen minutes from Cicero. As we came in the driveway and up to the main door, I saw some reporters out front and heard kids' voices calling, "There he is! Here he comes!"

Uh, oh, I thought. I've been here before. Nothing's going to change much.

But the school made the press stay back behind a low cement barrier, so they couldn't follow me inside. Wendy and Jill and some other student government officers met me right at the door, and helped me find all my classes. I'd kept to myself for so long, it was like being on another planet. When I walked into classrooms or the cafeteria, several kids called out at once, "Hey, Ryan! Sit with me!"

In my science class a slim, pretty, dark-haired girl around my height asked me to be her lab partner. She told me her name was Heather McNew, and she came from a big family—five boys and three girls. Heather is number five. Her family's house is the oldest in the county. Before the Civil War, it had been a stop on the underground railroad, a place where runaway slaves could hide safely. Heather said her family had a wood-burning stove and patchwork quilts on the wall, along with her track ribbons. She invited me to come visit them.

I guess I'm not in Kokomo anymore, I thought. My lab partner there was so upset when she was assigned to me that her parents started the separate school. Here everyone seemed to know who I was, and wanted to say hello. The school janitor gave me something he'd written, called "Ryan's Poem":

> *We are sorry for your fight*
> *But for every day that you are here*
> *We can see a little light*

As I left after my first day, a reporter asked me, "How do you like *this* school?"

"Oh, I think I'm going to like it here," I said. He must have noticed I was beaming. I'd been welcomed with open arms. I felt like I had hundreds of friends. It seemed like everyone said to themselves, "What if you were standing in *his* shoes? How would *you* feel?"

"In my wildest dreams I never thought it would be this easy!" Mom exclaimed when I got home. "I'm very proud we live here."

Things were so good all of a sudden. I had a regular teenage life, and other teenagers were part of it. Jill Stewart drove me to school in the mornings. She met me first, and then we went to pick up some other kids. By the time we got to school, the whole group was cracking jokes together. The first time, Jill and I didn't know each other all that well yet, and we were both nervous. It was worse for Jill: She was driving. She went right through a stop sign and we nearly crashed into a school bus. I let out a yell. That probably terrified Jill more than ever.

Sometimes I asked my new friends to help me stay as much like everyone else as possible. Once a news photographer wanted pictures of me walking into Hamilton Heights. I didn't want to be the center of attention, so I asked Jill and Wendy and a couple of other kids to walk in with me. The pictures turned out great, with the bunch of us cutting up in the corridors.

Another time, a TV producer showed up at school and announced to Mr. Dillon that he had come to interview me. Mr. Dillon called Mom. As usual she said, "Well, it's up to Ryan, what he wants to do." Mr. Dillon came looking for me, and told me about the producer who wanted to talk to me.

"Mr. Dillon," I asked, "do I have to?"

"It's up to you, Ryan," Mr. Dillon answered.

"Then could you tell him I don't want to?" I asked.

"Of course I will," Mr. Dillon told me. He said later that the producer's jaw had dropped over my message. He was totally amazed. He said, "Does Ryan understand that this is for national broadcast?"

"I don't think you understand," Mr. Dillon replied. "Ryan doesn't care what it's for. He doesn't want to be interviewed."

Whew. It was so great to be around other people who thought that what I wanted was quite normal. On most weekends there was a game at school and then a dance afterward. At first I was too shy to go. Between being sick and studying at home, I was out of touch with high school life. I wasn't sure I'd know how to act, and I didn't want to look silly. My social muscles needed exercise.

I did go visit Heather—quite a lot, in fact. I felt really comfortable with her and her family— no one had trouble with me at all. Heather's youngest brother, Sam, who has Down's Syndrome, was only three when I met him. I love Sam a lot. Once he threw a small truck—the kind I used to collect—and hit me on the side of the head. Everyone gasped. I guess they were afraid I'd start bleeding. But I just laughed, and so did Sam. It was no big deal.

Heather and I talked on the phone every day. I went to her track meets, and we passed notes back and forth in class when things got boring. I sent her sweet nothings like, "This class blows it out the rear!" I finally had a best friend—several, actually. I signed up to work on the yearbook, and at midterm my grades were mostly B's—though English was still my weak spot. I did really well in algebra. The first test I took, I got an A. I was real excited. Some kids don't care how they do, or pretend they don't. I cared! I wanted to do well. Next stop, the honor roll. When my school career started looking that good, Mom sat me down for a serious talk.

"It's Andrea's turn now," she said. Andrea was in junior high, and would start Hamilton Heights with me in a year.

"I have to even things out," Mom went on. "This next year is going to be your sister's. I want to help her get back into roller skating."

"Sure," I said. "That's only fair."

My family had thought I'd survive only a few months. But here we were, almost three years later. I was doing well. I had a chronic cough, but big deal. Now and again I felt extra worn out and had to stay quiet, or I came down with thrush in my mouth again, and had to whisper because it hurt to talk. Still, no one had to look after me twenty-four hours a day anymore.

Roller skating takes up a lot of time, and it's

expensive. A pair of skates, the kind Andrea needed now, cost five hundred dollars. When she was still growing and needed new skates every year, Steve often forked out for them. Now Mom could go back to work, so she could afford lessons and new skates for Andrea. She and Andrea could start driving to the rink in Indianapolis again for practice and lessons, and going away to meets on the weekends.

Andrea had to recoup all the practice time she'd lost before she could start winning again. But she was already a big hit at the rink. All the younger skaters idolized her; as far as they were concerned, she had always been a star. Besides, Andrea's really good with little kids. She would invite some of the girls to sleep over at our house, or she'd leave notes for them on their parents' cars when they were having trouble with a move. "Don't worry about your double lutz," Andrea would write. "You *will* get it."

That fall the three of us took another trip to California for a week. This time Grandma and Grandpa got to come too. We were invited out to Los Angeles by Athletes and Entertainers for Kids. This is a non-profit group of sports stars and various entertainers, who work with kids who are very ill or who might drop out of school and join gangs. For instance, Howie Long, from the Los Angeles Raiders, heads up Howie's Heros, a program which sends celebrities to visit kids in hospitals. Kareem Abdul-Jabbar, who scored more points than any other basketball star ever when he was playing for the Los Angeles Lakers, heads up Kareem's Kids, to keep kids in school and off the streets.

Now Athletes and Entertainers for Kids was launching a new program that they were going to call the Ryan White National Educational Program. It sent teams of celebrities and AIDS experts into schools to talk to kids—so there would be no more Ryan White stories.

Sounded good to me. They wanted me to be at the press conference that would launch the Fund. Andrea brought a video camera to the press conference and played TV reporter, taping Mom and Grandpa and Grandma in the audience. I was supposed to make a short speech, but I had laryngitis. Instead, Howie Long heaved me up over his head to make victory signs. Compared to me, Howie's about twelve feet tall, so I had quite a view of the crowd. Everyone cheered and whistled.

I thanked Howie for the lift.

"Nothing to it, man," he said. "I play football for a living. What *you* did—that was *something*."

What was really something, as far as I was concerned, was the earthquake that happened while we were in our hotel, early the next morning. We were watching local TV, and we saw the newscaster's desk start to shake! He looked all around, trying to figure out what was happening. Then he ducked under the desk and went on broadcasting! Finally the screen went black. The whole thing was hilarious, but

Grandpa and Grandma were too shook up to laugh.

"This is California!" I told them. "The complete experience!" I wasn't scared at all.

Grandpa did perk up when we went to a Dodger game. Dodger Stadium is high up in the hills above Los Angeles. You can tell you're in California because you can buy nachos in the stands, not just hot dogs. There's a famous vendor at Dodger Stadium who can throw you a pack of peanuts from behind his back, over his shoulder, any which way—even if you're sitting high above him. There was also a big video screen opposite our seats, flashing messages. One of them was "WELCOME RYAN WHITE FAMILY." We cheered, and people turned around and smiled at us.

Coming from Indiana, which doesn't have a major league team, we really appreciated being at a big game. The West Coast *is* different, though. Cubs fans are committed. The ones who live close to Wrigley Field watch games from their roofs. Cubs fans are colorful. They wear bathing suits and call themselves "bleacher bums." The chief announcer used to sit in the stands along with the bums to sing "Take Me Out to the Ball Game" during the seventh-inning stretch.

Not West Coast fans. Like you always hear, they're laid back. They don't arrive until the second inning, they leave during the seventh, and in between they sit on their hands. Grandpa was the most devoted Dodger fan there.

Dodger Stadium has something Wrigley Field doesn't. When the players step up to the plate, there's another screen staring right at them. The batter's face appears, with all his statistics, and how he's done so far in the game. Say you're up at bat and there's that screen, flashing "STRUCK OUT TWICE." This could be pretty demoralizing.

ALL ALONG, we had been keeping in touch with Linda Otto and the Landsburg Company. They had been writing and rewriting the script for our movie, and working on hooking a network that would air it. They wanted Lukas Haas, who had played the boy in the movie *Witness*, to be me. While we were out in L.A., Linda had a party for us at her house on the beach in Malibu. Heather was along as my date, but Linda asked if there was anyone I wanted her to invite. There certainly was.

"Do you think Alyssa Milano would come?" I asked. Maybe she was working. Maybe she wouldn't be interested. Maybe—maybe she'd be scared.

"I'll see what I can do," Linda promised.

When my family and I got to the party, we saw a ton of movie people. Bruce Willis, Demi Moore, Lukas Haas. Greg Louganis was there too. I felt a little lost in the crowd. Then I saw her. Alyssa was tiny—smaller than I am—and even prettier than I remembered. She had on jeans and a T-shirt, just like me.

I told her she was my idol.

"Well, I think you're a hero," she smiled. "And where I go to school, everyone else thinks so too."

"You mean they're not scared of me?" I asked.

"Oh, no," said Alyssa. "They admire you!" It felt good to know there was more than one high school where someone like me could fit in.

I had read everything I could find about Alyssa, so I knew a lot about her. I guess because I've spent so much time in front of TV, watching people act, I wanted to get behind the scenes. And I wanted to learn how actors and singers did their jobs. Alyssa was only a year younger than I was, but she'd been acting since she was eight—over half her life! She was close to her mom, just like me. I knew Alyssa'd said it was hard to be famous, because you get stupid stuff written about you. I'd hate to have the name of anyone I went on a date with in all the papers the next day. But at least she got recognition for her *work*. Not for being *ill*.

So I asked Alyssa every question I could think of—about the show and her job and what her day was like. As every teenager knows, Alyssa plays Samantha on *Who's the Boss?* That's Tony Danza's teenage daughter. Alyssa said she was able to work and stay in school because she got tutored on the set three hours a day. She said the cast are very good friends now that they've worked together for so long.

They rehearse Monday through Thursday, and then tape the show on Friday.

"Why don't you come to a taping?" Alyssa asked. "You could be my guest. You'd get to see where they place the cameras, how they get different shots, where we have to stand and move around on the set."

"Wow, I'd love that!" I told her. "What was your all-time favorite episode?"

Alyssa laughed. "Samantha getting a hickey!"

"Mine too," I said. "That was a good one! Did you have to go out and get a real one for the camera?"

"My hickey was the magic of Hollywood makeup," Alyssa answered, rolling her eyes and smiling.

"Did you get teased anyway?" I asked.

"No, because the script was about dealing with peer pressure." She looked at me. "I guess you know something about that."

I nodded. I did know what it could do to people.

Alyssa had about a million silver bangles clinking up and down her arm, along with a friendship bracelet—one of those bands of multicolored woven threads with long, loose ends. She took it off and tied it around my wrist. She told me to leave it on until it wore off. Then she shook my hand good-bye.

I was ecstatic. Still, there was something missing. I wasn't sure whether I was doing the right thing, so I needed a go-between.

"Mom," I said, "do you think I could ask Alyssa for a kiss good-bye?"

"Well," Mom said, "she can only say no." Alyssa was about to walk out the door, but Mom caught up with her. They huddled for a few seconds, and then Alyssa came marching back, grinning from ear to ear. She gave me a giant hug and a big kiss.

"I'll never wash that cheek again," I told her. I felt eight feet tall.

"You certainly can talk to anyone," Mom marveled. "You could make the President of the United States feel comfortable."

I didn't say anything. I was much happier I'd made Alyssa feel like I was an ordinary kid. After she left, I started to untie her bracelet.

"Ryan, what are you doing?" Mom exclaimed. "Aren't you going to keep it on forever?"

"I want to *keep* it forever," I said. "I don't want it to get dirty." When I got home, I hung Alyssa's bracelet on my bedroom wall.

IN DECEMBER I turned sixteen. Right away John Riser gave me a job, working at Maui Surf and Sport on Saturdays and weeknights. My first paycheck! Most of John's customers for boards were kids about my age. Usually they knew what they wanted. We had a whole wall covered with boards, all of them different shapes and designs in cool colors. The more of a concave your board has, the more tricks you can do. We had wheels in different colors too—but what counts with wheels is how hard they are. I'd talk to each customer, try to find out how much skating he did and how well, and then match his board and wheels to his style. The harder your wheels, the easier they slide. That's important if you spend a lot of your time practicing tricks on a half-pipe, which is a laminated ramp. For a street skater like me, hard wheels aren't as important.

"There's nothing we can't get," I'd tell customers. "If it's hot on the West Coast, we have it."

John liked to find obscure lines of clothing and gear from small outfits, so Maui would stay unique. Just to show you what I mean, we sold roller blades, but they weren't the big fad they are now. We kept up with trends, and stayed ahead of the pack.

Once I'd matched my customer with the right components, I'd custom-build his board on a workbench in front of him. First I'd cut the grip tape to fit the board's shape. Then I'd put the wheels on the truck—that's the mount for the wheels. Then the mount goes on the board, and you're set. The whole job takes about ten minutes.

Now and again I heard people gasp when they came into the store and spotted me walking around or back at the bench. I guess John took a chance taking me on. But nothing went wrong. When people spoke to me, they usually said something nice or wanted to know if it was really me. They'd go, "Haven't I seen you somewhere? You look *so* familiar." I just talked to them in a down-to-earth way, like I wasn't anyone special.

One day I was waiting on someone, and all of a sudden a kid who'd come in with his parents said, "Hey, Ryan!" I turned around. There was one of the two boys in whose names the Concerned Citizens had sued to keep me out of Western.

We didn't say anything memorable to each other, just the usual—"How're you doing, man? Good to see you! What's going on?" But he seemed really glad to see me, and so did his parents. By then I'd been out and around enough to know when someone was faking. This time I thought the whole family was saying, "Let's forgive and forget, okay?"—like they meant it. I was real pleased that they had seen me on the job.

John Riser and I had gotten to be good friends. We skated out back quite a lot. "Pretty good vigor there," he'd tell me. Afterward we'd go wolf tacos. Now that I was an employee, I had a discount, so I gave John some business myself. I'd finally gotten my learner's permit. When a group of Indiana car dealers gave me a black 1987 Chevy Cavalier with gray interior, sunroof, and stereo, I drove it over to Maui right away to show it off to John.

I told him I had a fuzz buster—a police radar detector. That was a secret I kept from almost everyone. It kind of made up for the pillow I had to keep on the driver's seat so I could see over the wheel. Having the car made me more interested in school games and parties and made me feel I now really looked sixteen. Someone who already had a license had to be in the car with me. So I'd offer to take a bunch of kids to whatever was happening over the weekend.

I was out of work for a while in January because I got my second bout of pneumocystis pneumonia—something everybody'd been waiting for since I was diagnosed. Still, I spent only eighteen days in the hospital—no big setback. According to the press, I was officially no longer dying. In fact, *People* magazine ran a lot of photographs showing the world how well I looked. In one of them, I was sprawled on my bed, doing homework.

The next week I got a funny phone call. "Helloooooo, Ryan," Matt Frewer said. "I like your *Max Headroom* poster." He'd spotted it on my bedroom wall in the *People* photograph. Matt has sharp eyes and a sharp sense of humor. Even his answering machine is funny. "I'm not here," he says. "Well—you know what I mean." He called up regularly, just to see how I was doing. I really wanted to look him up in L.A. He said he'd come out to Indiana too. One day I was in the family room watching *Doctor Doctor*, and there Matt was in an episode about a patient with AIDS. I shouted for Mom to come downstairs. At the very end we saw Matt come on screen and announce that the preceding episode had been dedicated to me. "He was treated badly by people who didn't know better," Matt said. It was Matt's little surprise for us—and it had been a big one!

Then I had to ask John for some extra time off. I was going to have a chance to talk to the President of the United States—at least, to his Commission on AIDS. They were inviting me and Mom to Washington to talk about prejudice against people with AIDS. And they wanted Jill Stewart to tell them about Hamilton Heights' crash course in AIDS education.

I got my time off—along with a strong dose of teasing. John didn't want me getting a swollen head. He would tell me, "I'll never say you were the best worker I ever had." Sure enough, he hasn't.

But now I was in major trouble. I had to write a statement to read to the Commission. Like I said, I never have done well in English. I did get an A on that one paper I wrote about Mom when we were back in Kokomo. It was the brief, very brief story of my life, one page exactly. And still I took two weeks to come up with something halfway presentable.

My paper for the Commission had to be around three or four pages long. *Aargh!* Mom had a good idea, though. She said, "Why don't we go see your English teacher, Mrs. Reeves? Maybe she can help."

When we got to Mrs. Reeves' office, she had a pile of essays she'd just marked sitting on her desk. We explained my problem.

"Well, Ryan," she said, "you just got an A

on this last paper you wrote, the one called 'My Odyssey.' I think it can get you started."

I looked over my paper, which had been about moving from Kokomo to Cicero. There *was* a lot of stuff I could use. I knew I had to mention the bad old days in Kokomo, and things like Ryan White jokes and rumors about my biting and spitting on people and the day my locker was vandalized. The Commission needed to know what went on.

But I also remembered Mom's approach to Dick and Charlie. You always have to live with what you say. It's important to be dignified—especially when the President might read what you write. So I planned to concentrate on how much my life had changed. Cicero and my new school had worked hard not to be like Kokomo.

Mrs. Reeves understood what I was after. I came up with an outline, and she and Mom helped me polish three and a half pages that seemed reasonably okay. Jill was used to giving speeches, being a student politician. But even she was nervous about our trip. I think she felt a little funny. This was such a good thing for both of us, but it happened because of a bad thing—my disease.

Jill, Mom, and I flew to Washington and took a look at all the famous buildings and monuments—even the *other* White House. I really liked the Vietnam memorial, the way you could see all the soldiers' names written on shiny black marble and your own face reflected among them.

The night before we were going to speak to the Commission, Ted Koppel had all three of us on *Nightline*. He's famous for asking questions nobody else asks. Sure enough, he said to me, "Here you are, sixteen years old, when most youngsters really don't have to think about death at all. That's something way down the road. How have you come to terms with it?"

"Well," I said, and took a deep breath, "I believe that when you die you go to a better place. And I believe in God and everything, and I'm not really afraid of dying."

You don't hear people telling Ted Koppel stuff like that every night. So he asked, "Are you a very religious person now?"

I simply said, "I'm very religious."

"Have you always been?" Koppel persisted.

I had to say, "Not as much as I should have been."

So then Koppel wanted to know what turned my head around. Had it been fear of dying, or prejudice, or what?

"Well"—I hadn't thought much about that. I don't talk about my faith unless I'm asked about it. It's just there when I need it—"I think it's a little bit of everything," I finished.

I didn't regret what I'd said, but I was afraid my answer sounded lame. Being thankful for each day and hopeful about the future was such a habit with me now. But I didn't know exactly how to explain it on national television.

The morning after, I was even more worried

about going up before the commissioners. Who knew what *they* would come up with?

We took a cab from our local hotel to Capitol Hill, and walked into a vast room with a high ceiling and wooden paneling on all four walls. The press was everywhere, snapping pictures and rolling cameras. I blinked at the TV lights. We sat in the center of the room at a plain wooden table with microphones and water pitchers on it. Jill had on a dressy dress and pearls, but I'd decided to wear what I'd wear to school: a loose white shirt, jeans, and untied high-top sneakers. I carried my statement with me.

When we sat down, there were rows of people sitting on chairs behind us. I wasn't sure who they were, but I guessed they wanted to hear the three of us. In front of us were the commissioners, sitting in a row on a small stage along a high wooden desk, like the judge's bench I remembered from courtrooms. A bunch of photographers sat on the stage below the commissioners and kept snapping away at us.

I had a couple of small coughing attacks and had to pause for a sip of water. I told the Commission about the hardships that go along with AIDS, and how I tried to turn the other cheek. But I also talked about the stars who'd helped me. I made sure to mention Elton, Greg, Matt, and of course Alyssa. And I talked about my dream of fitting in somewhere—and now I did.

"My life is better now," I wound up. "I'm a normal happy teenager again. I'm just one of the kids, and all because the students at Hamilton Heights High School listened to the facts, educated their parents and themselves, and believed in me. I believe in myself as I look forward to graduating from Hamilton Heights High School in 1991. My school is proof that AIDS education in schools works."

Then I sat back and heaved a big sigh of relief. The hard part was over now. Jill told the Commission what our school's program had been like, and how AIDS education was a permanent part of our curriculum. Governor Orr of Indiana had given Hamilton Heights an award for setting an example to other schools and making our state look good. I was glad we were taking the message all the way to the President.

Jill ended up by paying me a nice compliment. She said that as far as Hamilton Heights was concerned, when a student with AIDS comes to school, it's important to find out what the family and the person want. "But," she went on, "that's leaving out how much Ryan has done for us. He puts life in perspective. These things you can't measure."

Luckily the commissioners said Ted Koppel had asked Jill and me just about all the questions they could think of. They did want Mom to tell them how we kept our spirits up.

"For one thing, Ryan looks normal," Mom said. She knows what counts with me. "When he's been in the hospital, he's seen kids who were disfigured, or in a lot more pain than he was. Then I've always told him, 'You have to go out and reach for things in life—not just sit around.' "

WHAT MOM had said about my looking okay came back to me later on. In August we were going to spend a month in Statesville, North Carolina, a little town where the Landsburg Company wanted to shoot our movie. John Herzfeld, the director, came to visit us in Cicero and I drove him around.

"Whoa, Ryan!" he exclaimed. "Slow down! I want to live to make the movie."

Later we ate pizza at our kitchen table and went over the script again. We had gone through this before. There had been about four different versions. The first one wasn't right at all. It just had our names stuck in every now and then to make it sound like it was about us. But the next one was better. We made sure everything was in the right order. We ended up changing a bunch of lines because they didn't sound like Mom and Andrea and me talking. We got rid of all the seven-dollar words, dictionary words.

Let me tell you, rewriting a script is *slow*. One time we had a script meeting and Mom kept working, but I fell asleep. Heather was there and she took a picture of me to prove it.

There weren't any exaggerations in the script, though. Just the opposite, really. There was only time to show a few of the awful things that happened to us. Some stuff had to be clumped together, like court hearings and trips to the hospital, or you'd be watching all night.

Then John said out of the blue, "Ryan, how'd you like to play Chad?"

I couldn't believe my ears. "You mean it?" I asked.

"Absolutely," John said.

"Wow!" I said. *"Yeah!"*

Not everyone with a terminal illness looks good enough to be in a movie. I reminded myself one more time that I was luckier than a lot of other sick kids. But Mom was worried that I'd get upset playing someone who'd died.

"Mom," I said, "it's only acting."

I'd been on TV often enough so I wasn't nervous around cameras. I looked over my lines just once, the day before my scene. After all, I was the only one who knew what Chad had been like.

Besides, once we got to Statesville, I was incredibly busy. All three of us were. Some days we had to be on the set, ready to work, at 6:30 in the morning. Sometimes we were still filming after midnight. And when we weren't working, there were lots of people to hang out with.

We each had our own director's chair and we had our own trailer to rest in when we didn't have to be on the set. We'd thought we'd be spending most of our time there, off in a corner. Not so. John Herzfeld wouldn't make a move without us. He had to hear from us all the time. He wanted to make sure everything looked and sounded just the way we remembered. We were the resident experts!

At first we held back. We wanted to be polite, and we were afraid we might not know what we were talking about. Sometimes we didn't. Doug Whitley was the location manager—he had found Statesville and all the buildings where we filmed. When we arrived, he took us to see the house that John had picked to be ours.

We looked at each other. We didn't know what to say. It was a nice old house—once. Now it was really run-down, nothing like our house in Kokomo.

"Gol-leee," Mom began.

Doug read our minds. "Don't worry," he said. "John knows what he's doing. Wait 'til the art department gets through with the place."

The film crew moved out the family who lived in the house, and put them up in a motel while we shot. Mom ended up having a great time helping to fix the house so it looked like it was really ours. We brought my camouflage curtains and sheets and my I. U. pennants for my bedroom, and Andrea's skating trophies and ribbons for hers. I lent Lukas my I. U. sweatshirt and the shirt I had actually worn the day I went back to Western. Mom put up some of our own Christmas decorations for the scene where the robbery is discovered.

It was weird watching everyone work so hard to make it look like winter when the temperature was over a hundred degrees every day. People talked about how all they were going to remember about making our movie was the heat. When we needed snow, the crew made it out of wood chips. Once they overdid it and we had a small blizzard on the set—in about thirty seconds, two inches of fake snow fell!

John kept bugging us to tell him if things weren't right. "Ryan," he'd say to me, "I don't want you calling me up afterward and complaining about the movie. You're here—you can make a difference."

So we tried. Actors like to work in different ways. Judith Light was playing Mom. Whenever I saw Judith on the set, I'd say, "Hi, Mom!" I had already met her out in Malibu at Linda Otto's house. Back then I had just said a quick hello-good-to-meet-you, and then raced out to the surf with Heather and Andrea. "You certainly aren't star-struck," Judith laughed. Well, after all, it was our big chance to do some boogie boarding. You put your board under your stomach, turn your back on the wave, and then jump up to catch it as it's going by.

Before we had left for Statesville, Judith had spent three or four hours on the phone with Mom, asking her tons of questions about how she grew up, and how she brought Andrea and me up. She wanted to know how Mom handled my hemophilia. Mom told her how Grandma used to make me padded suits. One day Mom saw me trying to stumble around in one of them.

"I thought, 'Enough is enough,'" Mom told Judith. "'I've got to get this stuff off him.'"

"What if Ryan acted up?" Judith asked. "What did you do? Would you grab him and hold him tight?"

"Yeah, I'd even spank him!" Mom said. True enough!

Mom and Judith got to be very good friends. Mom watched Judith in every scene, except for the one where she has to tell me I have AIDS. That was too hard. I know how Mom felt—at least a little bit, I guess. The day they filmed Barney's accident, I had had to go back to Hamilton Heights to register for my sophomore year. I was glad I had an excuse to be gone.

That scene where I find out I have AIDS was filmed in an abandoned hospital in Statesville. The art department had to work hard there! Judith would go into my hospital room and do one take. Meanwhile, Mom listened in on a headset out in the hall. In between takes, Judith would come out to see Mom. They'd hug each other and cry until Judith had to get her hair and makeup fixed for the next take.

Lukas Haas and I were more casual. We never did have any heart-to-heart talks about the real me. Mostly we ran around together, along with Andrea and Nikki Cox, who played my sister; Casey Ellison, who was my old buddy Heath; and Kathy Wagner, who played Kris, my ex. You wouldn't think that Statesville would even have a hotel, but it did. So when we weren't working, the bunch of us spent a lot of time in each other's rooms, staying up 'til all hours, ordering from room service and playing Nintendo. Or we'd go up to the roof of the hotel and try to fly a toy airplane that never did work.

Or we'd explore the old hospital. The art department had fixed up only three rooms to use in the movie. Every other room was dirty and musty. Some had broken windows. We discovered a dentist's chair and some other equipment we could play with. In one room we found old pills scattered all over the floor. In another there was a dead bat! We chased each other through the hospital's corridors, yelling, "Did you see the bat? Did you see the bat?"

We had a great time, but I think Lukas also wanted to be around me a whole lot, so he could figure out how to act like me without being a carbon copy.

"I can't be just like you anyway," Lukas said. "You loved your school and I wasn't crazy about mine."

In the scene where Lukas is interviewed at home by a television reporter, he told me that he'd tried to make his voice and his eyes as relaxed and matter-of-fact as he could. "That's how you are all the time," he said.

Well, I try. When we first started shooting, I had had a bleed in my right elbow, and kept it all wrapped up in an ace bandage. It hurt to pick up anything. Everyone was very friendly and wanted to shake my hand. Normally when I have a bleed anywhere in my right arm, I shake hands very, very gently. I'm hoping other people will figure out that if you squeeze my hand tight, it hurts. But they don't always get my message. With my elbow out of action, I finally had to stop shaking everybody's hand—it was just too painful.

After a good actor has spent enough time with you, he can act more like you than you do! Like in the movie's opening scene, you see Lukas fussing with his shirt collar, first pulling it up straight, then flattening it down, then pulling it up again. That was Lukas's idea. He never did see me get dressed—but it *is* the kind of thing I might do.

Sometimes I would give Lukas some tips, though. In that opening scene, Nikki, who's playing Andrea, is trying to get Lukas away from the mirror and out of the house so she can make skating practice. After the first take, John asked Andrea and me if the scene sounded right. Andrea and I both said no—Nikki had to be a lot tougher. She should boss Lukas more. Nothing gets in the way of Andrea's skating!

It was fun to watch other people pretend to be us! I wasn't embarrassed or upset, but sometimes I just had to laugh and say, "Oh gosh, I can't believe I ever behaved like that! I was younger then!"

Andrea thought it was weird that she was being played by a redhead who didn't skate. Andrea did teach Nikki a few moves. Nikki had taken some lessons, but she was no skater. Andrea got to play one of the girls in the roller skating competition. She wore her own costume, a black and gold one. You can spot her in the rink, circling around in back of Nikki. She lent Nikki some medals she'd won, and her skating sweater.

A few people we knew got to be in the movie. Some of Andrea's skating friends came down to be the other contestants in the roller-rink scenes. Mr. Vaughan's son, who's his partner, played a lawyer, and Mr. Vaughan himself was a reporter. He lent the film people a picture of his father and a statue of a horse from his real desk for his movie office.

Mr. Vaughan must have been pleased that he was played by the biggest star, George C. Scott. Scott was in only a few scenes, so he wasn't in Statesville for very long. He's such a big name and acts like such a man of authority that Mom felt shy about asking him if she could take a picture of him with me. But he said, "Why *sure!*" and put his arm around me right away.

I know that when John cast me in the movie, he and Linda were trying to make a point. They were telling the audience, look, there's Ryan hanging around all these well-known actors. See, you can't catch AIDS from being close to someone who has it.

Every day I ate with everyone else working on the movie. I used the same toilets. No one in Statesville ever got upset. And none of the cast or crew ever objected. A lot of them had friends who'd died of AIDS.

I liked being a member of the cast, but the

best part for me was the way the cast and crew hung out together all the time, like one big family. You get to know everyone—or at least I did. I was amazed at how many people you need to make a movie. Because everyone was working long hours together, they made a big effort to be as nice as possible to each other. I appreciated that. I even got to be part of the crew.

The first time I met some of the crew, Mom and Andrea and I had just arrived in Statesville. I was standing in the hotel lobby, when Doug Whitley, the location manager, and a bunch of other crew members walked by.

"Hey, Ryan," Doug said, "we're gonna party. Wanna come?"

I found out that a party meant a trip to the hotel basement. The hotel didn't have a bar, but they'd tried to set one up in their storeroom. You had to walk through the kitchen, and then you found an old jukebox and some packing crates set on end with a few bottles on top.

Another movie company had just passed through and some of the crew had worked on their film too. I asked what it was about.

"Oh, an Amish family whose baby was killed," Doug said. "And now here we are on *The Ryan White Story*."

Everyone laughed, including me.

"Film crews have a sense of humor about everything," Doug told me.

"So do I," I said.

Then a crew member I didn't know came over. "Hi, I'm Kurek Ashley," he said to me.

Kurek seemed like a tough street guy— "twenty-seven with a twelve-year-old attitude," he told me. He had worked with John on all his movies, but I found out he had other talents. Because of the heat, he was wearing a sleeveless T-shirt. My eyes kept wandering to his amazing biceps.

"Where'd you get those muscles?" I asked.

"I need them," Kurek said. "I'm usually a stuntman. Right now I'm a grip. I have to move the cameras around. Want to work out together sometime?"

"Sure," I said, even though I knew I'd have to spend most of my time watching. "Too bad there aren't any stunts in this movie."

"We can still do some," Kurek said. He showed me how to fake a punch and a couple of kicks.

A few days later, an NBC news team showed up to do a story about the movie. Kurek and I worked out a great stunt scene for them. Kurek came up to me shouting, "Hey, Ryan! Tom Brokaw's here! I told him he could interview you."

"You idiot!" I screamed. "What gives you the right to speak for me? No interview! I'll never do it."

Then I punched Kurek the way he'd shown me. We had someone off camera clap, so my punch *sounded* real. Kurek reeled backward and fell over a chair. We were a big hit with NBC and anyone else who happened to be around.

All the kids in the cast spent a lot of time with Kurek. He looked out for us. He even took Lukas and Casey to the hospital one day when they were working in heavy jackets in 107-degree heat and felt faint. You can see Kurek in the movie. He plays a plant worker who tells Judith she shouldn't be drinking coffee with everyone else at work because her son has AIDS. Then he gets into a fight with another guy who supports her.

The day we filmed that scene, Mom went up to Kurek afterward and said, "Kurek, you know I really love you. But when you did that scene, you were scary. I *hated* you!"

"That's a compliment, ma'am," Kurek said cheerfully. "I wanted to be the epitome of Kokomo."

Another day Mom was sitting watching the crew as they set up a shot. Suddenly a tall woman with long black hair came up to her out of nowhere and said, "Hi!"

Mom stared. She knew she'd seen the woman before, but she couldn't think where or when.

"Mom, it's me!" Andrea yelled. "Don't you know me?"

The makeup team had given Andrea a giant black wig and had used every kind of makeup they had on her.

"You should be in a magazine," I said. "'Before or after—which is worse?'"

Andrea tried to punch me, so I moved fast. I knew she hadn't been studying fake punches with Kurek.

I was hanging out with the crew so much they gave me a job—second assistant director. You're called second AD for short. There are usually a few second ADs, so I guess I was the third or fourth second. The first AD stays on the set with the director, the producer, the actors, and the camera crew. When everybody's ready for a take, the first AD says, "Roll camera!" As the second AD, I was outside, but I could hear the order over a walkie-talkie.

Then my job was to act like a traffic cop. I shouted, "Rolling! Very quiet, please"—so the rest of the crew and the people from Statesville who'd come to watch would shut up during the take. When I heard "Cut!" over my walkie-talkie, I knew they'd finished the take. Then I'd yell, "Cut!" again, so everyone could start talking or gunning their cars or whatever.

I had packed my skateboard and I used it to whiz around so everyone close by would hear me. Sometimes I fetched missing props, or found somebody to bring Judith a chair if we were shooting at night and she looked tired. I liked wearing two watches on the same wrist. My job made them look real official, not just trendy. I loved my job. I wanted to do it forever.

"You're military, man!" Kurek grinned at me. The crew gave me a T-shirt with everything the second AD yells listed down the front. "Rolling—Quiet! Cut. Going Again. . . . Rolling—Quiet! . . ."

Second ADs have to do a lot of paperwork

and behind-the-scenes stuff that I didn't know much about. One of the other second ADs, Annette Sutera, was only twenty-five. To work on movies, directors and ADs have to join a union called the Directors Guild of America, or the DGA. They have a training program for ADs. Annette was in it. I really liked her, so I volunteered to be the apprentice's apprentice.

One thing Annette had to do was make up call sheets. Everyone in the cast and crew gets one at the end of each day so they know what time to be on the set, ready to start work the next morning. I'd hang around Annette's room, reading comics on her bed or looking at TV, and watching with one eye how she did her job.

A couple of times I had a big coughing fit. When that happened, I could see I was making Annette nervous.

"It probably means I forgot to take my cough medicine," I told her. Most days I felt unbelievably well—so well I wondered whether my AIDS had gone away. All day long I'd go and go and go.

Annette liked shopping as much as I did, so in our spare time we explored the malls around Statesville. She loved my orange Oakleys, the sunglasses I had bought at Maui Surf and Sport, so I found her a pair. She told me exactly how to become a real AD.

"Come out to Hollywood," Annette said. "I'll help you join the DGA. Then you have to work a certain number of hours as a trainee. When you've finished that, you have to go before some members of the DGA board and pass an oral exam. They do everything except shine lights in your face."

"That bad? What happens?" I asked.

"They work hard to make you mad," Annette explained. "They want to see how well you can think on your feet. They give you problems to solve—situations that might come up on a set. Whatever you suggest, they don't like it. They say, 'Think of something else.' "

"How many times did you take the test?" I asked.

"I passed it the first time," Annette said. She sounded like she still couldn't quite believe it.

"Then I will too," I said.

I had to make my acting debut first, though. On the morning when I was supposed to do my part, I got a big surprise outside the hotel. There was a white stretch limo waiting for me at the curb. The limo had a TV and a bar, and it was full of balloons! The whole crew had rented it to take me to the set. When I rolled up, we opened all the limo doors, and balloons came flying out. Everyone applauded.

Russ, our transportation coordinator, said, "You've treated us with respect. So we wanted to show some for you."

Lukas and I put on those awful hospital pajamas that I never will wear. Then the wardrobe and prop people taped fake IVs on both of us. The tape was too tight, so we actually got bruises on our arms. Our hands started swelling up, just the way they tend to do when you have a real IV.

I had had a fever blister on my lower lip all week. Mom and I had been slaving away, putting all kinds of medication on it every hour on the hour. It had finally dried up just in time before I did my scene. Then the makeup people decided I needed three *fake* fever blisters! Not as cool as Alyssa's fake hickey!

I gave Lukas some pointers on talking back to Dr. Kleiman about the feeding tube. "Yell it out, man. Say *'No way!'*" I told him, "You don't want that thing in you *ever*."

Our scene went well. It was funny to hear Lukas lecturing me about my bad attitude, but I managed to keep on dragging my feet and being Chad. Afterward, everyone on the set gave me a standing ovation. It was so nice, I was embarrassed.

It felt even better when Lukas told me, "I've never worked with anyone as good as you their first time."

But soon I had to give the last order on my AD T-shirt: "That's a Wrap! Let's Party!" A wrap means you're done shooting. After the wrap party, you can go home. We were all done in four weeks. It had happened so fast!

The party was in the hotel's basement bar, of course. Where else? I danced with Annette, and when it got late and most people had left, the crew slipped me a beer.

"Your eyes are getting rounder and rounder," Doug told me.

I just took a few sips. I think alcohol tastes like what it looks like. But standing there holding a beer, I was really part of the whole gang. I had so much energy I stayed up all night.

The next morning I was real sad. We went around and said good-bye to everyone. They gave Mom a bunch of stuff from our movie house. The beautiful crocheted tablecloth from the movie is on our dining room table right now. I got to take home the Hollywood Herbie. He ended up outliving the real Herbie. Judith Light gave Andrea a little gold skate on a necklace and I got a gold cross.

All our new friends would be off working on another movie somewhere, but we had to go home. Andrea and I were due at school. Well, I thought, I just gotta find a way to do this again. At least I know what to look forward to now.

It was especially hard to say good-bye to Annette and Kurek. I told Annette I'd call her next time we visited Los Angeles. In Kurek's scene in the movie, you can't see that he always wears one earring. Sometimes it's a classy-looking gold ring. Sometimes it's a dangling plastic skeleton or a painted wooden parrot. I'd asked Kurek if he'd take me to get my ear pierced like his. I wasn't planning on changing my earring. I really wanted to wear a diamond stud all the time.

"Fine," said Kurek. He found a jeweler in Statesville who said fine too. But John Herzfeld squashed our plan. I was going to have to give

TV interviews about the movie. John didn't want anyone in Kokomo spotting my earring and saying, "See, I told you he was gay. There's the proof."

We went back home, and I started my sophomore year without an earring. I gave a lot of interviews and I never did pierce my ear. One day I was working behind the counter in Maui Surf and Sports when John and Doug drove up.

They'd brought a very small crew—just about a half-dozen people—to get the shots of Kokomo and Indianapolis that you see at the very beginning of the movie. We had a mini-reunion. They hung out for a while and admired the merchandise. I recommended some Oakleys.

After their van pulled away, I started sorting some T-shirts from California that John Riser carried. I really liked those shirts. Each one had the company's logo, a black and white yin-yang symbol. John had told me that it meant there was some evil in every good, and some good in every evil.

I remembered how Jill Stewart had felt about our trip to Washington. Some good things had happened—definitely. Jill and I had gotten to talk to the President's Commission, and my family and I had had a great time helping make a movie about what had happened to us. If enough people saw it, maybe other kids with AIDS, kids I'd never know, would be treated better. All this because of something bad—my AIDS.

Besides, I'd had another great job. Now I knew I was good at something besides being sick. I looked out the front window after the movie van. I thought, There go the best days of my life.

6

Going to a Better Place

"HOW DO YOU FEEL knowing you'll never have sex?"

I'm at Boys Town, my first time out answering kids' questions about AIDS. Right away they hit me with this. I've gotten it before, and it's sure the one I hate the most. It's the worst. It makes me wish the floor would open up and swallow me. I always find a way around a straight answer.

Boys Town is a home in Nebraska for kids who have no one to take care of them properly. Maybe you've seen the famous old movie about it on late night TV. Right now girls live at Boys Town too—and some of them have come out to hear me. So I feel even more embarrassed.

After Jill and I went to Washington, I started getting two, maybe three offers to speak every week. I couldn't go everywhere, or I'd turn into a high school dropout. Anyway, I don't speak. I can't even write an English report, let alone a speech. So when I do have time to show up somewhere, I stand in front of a room and take questions.

At Boys Town, there were two rooms full of kids. When Mom and I got there, the priest in charge told me, "These are the kids who probably would have made trouble for you if you'd been at *their* school." But they never ran out of things they wanted to ask me. They were fascinated. Finally we ran out of time.

I did say I'd give one speech—to the annual convention of the National Education Association in New Orleans. For one thing, I'd be speaking at the Superdome, where I. U. had won the National Basketball Championship the year before, in 1987. Then there was the fact that I'd be talking to about 10,000 teachers. They could help hundreds of thousands more kids understand AIDS. It was a big chance, so I said yes. Besides, people run around with a lot of misconceptions about AIDS, but the biggest one is that you can't do anything except lie in a hospital bed. I wanted those teachers to see that you can do a lot of things. I do.

Instead of a new speech, I ended up saying in New Orleans pretty much what I'd told the President's Commission on AIDS. I was a major hit. The teachers gave me a standing ovation that never seemed to end. I nearly fell over backward! I wasn't sure what to say or do.

Afterward, the NEA wanted me to talk to

some reporters and then take Mom and me to a fancy restaurant. But that much attention is irritating. At least I think so. I get real tired of answering questions all the time, even for a good cause. I don't care about fancy food. I prefer my privacy. So I asked to be excused from the restaurant and walked around the French Quarter on my own for a while. The French Quarter is the oldest part of the city, and it's where you go to hear New Orleans jazz. It was a hot July night, so there were crowds of people doing the same thing I was. All the jazz bars and clubs along the old streets keep their doors open, and some musicians stay on the sidewalk and play. So even if you're just standing outside, you can hear music everywhere. That was the best part of the trip— strolling around, and then picking up Mom and stopping at Burger King on the way back to our hotel.

After the teachers in New Orleans, I realized that even though kids may listen to me more than adults do, they're harder to talk to. I don't think they realize how much they stare. They're so curious they don't care. You know the look— "There he is—he's got *AIDS*." And sometimes once kids find out who I am, they have a problem with me that they didn't before. When I walk into a classroom, some of them look at me with their eyes out on stalks practically. Like, "I can't believe he's *the one*. I just passed this kid on the stairs!"

After I start talking, though, they begin to

think, Hey, this guy does the same things I do. He likes to skateboard and he likes to watch TV and he loves cars. That makes him not so different from me.

I let them know I don't feel like I'm anybody special. I admit—I got a D in English my freshman year. That makes me about as average as you can get.

The other tough part about going public is how stupid a lot of people are! They never bother to put themselves in a sick person's predicament. The mean ones think, AIDS is not gonna get *me*—meanwhile, let's get all of *them*.

When the movie was broadcast, the NEA sponsored a special screening in Washington and recommended that teachers use it in schools. I wanted to make the movie because I was hoping that what we went through will never happen to anyone else again. But plenty of people in Kokomo complained anyhow. They called Dick and Charlie and said, "Why didn't the movie show our side?" They didn't seem to learn anything from anything. Some of them still believe all those old rumors about me. They're glad I'm gone.

Other people—not just in Kokomo—can't seem to get it right. Most of the time you can't tell who has AIDS and who doesn't. You never know when you might be next to someone who does. Some people still believe that the AIDS virus is airborne, so they keep thinking they can't be in the same room with me. They're totally afraid to sit next to me but they'll sit next to someone who did. Now that's just plain stupid—and it hurts!

The point is, you've got to try to change people anyway. Lots of times I get the same questions over and over. So I work hard to be patient, I really do. It's perfectly safe to go to the same school as someone with AIDS, I say. Perfectly safe to kiss them or to go to the same movie theater or drink out of the same water fountain. If I kiss your dog—I might; I like dogs—he won't give you AIDS. I keep reminding myself that education takes time. Ignorance dies hard. But I guess this is going to take a lot longer than I ever dreamed.

Kids almost always want to know why I didn't tell a good chunk of people in Kokomo to buzz off. My answer is "Well, lots of times I wanted to say, 'Don't you think I have feelings too?' But I never did. I just ignored what people said." I could do it because I knew they were just ignorant.

Another question I get a lot is "How does it feel to have AIDS? What are you able to do?" So I say AIDS runs you down. You lose weight and you can't put it back on. In Africa, where lots of people have AIDS, they call it "the slim disease." I guess this is why. But I've always done everything I can. Always have, always will.

Then I hear, "Are you scared of dying?" You'd think this one would be tough, but it's not. "At first I was," I say. That's the truth. "But now I'm really not, because my mother told me we're all going to die sometime, so just step up to it." For some kids, that's a shock—to hear they're going to die too. If you're a teenager and you're not sick, you never think about dying.

Besides, I say, if you think, Well, I'm never going to make it, then you're not. I do think I'm going to make it. From the very beginning I've said I was going to fight this disease, and I was going to win.

But there's one place I can't win. That's where I am when I get that horrible question, the one they asked me at Boys Town. I was sixteen now, going on seventeen. I was thinking about working in film, or being a TV broadcaster, or working behind the scenes in TV. I sure had experience. My AZT was still doing me good. I felt fine. I thought a lot about girls, and I wanted to date.

I knew it wouldn't be easy. Mom and I still talk about most everything, even this. Mom said, "It'll be hard to meet a girl straight on. A lot of parents won't want you to have anything to do with their daughters."

As I said, I'm terribly shy. I would never force myself on a girl. I don't want to get hurt. I've just got to hope she loves me that much, because I would really, really like to get married and adopt children. Steve Ford has been a real dad to Andrea and me, so I know you don't have to be related to a kid to be a perfectly good parent.

But I worry that no one will ever love me

enough to be my wife. Then I start wondering if I have the courage to adopt and set up a family all by myself. I can tell that being a single parent has been real hard on Mom sometimes. It gets pretty lonely. You need someone to help you decide what school to send your kids to, or just tell you jokes when things start to get you down. I would love to fall in love—I'm really looking forward to it. But lots of times love songs make me sad. Even Elton's.

> *I guess that's why they call it the blues*
> *Time on my hands*
> *Could be time spent with you*

I'm not one to sit around singing, "Why me?" for too long, though. After all, I have a lot to distract me. I do feel very comfortable with girls. I understand their point of view. Comes from hanging out so much with my mother and sister, I guess. I like girls as friends. For one thing, they can help you find out whether the girls you like like *you*. I tease girls a lot and give them a hard time. But I think I'm good at being a friend. I remember birthdays. I don't let myself get too busy to stay in touch. I make time.

I mentioned that thanks to AIDS, I look very young—much younger than sixteen and a half. I'm only five feet. Andrea's been taller than I am for two and a half years now. Looking so young can be really obnoxious. Sometimes adults who don't know me talk to me as if I'm a child.

Every now and again, I get stopped in my car because the police think I'm underage. Then I drive up to a McDonald's window and the take-out person says, "How *old* are you, anyway?" Or I walk into a restaurant and get handed the children's menu.

I began to feel much better about my height after I started going out to California. There were plenty of celebrities besides Alyssa Milano who weren't any bigger than I was! And everyone in Hollywood wants to look as young as possible.

Sometimes I think the way I look even helps me with girls. If I were a girl, I might be intimidated by big beefy guys. There are millions of them here in Indiana because everyone is so into sports. A girl certainly doesn't have to think twice about being scared of me, or worry about whether I'll put pressure on her.

So I had a lot of dates. I went out with girls who were good friends, and I did things with groups of kids. Around here, you do pretty much the same things whether you're on a date or just hanging out with a friend or friends. Like I'd go over to Wendy Baker's house and watch TV or rent a movie and order pizza. She'd always wanted to be a cheerleader, but she wasn't sure she was pretty enough to try out.

"Sure you are," I told her. "Go for it." She did. She made the squad.

"See, I told you so," I said.

Sometimes Wendy was upset with her boyfriend. She'd tell me about how he didn't call when he said he would, stuff like that.

"He shouldn't make promises he can't keep," I would tell Wendy. "That's not right. You should be with somebody who treats you nice."

"Not everyone is a perfect gentleman like you, Ryan," Wendy answered. She was smiling, but she sounded a little sad.

"Well, they should be," I said.

Whenever Wendy was down, I'd call her. "Are you okay? Do you want to do something?"

I'd ask her if she wanted to drive into Castleton with me when I went to pick up my paycheck from John Riser. Afterward we'd go shopping or stop at Chi Chi's.

"Don't worry about him, Wendy," I'd say. "The guy looks like a yak."

She'd sock me in the arm, but at least she'd start laughing.

Heather and I kind of went back and forth between being best friends and being boyfriend and girlfriend. I mean, we really liked each other a lot, we talked on the phone every day, and we spent a lot of time together—as friends and on dates. I always wanted to take a date when we went to AIDS benefits and public events, so Heather came to just about every one. Whenever she was baby-sitting, I'd go help her, and we'd do our homework together. A lot of the time we went out with a group of kids, including Andrea, so she and Heather got to be good friends too.

But I also liked to flirt. Sometimes Heather

would pay me back. I can't say I enjoyed that. I'd send her notes like, "I was mad and sad to see you with Brad. After Detroit I thought we had something going."

Detroit was one of the trips Heather and I went on together. We went to New York twice, California twice. This time, Elton had invited Andrea and fourteen of her friends to his concert in Detroit for her fifteenth birthday. Luckily Andrea thought Heather and I both qualified. We got special passes to go backstage and visit Elton in his dressing room. He's always really excited to see us, and gives out plenty of kisses and hugs.

By that time we were old hands at this kind of thing. Mom, Andrea, Heather, and I had been in Los Angeles for an Athletes and Entertainers for Kids benefit where Elton played and sang. I was a special guest, along with Jason Robertson. He was seven, from Granite City, Illinois, and had gotten AIDS from a blood transfusion. He'd had a hard time in school too.

This benefit wasn't the first thing Elton had done to fight AIDS. He was on "That's What Friends Are For," the record that raised money for AIDS research. But this *was* going to be the first time he'd sung in a while because he'd had to have throat surgery the year before. You could tell he was all excited about being back on stage.

Elton has a song called "Candle in the Wind," about Marilyn Monroe. Whenever my family and I are there to hear him, he always dedicates the song to us. Mom cries every time.

"Don't start," I tell her. "You'll get me going."

I didn't dare get weepy this time. When Elton started "Candle in the Wind," he wanted Jason and me up on stage. We sat beside him on the piano bench while he played. The stage was dark except for one light on Elton and us. We didn't have to do anything—just sit there and listen. Elton turned to smile at us whenever there was a pause in the song. We tried to keep smiling back. It's a nice, sympathetic song to have a star sing to you. But poor Jason was having a hard time. He kept putting his fingers in his ears. Being that close to the piano music made them hurt badly. I felt for him. Now and again my ears act up if I'm not very well.

When the song was over, Elton hugged us both and walked us off the stage before he went on to the next number. My main memory about the party, though, is that only Andrea was served champagne. When Heather and I held out our glasses, we got carded!

The next day, Matt Frewer took us out to lunch in Marina del Rey. It was the first time we'd met in person. Up 'til then, we'd just been phone friends. He teased me when I wanted Mexican food—"More burritos, please please!"—and he told me that when I walked in all the girls were looking at me and going, "Oooh, it's Ryan White!"

"Just give them a wave like you're a rock star," Matt advised.

We got to see Greg Louganis again—this time at his house. It's high up in the hills around Malibu. The road up from the highway along the coast twists and curves like you wouldn't believe! Greg's house was very new, and he was still fixing it up. His garage was built to hang right out over the hillside. I wondered what an earthquake might do to it. His pool *was* earthquake proof. It said, "Custom Designed for Greg Louganis" right on the side.

"Ever need a house-sitter?" I asked Greg. The view all the way down to the beach was unbelievable. I was ready to live on a surfboard for the rest of my life.

Greg laughed. "Come by again on your next trip—even if I'm not in town. You can spend the day and enjoy yourselves."

We took him up on it, and came back with my grandparents. I felt very comfortable here because I could get away from being watched all the time. No one stared at me. No one teased me about being a hotshot. No one bothered me at all. Celebrities needed the same things I did: peace and quiet and privacy. One thing I'd had because of AIDS was shingles. I got itchy, painful blisters which had left scars on my back. If I was in a bathing suit, I felt much more comfortable now at Greg's pool then I ever would again on the beach in Florida.

I loved going to New York and California, and I was really happy that I could take Mom and Andrea and my grandparents and Heather. Sometimes Andrea even got to bring a skating friend. But the rest of the time, being well-known was more of a nuisance than something nice. Nobody at school ever bugged me about AIDS anymore, but I could tell that some kids were jealous of me, especially after the movie. Believe me, I *never* sit down in the cafeteria and start babbling about Greg's view, or how I had been on Phil Donahue and then he'd phoned the other night, or the time Andrea and Heather and I went to the Hard Rock Cafe in New York and Cindy Lauper called us there to give us shopping tips. I never try to be anything but as normal as possible. I certainly don't plan on spending all my time with celebrities, even though I'd love to move to California.

Besides, I'm a strange kind of celebrity. Even when Heather and I are just hanging out at Pizza Hut in Noblesville, someone always recognizes me. Sometimes they come over and shake my hand and say something really nice. That's great, even though shaking hands is not what I want to do most when I'm eating pizza. But sometimes people just gawk. When they stare at me, I remind myself that I'm acting normally, just going about my business. They're the ones who are being weird. But sometimes I wonder what they're expecting. If I were Elvis Presley, they'd want to tear my clothes off. But since I'm only Ryan White, they don't know what they want from me.

Whenever Heather and I spotted anyone staring, we'd start laughing. "Maybe I should moon them," I joked once. "Really give them something to look at."

When we still lived in Kokomo, I got a great letter from Tina Yothers, who's on *Family Ties*. She wrote me, "Because I am in show business a lot of people don't like me either. You just have to be strong and don't let people get you down." She was talking about fame, but she's right—it's a good way to think about AIDS too.

If I suddenly stopped being famous, I'd be so happy! I'd never miss it. I'd rather be Mr. Anonymous and do whatever I wanted. That's so much more fun. When we were staying in Los Angeles, Andrea, Heather, and I rode around in a limo taking pictures of each other making faces and fooling around. We had a big bunch of balloons trailing out the window. The other cars kept honking because our balloons were getting in their way. We drove over to Venice Beach where everyone does tricks and fancy skating on the boardwalk. Back at the hotel, Andrea skated and I skateboarded in the parking garage. No one bothered us.

"I'm jealous," Heather said. She doesn't skate—just runs.

"Hey, we want to enjoy this while it lasts," I protested.

But I made it up to her. She woke up in the middle of the night in the hotel with a terrible toothache. We had to take her to a dentist who said she needed a root canal. I've never had much tooth trouble, but I do know that root canal stuff is supposed to be horrible and real painful. So I held Heather's hand the whole time and talked to her.

"You think this is bad," I said. "Your birthday's coming. We're really going to give you a toothache." Heather's birthday is in November. I always take her to Ben & Jerry's. She has mint chocolate chip, and I have Cookies 'n Cream.

When we got back to Cicero, Heather had to have dental surgery all over again because the dentist in L.A. had messed up. I sent her notes while she was sick, just to let her know she wasn't missing anything at school. "Yearbook's about the only thing worth coming for," I'd tell her. And I'd sign off, "Totally bored but in a good mood."

I never let trips get in the way of stuff I had to do for school. I didn't want to ask my teachers to make exceptions for me—ever. Hamilton Heights has a program where you can be a teacher's assistant. I helped Mrs. Schwartz, my science teacher, with a biology class. Sometimes I took attendance, or I helped give quizzes, or I did Xeroxing for her. If I couldn't be around, I always let her know. If I was away and missed quizzes in my own classes, I always made them up, even if I had to take two or three at once. I was on the honor roll now. I wanted to stay there. And I couldn't wait to take auto mechanics.

Andrea had some good times because I got so much attention, but she didn't like it either. Andrea's modest. She would never tell you about her skating trophies. She doesn't even keep some of them in her room. She never gossips. She hates it if people get critical or make fun of anyone behind their back. She'll jump in with something nice about them.

Now everyone at school knew Andrea from the movie. She had almost as much fun making it as I had. But after it was broadcast, she got several letters telling her she sounded real spoiled. How could she think about roller skating when her brother was going to die? It wasn't just letters. Kids even said to me sometimes, "Boy, your sister sounds like a brat." It really upset me.

They didn't understand how much skating kept Andrea going, even though I was sick. Skating gave her some time alone with Mom. It helped her get away for a while from "that issue," as she calls AIDS. I certainly didn't blame her. I was glad Greg Louganis had gone to one of her workouts. He had been real worried about Andrea back when she'd had to stop skating, and later continued to follow her progress.

"I'm going to encourage you, not give you advice," he told her. "Keep it up. Enjoy it. Do it for yourself."

So I was really glad when Andrea and her skating partner, Scott, did their routine for the whole school. I knew she'd be back at the nationals soon. Now she wouldn't be just Ryan White's sister full-time, forever. Anyhow, sometimes I couldn't believe she *was* my sister, she was looking so good. She'd started letting her hair grow while we were in North Carolina working on the movie, and now she'd gotten it permed. She was no tomboy, and she wasn't quite so interested in squirting you with trick ketchup bottles anymore.

Even Steve noticed the transformation and he loved to tease Andrea about it.

"How come your hair's all messy?" he'd laugh.

Steve and I were always visiting and entering car shows. He had his Mustang and I had mine—I had traded in my Chevy for a new black and gray Mustang. I spent hours studying *Mustang Monthly* and *Wheels and Deals*. That's a trading paper that tells you what you need to soup up and modernize your car. I'd started daydreaming about going to school in California to learn to be a race-car driver. I could do that in the summer. Then I wouldn't have to wait until after college to head west.

"I think you have enough to worry about just buying gas," Mom told me.

"You can tell the men from the boys by the price of their toys," I said.

"He's sixteen, Jeanne," Steve said. "At his age I was car-crazy too. I used to drag race."

"Well, Ryan," Mom said, "I can't stop you— but I can sure try."

One day after school started I was driving out of the Pizza Hut parking lot in Tipton— another place Heather and I stopped by all the time. Tipton is a big cruising town. All of a sudden a kid waved me down. I knew John Huffman to say hello to at school—but that was all. He was a junior who lived in Cicero.

"Can you give me a ride home?" he asked me. "My car door fell off."

Well, his car was a red Mustang, so I said okay. I think that was the start of a great friendship. On the way to his house John told me his dad and his older brothers were all incredibly into cars. His dad even had a '68 Mustang—a real prize. They had all the Ford motor books and read the same magazines I did. When I dropped him off, John asked if I'd come back and take him to pick up parts while his car was in the shop.

After that we started cruising together. Just about every town in Indiana has a cruising strip. Around here, Noblesville is *the* place to show off your car on Saturday night. But Cicero does have its own strip, between the Dairy Queen and the bank. John and I'd pile Andrea and Heather and John's girlfriend, Dee Louks, into our cars and take off to see who we could see and what they were driving. Then we'd go down to Castleton to catch a movie or some salsa and chips.

I went by the Huffmans' as much as I could. John's bedroom was covered with performance stickers and posters for Mustangs and Oakleys. And he and his brothers and his dad all worked on their cars constantly. Whenever I stopped in, they might be looping a chain over a tree branch to haul an engine up into the air to repair it. I never knew what they might be getting ready to do next.

John was kind of a wild man, always collecting speeding tickets. I kept bugging him to slow down.

"You're a worrywart," he told me. "You drive fast enough when you get the chance."

"Yeah, but I hardly ever drink!" I said. "I certainly don't when I'm driving, and I won't drive with someone who does." I don't know why people drink anyway.

One weekend Mom and Andrea were away at a meet, and John's parents took a trip to Illinois. So John had an all-night party. Almost everyone stayed over, including me. Saturday morning I was sitting on the couch watching TV with a couple of girls. All of a sudden John's parents pulled into the driveway. They'd come back early.

The girls screamed and ran into the garage to hide. Another kid rushed around hiding empty beer cans. But I sat still. When the Huffmans walked in, I smiled at them. What else could I do? They caught us. Thank goodness Mom never found out—until she read this!

I turned seventeen in December. In the spring John and I planned to go down to the Speedway in Indianapolis to watch the cars and drivers warm up for the Indy 500. Since that was a while off, we spent our time at electronics stores, looking at new stereos we wanted.

Then one day Michael Jackson called me. Wow! I didn't know why he had, except maybe because he's from Indiana too. He was in his car, he said.

"If I lose you, man, I'll call you back," he told me.

So I told him what I was doing, what movies I'd seen, what school was like, how John and I had been window-shopping for stereos—stuff I'd talk about to anyone. I said I was playing his albums. I liked "Man in the Mirror" the best. Michael's not flaky or weird, like you read in those newspapers you can buy in the supermarket. He's real quiet and soft-spoken. Sometimes he takes a while to say things. He's just kind of gentle and peaceful. He was a nice new friend for me to have.

"Next time you're in L.A., we'll get together and have some good old fun," he told me. Well, I couldn't wait. But it was going to take us a while to get back to California.

Meanwhile life in Cicero was interesting. One day John came over and told me he'd broken up with Dee.

"That's too bad," I said. "She must be upset."

John shrugged. "Yeah, I guess," he said, looking away. He looked like he wished he hadn't said a word.

So I called Dee, just to be friendly. "How're you doing?" I asked her.

"Not too well," she said. "I'm glad you called."

"Don't worry about it," I told her. "Want to drive around for a while?"

"Sure!" she said. I think she was halfway hoping we'd run into John.

We went cruising quite a bit, just as we always had. Sometimes we saw John; sometimes we didn't. Mostly we just hung out together. Business as usual.

"You know," Dee said to me one time, "I never thought I'd see you anymore."

"Why not?" I asked. I was real surprised.

"Well," Dee said slowly, "John and I are broken up. You're John's friend."

"So?" I said.

"When a guy breaks up with a girl, his friends usually stick with him, not her," Dee explained.

"That's dumb," I said. "You're my friend too. Why can't I stick with both of you?"

We'd been close before, but we were a lot closer after that.

Spring was coming. Soon it would be May, which meant the prom, the greatest night of high school. Kids in Cicero look forward to it all year long. You may never get that dressed up again, your whole entire life.

I'd gone to black-tie parties before, but not to a high school prom. I definitely did not want to miss this one. Next year I might be in the hospital for mine! I was a sophomore now, but since I was older, most of my good friends were juniors and seniors. Sophomores couldn't go to the prom unless upperclassmen invited them. Heather was a sophomore too, and she was going with a junior. Dee was a senior.

I would have liked to have been going to my own prom, with someone I felt romantic about. Dee would have liked to go with John, but now he'd moved on down the line. Still, Dee and I had each other and lots of kids go to the prom with a good friend.

So I started lobbying. I think I must have said, "Let's go to the prom! Let's go to the prom!" every five minutes the whole month of April.

At first, Dee didn't get it. She thought for sure I was joking. "Are you serious?" she said at last.

"Yeah, I really am!" I exclaimed. "You know we both want to go. I can't ask *you*, but you can ask *me*."

So we made it mutual. We were both really happy to be going with someone we knew well. I called Dee to find out what color dress she was wearing.

"Pink," she said. "My favorite color."

Well, it's not mine. I've never cared for pastels. I like strong colors, like black and white and red. They're cooler somehow. And I like the way red glows.

But I went out and bought myself a pink bow tie and a pink cummerbund. Dee had mentioned that her dress had spaghetti straps, so there was no place to pin flowers on it. "I hate those things you pin on, anyway," she said. So I got her a wrist corsage of pink carnations, and another carnation for my tuxedo lapel.

The day of the prom finally arrived. It was

overcast and a little chilly, but Dee and I hardly noticed. I have to say we looked pretty great— so well coordinated. Mom took a bunch of pictures of us with the lake in the background, and then we met some friends who drove us to Indianapolis. The prom was going to be in a big club there.

The club had several levels, and the prom was on the top. When we walked in, we had our picture taken together right away for our souvenir. The photographer had us stand against a glamorous-looking backdrop, kind of like the New York skyline at night, with towers and skyscrapers and bright lights in the windows.

Then we walked into the prom. The club was roomy, but Dee's class was the largest ever to graduate from Hamilton Heights. So the room was packed. There was a band on stage at one end, and tables of food along the walls. As far as I was concerned, there wasn't nearly enough food—just stuff like piles of fancy fruit and miniature meatballs. I'm not the world's best dancer, but Dee and I danced one fast number and one slow—just to be out there on the floor. Mostly we hung out and made each other laugh and fooled around with our friends. A lot of people said to me, "It's so great that you're here!" They were glad I'd had a chance to come.

Around midnight we left the prom and went to the afterparty in a bowling alley in Cicero. *There* they had plenty of food, especially pizza. I dived in. We played video games and bowled until nearly four in the morning. I scored pretty well—better than Dee, I have to point out.

When I finally got home, it was almost light and birds had started cheeping away. Everything about the prom had been just about perfect. I'd lived a true chapter of teenage life and I could say it had been really wonderful—almost as great as I'd always hoped. I was happy.

In June Mom, Andrea, Heather, and I were due back in L.A. Athletes and Entertainers for Kids was having a benefit for Kareem Abdul-Jabbar, who was retiring from playing for the Lakers. I was supposed to introduce Kareem. We would make a great photo. Kareem has to be the tallest person in the world—and then there's me.

We called our friends to let them know we were coming. Matt Frewer was going to take us to a hamburger place in Hollywood. Annette Sutera, my old friend from the movie, promised she'd call a friend who was working on *Cheers*. Maybe I could visit the set. And Michael invited us to spend the day with him at his ranch outside of Santa Barbara. We'd be picked up in L.A.

The Kareem tribute turned out to be a big, fancy party with crowds and crowds of celebrities. The whole thing was broadcast, so I had to use a teleprompter to introduce Kareem. It wasn't hard at all. What he did with Kareem's Kids was great, I said, because now "kids know that someone important thinks they're important."

Kareem loves Indiana because we love basketball. He's from New York City, but he went to U.C.L.A., and his coach there was John Wooden, a really big name in Hoosier basketball. "So I have wonderful roots," Kareem told me. "New York City and Indiana!"

When I was actually standing beside Kareem, all of a sudden I thought, Wow! Maybe it's as tough to be seven foot two as it is to be only five feet. Turns out that when he first started growing, his mother told him to stand tall and be proud. Kareem's mom told him the same thing mine did: "Don't let anyone intimidate you."

At the tribute I met Billy Crystal, one of my favorite comedians—after Matt Frewer, of course. I'd seen Billy so many times on *Saturday Night Live*, I felt like I was in the middle of one of their routines when I talked to him. I met my namesake, Ryan O'Neal. He was there with Farrah Fawcett. It's hard to get more Hollywood than that. The next day we went to see a Hollywood landmark—the stars' handprints and footprints in the cement on the sidewalk in front of Mann's Chinese Theater. Mom took a photo of Jeanne Crain's handprints.

"Wait 'til I show Grandma!" she said.

Athletes and Entertainers for Kids also asked me to help some teenage TV stars open a new ride at Disneyland called Splash Mountain. Now it's the most popular thing there. It's a little like a roller coaster. You ride along a track inside a fake mountain through swamps and bayous—and all of a sudden you whoosh over a waterfall at forty miles an hour! The first time, you aren't prepared for what's coming, and it just takes your breath away. You can't see the bottom when you go over the falls. There's too much fog and water spray in the way. Well, we took turns going down the flume and getting a little damp. In the pictures we look like we belong at the beach. I had had the good taste to wear a T-shirt that said, "Life's a beach."

While we were at Disneyland, we checked out the 3-D movie of Michael as Captain EO, which I had already seen before. I planned to talk to him about it.

On the day we were going to spend with Michael, a limo picked up Mom, Andrea, Heather, and me very early at our hotel. After we climbed in, we were told that we couldn't take any cameras with us because we weren't allowed to take pictures. About three hours later, about ten in the morning, we drove up to the entrance of Neverland, Michael's ranch. We had to stop and let the security guards check us out again. They escorted us to the main house. Michael was busy, we were told; he'd be there in about a half hour.

So we had some sodas and Heather, Andrea, and I found a game room. The girls started on the video games. I climbed into an airplane that rocked around just as if it were really flying. All of a sudden, I caught a glimpse of Michael, playing along with the girls. I kept trying to look around at him and say hello, but I was trapped! I couldn't figure out how to stop the plane. No one else could either, so finally Michael had to stop laughing and unplug it!

Michael was wearing black pants and a red and black jacket and a black hat. He always wears my favorite colors. He showed us around the main house. Just like me, his dream is to have kids, so the house had a bedroom for a little boy and one for a little girl, plus a play-room with all kinds of toys and arts and crafts—even a miniature merry-go-round. Just like me, he collects things, especially dolls that are about three feet tall and look very lifelike. Mom loved them.

Besides the main house, the ranch has a pool, four bungalows for guests, and an old-time movie theater, with a popcorn machine and candy and a soda fountain. You use golf carts to get from one building to another, and to see the animals that are outdoors. There's Michael's giraffe, and cows that graze on his land but really belong to other ranchers.

At lunch—chicken, corn on the cob, and pumpkin pie—we met Michael's monkeys. His famous one, Bubbles, wasn't there, but the others made up for him. They all wore diapers and T-shirts in different colors. They have their own baby-sitters, and they go to school every day to learn manners. Their manners were pretty good! They hopped around and played with our shoelaces while we ate. Every now and again

Michael fed them a treat. I never wanted to say good-bye to them.

I felt very comfortable around Michael because I could see he was just as shy as I am. He seemed like a regular person to me. I certainly could relax with him. At lunch there was juice and Pepsi. Mom asked if there was any Coke. Then she remembered Michael's Pepsi commercial. She really thought she'd blown it.

Michael smiled. He knew what she was thinking. He said that Mom was just like his mother. So Mom got up the nerve to ask a mom-type question. "Michael," she said, "is it true that you sleep in an oxygen tank?" That's something the tabloids have said about him.

Michael laughed. "Now Jeanne," he said, "you know all the stuff that's been written about you and Ryan."

"Oh gosh," Mom said. "I understand!"

After lunch Michael asked me if I'd like to ride around part of the ranch in his four-wheeler. "Yeah!" I said. Andrea was going to try his trampoline, and Heather and Mom were checking out his outdoor hot tub that had a video screen on one side.

Michael and I set out over the ranch's dirt roads. I was at the wheel and he rode in the back. I took off and Michael yelled, "Slow down, Ryan!" After we'd gone a few miles he asked me if I could find my way back to the house.

"Sure," I said. I listed a few landmarks.

"Good for you!" Michael said. "But now let me drive!"

When we caught up with Mom and the girls, it was getting late. We had homemade pizza for supper, and then it was time for us to drive back to L.A. I told Michael that I really, really wanted a photo of us together. So he sent someone out for a Polaroid camera, and drove down with us to the ranch's entrance. Mom got some good shots, and then we said good-bye.

As the limo headed for the highway, Heather covered her face with her hands, shook her hair back and forth, and started laughing and laughing and laughing. She'd gotten excited when we went to see *Cats* in New York and the actors dressed as cats came down into the audience. But not like this.

"I just can't believe it! I just can't believe it!" she cried. "We spent the day with Michael Jackson. *I can't believe we were with Michael Jackson.*"

BACK HOME Andrea was making a giant comeback in roller skating. Five years ago she'd been one of the top five skaters in her age group. Then I was diagnosed. But in June Andrea won first prize in her age division for the state. In July she finished first at the regionals in Detroit. That meant she was eligible for the nationals, which were going to be held in August in Fort Worth.

Matt Frewer sent Andrea her plane tickets.

He wanted a video of her performance. He called afterward and asked, "How'd she do? How'd she do?"

Andrea did great. She finished third. She was pleased, she said, because the girls who took first and second were better than she was. Finally, there was another White in the newspapers and magazines.

Right around then, a car salesman in Noblesville called me. "I have a red Mustang here for you," he said. "It's from Michael Jackson."

Mom wasn't overcome with shock. She had some idea what was coming. Michael's office had called and asked her, "Now what was the car Ryan told Michael he liked?" Michael and I kept up with each other on the phone. Sometimes we talked twice a week, a lot of the time about cars. And when I thought back, I remembered that Michael had seen me by the pool at the ranch, leafing through *Mustang Monthly*.

Mom, Andrea, and I rode over together to pick up my new car. I started grinning like a Halloween pumpkin when I saw it. It was exactly what I wanted: red with a black and gray plaid interior and a sunroof. It even had oversized tires and deluxe wheels—really fancy for a Mustang. I put on my Oakleys and took off. I wanted to show it to everyone I knew. I had an appointment with Dr. Kleiman at the hospital in Indianapolis, so I whizzed down.

In the hospital parking lot, I had to back up in a hurry. I forgot to check my rear view. All of a sudden I felt a thud and heard a loud crunch. Uh-oh. I looked in the mirror—a little bit late. I could see a man with a beard pounding his fists on his steering wheel.

I got out and walked back to his car. "I'm *real* sorry, Dr. Kleiman," I said. This wasn't exactly how I'd planned to show off my car. Thank goodness there was no damage! Whew.

"I think Dr. Kleiman's mad at me," I told Mom that night. "You won't believe what I did. . . ."

Time to write to Michael. "Thanks a million for the Mustang," I started out. "Gee, IT'S GREAT. It really brightened up my summer. It came just in time too. The local Mustang club is having a show with hundreds of old and new Mustangs." Steve Ford and I had been looking forward to it. I told Michael, "Now I can enter mine and join the club."

I added, "I *hope* to get the windows tinted really dark so no one can see in. Maybe if you come here we can go for a ride."

I even made the ultimate sacrifice and took the car up to Kokomo to show my relatives. Grandpa and I were out cruising when I realized there was one person I really wanted to see my red Mustang.

"Grandpa," I said, "can we drive past Dad's house?"

We did, but there was no one home. I went back again. This time, there was a "For Sale" sign out front. As far as I could tell, Dad had moved, and I didn't know where. He had never seen Andrea skate. He didn't realize I had friends who cared so much for me. I wanted to tell him he was missing a lot.

I STARTED my junior year, but that didn't keep me off the road. I was in my car every spare minute. Everyone in town knew my car and how I'd gotten it. *It* was famous! Kids asked, "What's Michael Jackson really like? How about Kareem?" Adults asked too. I said, "Oh, he's nice." Or I mumbled something I hoped wouldn't attract much attention—I knew some kids were jealous, thinking I had such a great life knowing celebrities. I guess they forgot I was also sick.

One day Mom was in the school office borrowing a copy of *USA Today*. She wanted to see a photo they'd run of me. Someone had scrawled in the margin, "I hope you DIE!"

"I'd like to ask that kid if he'd swap places with you," she said. "I bet the answer would be the longest silence."

EVERY SUMMER I feel like I'm over AIDS, and in the fall, when it turns cold, I always feel chilled and I'm sick again. This fall I had a hernia, which meant that it hurt to sit, stand, or walk. My liver was acting up, and sometimes my stomach was so bloated I couldn't see my feet. I looked like I was having a baby. I was having fevers again, and I felt like I'd been coughing my whole life. For a third of it, I had. I sounded like a weak car battery, turning over and over and over again.

By October I was too worn-out to go to school for more than a couple of days in a row. Just carrying my books from my locker to class was enough to drag me out. It didn't help to think that I should have graduated by now.

To top off my troubles, Heather and I decided to go our separate ways. I missed her. I hoped we'd end up being best friends again. I knew she'd put up with some bad stuff on my account. She had had nasty notes left in her locker too. One time I called her at her baby-sitting job, and some other sitter answered. I tracked Heather down at home.

"How come you're not working?" I asked.

"I lost the job," she said.

"What'd you do?" I asked, just to be pesky.

"I'm your friend," she reminded me. "The woman said she couldn't take the chance."

That was Heather's second baby-sitting job gone for the same reason. I felt sad she'd had to pay for hanging out with me. And I felt almost eighteen and very lonely.

I had to go into the hospital so Dr. Kleiman could decide what to do about my hernia. I was lying around waiting for the next test when another doctor walked into my room.

"Well, Ryan," she said in a super-cheerful way. "Any girlfriends?"

For a moment I looked at her blankly. I couldn't figure out what she was driving at.

Then something clicked in my head. I was going to get a lecture on safe sex.

I don't get upset over IVs and all the stuff that happens to you in the hospital. But now I was fuming.

"Where's Dr. Kleiman?" I yelled. I could hardly speak. "*He's* my doctor!"

The woman doctor left in a hurry. When Dr. Kleiman showed up, I said, "I don't ever want her coming near me again."

"She won't," Dr. Kleiman promised.

After all the tests, Dr. Kleiman said the doctors couldn't operate on my hernia because thanks to AIDS, my blood platelet count was too low. Even with Factor and transfusions of platelets, my blood wouldn't clot enough. Surgery was too dangerous. There was nothing anyone could do. I just had to live with the pain. Well, I would. I had bad days, when just taking a shower and getting dressed was enough to exhaust me. But I always got dressed. I never was bedridden. I knew I had good days too, and I wanted to be ready. Plus I was still waiting to meet the right girl.

One halfway decent day I was up to going to Tipton and cruised by the Pizza Hut. John Huffman was there with his new girlfriend and her best friend, a pretty sophomore named Steffonie Garland. Steffonie had brown hair down to her waist. She had done a lot of gymnastics, and now she was a varsity cheerleader.

I asked John to tell his girlfriend to tell Steffonie that I liked her. She came to a surprise party we had at Pizza Hut for Andrea's sixteenth birthday. And on Steffonie's birthday, John and his girlfriend and Andrea and I took her to Chi Chi's. I made Steffonie stand straight up on a chair while we all clapped and cheered.

When I turned eighteen in December, I was in poor shape, though I did manage to go out for Mexican food. My nose was always runny, and I had laryngitis again. One day I could hear; the next day I couldn't. I had bloody noses and had to have Factor almost every day. And I was sick and tired of people asking me how I was, especially my relatives.

"I'm doing okay," was all I'd say.

"I'm your uncle," my uncle Tommy answered me back. *"I want to know."*

Well, he had to go get the list of my problems from Mom. Most of the time I was still well enough to bug my family to go to the movies. One night Uncle Tom, Aunt Deb, and all my cousins piled into our van with Mom, Andrea, and me. I was sitting up front and I turned the heater up full blast. The others all had down parkas and heavy winter coats on, but they didn't say a word.

On bad days I had to rely on the phone for social life. Michael called to say he was busy working on an album. He was in the studio every day. In between he had to pose for pictures.

"Oh yeah!" I said. I knew what *that* was like. "You have to smile for so long! Then the photographer says something corny like, 'Smile just like you smiled earlier!' I always want to say, 'Give me a mirror so I can check.' "

"We've got to get together and goof off again," Michael said. He wanted to know if I could come back out to the ranch after Christmas.

Well, when Michael invites you, you don't say maybe. Dr. Kleiman knew I wanted to keep going, and that trips to California kept me going. I could count on him to get me on that plane. So I told Michael, "You can bet on it."

Carrie Jackson Van Dyke wasn't a TV reporter anymore. She worked for the State Department of Health now. She asked me to make some public service announcements for TV and radio about AIDS, and to pose for a poster. I'd earn some money I could spend in California.

I was worried about looking sick on camera, so I got a little help from Carrie's makeup. "I didn't have a choice, but you do," I told kids. "AIDS is spread by ignorance."

Carrie brought my check for doing the announcements to Riley, where I was waiting for Dr. Kleiman to declare me fit to travel. I wasn't sure what he'd say. I had a big stomach that day.

"Carrie!" I said, pulling up my shirt. "I look like you did when you were pregnant!"

Now, Carrie's seen it all, but for a split-second, she looked shocked. That's just what I'd been hoping for.

Dr. Kleiman saw no reason why I couldn't visit Michael. I love Christmas, but this year I couldn't wait for December 28, when I was taking off. Mom and I hung all our favorite ornaments and watched *Miracle on 34th Street* for the five hundredth time. I still loved seeing the little girl who didn't believe in Santa and how she found out that he's real. Andrea could care less about fussing over Christmas, the way Mom and I like to.

"Remember how long I believed in Santa, Mom?" I asked her.

"Yes, and I remember how Andrea used to laugh at you," Mom said.

"I wonder whether she ever really believed at all," I sniffed.

This year, as usual, I had a long list for Santa.

"You always want more things and *better* things," Mom complained.

"Christmas isn't about receiving, Mom," I kidded her. "It's about giving."

At last I left for L.A. in a new leather jacket that I thought looked pretty cool. Michael's security people met me in a limo. I called Mom from the limo to let her know I had arrived okay. We picked up Michael at his apartment, and then headed south for the ranch. Michael said he thought I looked better than I had on my last visit in June. I hoped he was right. Maybe the jacket helped.

The drive took about three hours. The limo dropped me off at Bungalow Three for a rest. Michael said, "See you at seven." That was suppertime. I was worried. My stomach ached and I was having cramps. I called Mom.

"I shouldn't have come," I told her. "I don't want to be sick here with Michael."

"Well, you haven't eaten in a while," Mom pointed out. I usually needed at least a snack every couple of hours or so. She said, "Why don't you see how you feel after supper?"

I took a nap and went up to the main house for supper—chicken, beef ribs, and baked potatoes. Then Michael and I went to his private theater and watched two and a half hours of *Three Stooges* reruns. We ate popcorn from the theater's own machine, and had pizza delivered from the house. I felt a lot better and had a great time. Now I was glad I had come.

Michael had told me to call the house the next morning when I woke up. Mark, the ranch manager, and his wife did all the cooking. They gave me a list of choices for breakfast and told me, "Anything you want, we'll fix it." I picked French toast and bacon. My room was a little chilly, even though I'd brought my heater with me. So they brought me another portable heater and an electric blanket.

"I like your jacket," Michael told me, "but I want you to have a heavier one."

So the two of us drove to a nearby town in Michael's Bentley. I can't name the town, because Michael likes the ranch to stay a private place. We couldn't find the jacket Michael had in mind, but he did buy four or five dolls for other kids. The best part was, the man in the shop didn't believe that Michael and his credit card were for real! Michael gave him the ranch's security number, and he called to clear the card and to double-check that Michael was who he said he was.

I was very happy that dinner turned out to be tacos. Afterward I showed Michael a video that Mom, Andrea, and I had made for him of our whole house—every room, every poster and decoration we have on the walls, Andrea's skating trophies and my collections. In the video, we took him on a guided tour, waving and clowning at the camera.

"When you come to visit now," I told him, "you'll know your way around our house."

That night we watched the new Indiana Jones movie, *The Last Crusade.* How lucky can you get, I thought. The lines were too long to get in at home, but I was getting a private screening.

The next day Michael had business meetings, so Mark took me to pick up a bomber jacket, the heavier one Michael wanted me to have. When Michael was free, we went back to town to pick out some presents for Mom and Andrea. I got Mom a great big Santa, and magic stuff for Andrea. Michael had a video crew come in, and we made a tape together about our friendship—kind of the flip side of the video we had made for him.

At dinner on New Year's Eve, Michael gave me a wonderful watch. It chimes every hour and has a built-in alarm. It tells you the day of the week, the date, the month, and the year.

"*Thanks!*" I said.

"I have to leave early tomorrow—before you go," Michael said. "I'm sorry I won't be around. And I'm sorry I don't have the autographed photo you wanted. But I'll mail it to you."

When we hugged good-bye, Michael said, "Never give up. Do it for me."

New Year's Day: my last day at the ranch. I played with Max, one of Michael's pet monkeys. I was glad to see him again, and he was glad to see my shoelaces. I puckered up for a kiss, and Max gave me a big one.

I called Mom to tell her I was on my way home.

"There's a big box at the ranch entrance for me to take home," I told her. "It's driving me crazy. What do you think it is?"

It was a whole new stereo system and disc changer. A few days later I got a photo of Michael signed "To Ryan." He was wearing red, black, and white. Thanks, Michael!

AFTER NEW YEAR'S I had days when rinsing shampoo out of my hair in the shower left me weak and breathless. I'd have to lean against the tile for a few minutes before I had enough energy to dry myself off and get dressed. Between my swollen stomach and my hernia, I often walked half bent over.

My shingles had cleared up, but now I had open sores on my legs. Mom had to change the bandages every few hours. My throat was very sore and I could hardly breathe in the cold. Because of my hemophilia, I'd get blood clots in my nose, and then I sniffed so much people thought I was making faces at them. Michael had invited me back in the spring. Now that my legs looked so bad, I'd never be able to go out on the public beach in Florida over spring break.

I was having trouble with my liver, so Dr. Kleiman put me on a protein drink. Otherwise, he said, I'd have to have nutrition through an IV. I'd have to stay hooked up for hours every day. I was supposed to mix the protein drink with juice or Sprite. Even so, it tasted sickening. Dr. Kleiman wanted me to have it seven times a day, but I'd only managed to get up to four.

Between coughing and struggling to breathe, I was also having trouble sleeping. When I lay awake, I worried about school. I didn't know when I'd be going back. When I did, I'd be way behind. But I didn't have the strength to keep up with assignments at home. I watched TV and buried myself in my car magazines. Sometimes I read car-parts catalogs until three or four in the morning, when I could finally sleep a little.

I had big plans. I spent hours polishing the Mustang Michael had given me. I flew off the handle if the cat walked over it and left dusty prints on the roof. I had gotten tinted windows, but I wanted to customize the whole thing. I spent hours talking to Steve, John, Michael—anyone I knew who cared about cars.

Early one evening I was sitting downstairs watching a *Lucy* rerun I practically knew by heart. Mom came and sat beside me.

"Ryan!" she said. "You're sitting down here and getting old along with Lucy."

I didn't say anything. Lately I didn't want to talk about much except cars. They weren't Mom's favorite subject.

"Ryan," she said, "what's happening to you? All you ever talk about is *things*. You have a terrific car. You have a great stereo. You've been given so much, but you just go on and on about how much more you want."

I stayed quiet for a while. At first I wasn't quite sure what to say—or how much.

"Mom," I said finally, "you don't understand. I don't have much time. I don't want to miss out. There are still so many things I want."

Mom didn't say anything. She knew wanting things kept me going. But she knew there was more to it. She was right.

"I'm scared," I said.

For the last five years I'd been so strong. I'd have to go into the hospital, things would look bad, but then I'd be out again and I'd be fine. Now I'd been sick since September—the longest ever—with all these chronic problems I couldn't get rid of, like my hernia and my liver. Every week I seemed to have something new, like those sores on my legs. My body felt like it was rotting away.

"All I do is think about dying," I told Mom. "Reading another car book, pricing a new car—those are the only things that get my mind off it.

"I can't sleep because I'm scared I might not wake up," I said. "It's never been like this before. I don't want to go without saying goodbye."

"Remember your guardian angel," Mom answered. "You always have your night-light, and you always have your angel watching over you."

Mom knew I wanted to be buried in the Cicero cemetery. She knew I wanted the Reverend Ray Probasco to conduct my funeral. He had known us in Kokomo and he had visited me in the hospital when I was diagnosed. But Mom and I had never discussed the really important stuff: What I should wear.

"I'd like to see you in your prom tux," Mom said quietly. "You and Dee looked so great that night."

"No, Mom," I said firmly. "I want to look like me. I want to wear my Guess? jeans, a surf shirt, boxer shorts"—I wanted to be comfortable—"my Air Jordans, and my Oakleys. And the watch Michael gave me."

After that I felt better. I guess just saying I was that scared helped. Plus I always feel better if I make plans. I started looking ahead again. In February Dr. Kleiman said I could go back to school, and we had another trip coming—to California and Florida. Two weeks of warmth! First, Athletes and Entertainers for Kids wanted me to give an award to former President Reagan at a special party on the night of the Academy Awards in L.A. He'd made a public service announcement about AIDS, and he'd sent me a couple of nice letters from the White House, so I wanted to meet him. And the party would be good for the cause. Then we were going to Miami for spring break. A kind man who owned a broadcasting company sent us plane tickets and put us up at his hotel. I wasn't quite so bloated anymore. I'd look okay in a bathing suit.

My junior prom was coming up April 28. I planned to be there. One Friday night Steffonie came to visit Andrea and me and watch TV with us. She ended up sleeping over, and the next morning I lent her a shirt and a pair of overalls. She was just my size.

We sat on the couch in the living room and leafed through an album of photos of our trip to California last summer, including the one and only shot of Michael and me. Steffonie told me about a class project she was working on, designing a dream house. She showed me some floor plans she'd drawn. She had had to decide which rooms went where. She'd picked out colored swatches of rugs and curtain fabric and glued them to her sketches.

"Now here's the sauna," she pointed. "And here's the wet bar."

I wouldn't mind living here at all! "This'll be our house," I told her. "Here's our kitchen. Here's our living room. We'll put the couch here, so we can sit like we are now."

Steffonie laughed.

"How would you like to go to the prom with me?" I asked.

She smiled and looked at her sneakers.

"If I went with anyone, it would be you," she said. But she was only fifteen and her parents wouldn't like it. They thought she was too young to date.

I wondered whether that was the real reason why they wouldn't like it, but I didn't say anything.

That was a letdown. I let the prom drop for a while after that. Finally a couple of weeks before we were going to California, Mom said, "Why don't you ask Heather? If you don't, she'll probably ask you."

I thought it over. Heather had kept in touch, and I felt like enough time had passed. We could be good friends again. So I picked up the phone.

"What are you doing April 28?" I asked.

"Nothing," Heather said.

I had to pick up some new jeans for California, so Heather and I spent a day shopping. There was nothing in my size, and I got fed up—I wasn't feeling very well. "Let's get out of here," I told Heather. I'd see what I could find in L.A.

When I dropped her off, I said, "Don't forget. April 28."

"Don't worry," Heather said. She didn't tell me then that she'd turned down two other dates to go with me.

The week before we left, my throat got very sore and I started running high fevers at night. But they were usually gone in the morning. Dr. Kleiman said I had an infection in my throat, but I could still travel.

I ran a few more errands and took Wendy Baker for burgers at the Dairy Queen in Cicero. It's right near a four-way stop—the only one in town. Wendy and I always seem to drive up at the same time and spend about ten minutes waving at each other.

"After you!" I yell.

"No, after *you*!" she shouts back.

We have the same game going over lunch tabs. We always talk about school, who likes who, the usual stuff—and then fight over who pays. This time I won.

On the way back to her house, both of us suddenly got real quiet. I don't know why. We each stayed in our own thoughts until I pulled into her driveway. She hugged me good-bye.

"Just remember," I said. "You're buying next time."

THE FIRST THING I did in L.A. was go on *The Home Show* with Howie Long to tell everyone about the party Athletes and Entertainers was

having. In L.A., Oscar night starts very early—
like about two in the afternoon. You see people
eating in restaurants and driving around in evening dress, even though it's broad daylight.

But I felt bad, very bad. I had a fever. My
throat was the worst I could remember. I had
coughing spells that lasted hours. Thanks to my
hernia, I could hardly walk.

As we set out to meet President and Mrs.
Reagan, Mom said, "I know you don't feel
good. Are you okay? You're being so pleasant."

She knows how irritable I can be when I'm
sick. I said, "Mom, my chest feels really, really
tight. My body just doesn't feel right."

I had my picture taken with the Reagans. The
President said I was brave and gave me a yo-
yo with his signature and a picture of the White
House on it. I went back to our hotel and rested
for a while. Then Mom, Andrea, and I went to
the Oscar party. I had on a new tux shirt that
looked like it was splattered with thin streaks
of red, yellow, and blue paint. I almost didn't
recognize Andrea. She was wearing a black
derby and a short black strapless dress with a
full skirt and a big bow on it.

I had to get up on stage with Kareem and
Howie Long. My job was to thank all the volunteers. I hoped they could hear me. I hardly had
any voice left, even with the mike.

Then I turned to Howie. "Get me out of
here," I said.

Howie gathered Andrea, Mom, and me up

and cleared our way out to a limo. I spent the whole next day asleep.

Mom called some hospitals in L.A., but she had no luck. In a way, I was glad.

"I want to go home and see Dr. Kleiman," I said.

Mom looked at me. She was scared. I never *want* to see Dr. Kleiman.

"But first—Mom, could you call Elton again?" I had been trying to reach him and Michael. "I want to talk to him real bad."

"Why?" Mom asked. "Why do you need to talk to him?"

I didn't say anything.

We caught the first plane we could—an overnight flight that got into Indianapolis at dawn. There were hardly any passengers. The plane was dark and quiet. I could lie flat across the seats, and no one stared at me when I started coughing.

"I love this," I told Mom. "From now on, we fly at night all the time."

Dr. Kleiman admitted me to Riley right away.

"I was hoping I wouldn't see you again so soon, Ryan," he said.

"Me too," I said. Hospitals smell like no place else. It's not a bad smell—disinfectant, bandages, clean stuff. But right then, I felt like that smell had been following me around all my life.

"I'm so tired of fighting this thing," I added.

I realized I'd never said that before—to Dr. Kleiman or anyone. That night, my first in the hospital, I called Grandma in Florida. I hardly ever talked to her down there.

"I'm in the hospital, Grandma," I told her. "I don't feel so good."

She asked me about Mom and Andrea, about California. I didn't ask her to come see me—because I knew Uncle Tom, Aunt Deb, and my cousins were on their way to visit her for spring break—but she said she was flying up.

"Grandma," I said all of a sudden, "remember how we'd go to the beach and Andrea and I used to write our ABC's in the sand? Right by the waves? The tide would always come in and rub them out. We never did get them right."

"I remember," Grandma said. "But those were beautiful ABC's. You got them right."

That was just about my last phone call, because I was having so much trouble breathing I had to have an oxygen mask. I felt like Frankenstein—part kid, part machine. But even on oxygen, I could tell I wasn't getting better. Everything inside me seemed to be breaking down. AIDS was wearing down my liver, my spleen, my kidneys. And fast too. Mom left me for ten minutes to say hello to the Stewarts and the Bakers, who'd come to see us. When she got back, she saw nurses and doctors huddling next to my room. She started running. Dr. Kleiman was having me rushed to intensive care. Mom moved my guardian angel right along with me. Grandma flew up from Florida as soon as she hung up. I was happy that she was coming to see me.

Dr. Kleiman wanted to lay out my situation for Mom and me. "Ryan," he said, "you're fighting so hard to breathe that you're wearing yourself out. The best chance you have is to go on a ventilator. Then the medicine we're giving you can work."

I had to write notes again. To help you breathe, a ventilator tube has to go in through your nose and mouth and down into your chest. That hurts. "Knock me out to do it or forget it," I scrawled.

"You'll be out," Dr. Kleiman said. "You won't feel any pain."

I looked at Mom. She was smiling at me.

"No feet," I wrote Dr. Kleiman.

"No IVs in your feet," he agreed.

This was the big one. I knew I might not wake up, but I pushed that thought away. I wrote another note. "Go for it," it said.

Mom clasped my hands and started the prayer we said every day. "Lord, let everything come out okay. . . ." Then she kissed me and said, "Honey, everything's going to be all right."

I hoped so. I wanted *her* to be all right. She'd have to watch whatever happened to me. Suddenly I knew from now on, it was going to be much harder to be her than to be me.

I wrote a new note. Just one word: "MOM?" She smiled some more. She knew what I meant. "Everything's going to be all right, Ryan," she said again, softly.

As the drugs took hold, I drifted back to a question some kid asked me once.

"Would you give up all your fame to get rid of AIDS?" he wanted to know.

How dumb can you get! I snapped my fingers at him. "Like that," I said. "I'd give it up like that."

EPILOGUE:

Ryan's Final Illness and Funeral

FOR THE NEXT WEEK Ryan remained unconscious, in critical condition in the intensive care unit of Riley Hospital. Dr. Kleiman told Jeanne he was sure Ryan was not in pain. But Ryan's chances of pulling through, he said, were only ten percent.

"And that's optimistic," Dr. Kleiman added. "He's Ryan White. That's why I said ten percent."

During the next days Ryan was never alone. Jeanne and Andrea remained with him in the intensive care unit, listening to the pumping of his ventilator and the beep of his heart monitor. Laura Kreich Block, Ryan's favorite nurse, was working at another hospital, but she volunteered to come back to Riley and help look after Ryan. His grandparents had hurried to Indianapolis right after his phone call, along with his aunt Janet, his uncle Leo and their kids, Uncle Tommy and Aunt Deb and their kids, and his stepfather, Steve Ford. They all arrived too late to talk to Ryan, but they spent many days with him and tried to keep each other strong. His father, Wayne White, came to the hospital several times.

As news of Ryan's condition spread, thousands of letters, telegrams, and presents from all over the country and the world flooded into the hospital. Every day, the hospital switchboard was jammed with calls, and the lobby was overflowing with reporters covering the front-page story. Former President Reagan and President Bush both publicly praised Ryan. Elton John flew in and told Jeanne, "I'm here to help you." He brought in bodyguards who stood watch at the intensive care unit. The Reverend Ray Probasco, whom Jeanne had asked to pray with the family at the hospital, noted that the guards were "725 pounds between the two of them." Jeanne was relieved that now Ryan could feel absolutely safe in the hospital.

One of Elton's main duties was to keep track of all the phone messages and mail Ryan and his family got. Some schools sent homemade posters lettered with "Hang in there, Ryan!" and covered with kids' signatures. Jeanne, Andrea, and Elton hung them on the walls of Ryan's room, along with quilts and pictures from well-wishers. Ryan received so many flowers that his family and friends gave them away to other patients. Elton gave out his own presents to other kids in the intensive care unit, and even sent for a pair of sneakers Jeanne needed.

There was no phone in Ryan's room, but when Michael Jackson called, Elton and Jeanne asked the hospital for a special hookup. Michael would have two minutes to speak. "Ryan," Elton said, "you can't turn down a superstar like this. I'm grade B compared to Michael." He held the phone to Ryan's ear so Michael could encourage him.

John Cougar Mellencamp and The Reverend Jesse Jackson came to the hospital to pay their respects. Jill Stewart and Wendy Baker and their parents, along with Heather McNew, Steffonie Garland, Dee Louks, and John Huffman and his mother all spent long days keeping Ryan company. They talked to him as much as they could, reminding him of things they'd done together, of how they wanted to cruise with him again, of how much they loved him. They played his favorite music tapes. Every now and again Ryan's eyelids flickered. Even though Dr. Kleiman said that Ryan was unaware of his surroundings, some friends felt strongly that he was with them.

"I said things I'd never thought about saying to anyone," Jill remembered.

"We're sticking by you, Ryan," Dee said to him. "Keep trying."

"Get up—we gotta go to the prom," Heather told him. "And don't forget my birthday. You've been promising me forever." Ryan had been too sick in November to take Heather to Ben & Jerry's. He'd said they'd go when he got back from California.

Jeanne knew how much Ryan always liked to look good, so she had been carefully moussing his hair as he lay in bed. But some of his visitors commented that the boy in the bed "doesn't look like Ryan." His medication had discolored his skin and had made his face and body swell. So Jeanne took his yearbook picture, which she had had blown up and framed, and hung it over his bed. There was Ryan smiling and healthy, as she knew he wanted to be remembered.

One evening in the hospital, Jeanne, Elton, Ryan's grandparents, and Uncle Tommy watched a short TV special on Ryan. At the end of the program, Jeanne saw Ryan say he'd trade his fame for health "like that"—snapping his fingers.

Jeanne laughed. That was so like Ryan. She felt a lift, seeing him looking so well and so sure of himself. Then she looked around at the others and noticed that they were crying. I should be sad, she thought, but I feel proud. He looked so good there.

The following Saturday evening, when Ryan had been unconscious for a week, Elton left the hospital briefly to join John Mellencamp and Jesse Jackson at the fourth annual Farm Aid concert. On stage he announced, "This one's for Ryan," and began singing "Candle in the Wind." Andrea and Heather were watching in the wings. As the song ended and the crowd applauded, they waited for Elton, but he rushed past them without saying a word. They knew he had been calling the hospital every fifteen minutes, so Ryan must have gotten worse. They raced back to Riley.

By the time Andrea, Heather, and Elton got back from the concert, Dr. Kleiman was convinced that Ryan would not last much longer. His blood pressure had dropped to dangerously low levels, and was still falling.

At about one o'clock Sunday morning, Michael Jackson called again from Atlantic City. When Jeanne told him Ryan was not expected to live, Michael declared he was flying to Indianapolis right away.

At about two in the morning, a nurse opened Ryan's eyes and flicked the light switch in his room on and off several times. Jeanne saw that there was no change in Ryan's eyes. They had stopped dilating. "That's when I knew," she said. "He wasn't going to make it this time."

But Ryan's heart had not stopped. Jeanne was afraid that he might struggle to hold on to life for her sake. So she told him, "Just let go, Ryan. It's all right, sweetheart."

RYAN DIED at 7:11 A.M. on April 8, 1990. It was Palm Sunday. Jeanne gave him one last kiss and then turned off his guardian angel nightlight. Andrea hugged him for a long time; she did not want to leave him by himself. So Laura told her, "I'll stay with him until he's ready to go to the funeral home." In a room near Ryan's, Reverend Probasco gathered Jeanne, Andrea, Ryan's grandparents, his uncles, aunts, cousins, Elton, Heather, and some other friends in a circle. They clasped hands to pray and say good-bye to Ryan.

As soon as Michael Jackson arrived, he went straight to the Whites' home in Cicero. He was very upset that he hadn't gotten there before Ryan died. He went up to Ryan's room, which was full of his collections, posters, and souvenirs, including his director's chair from the movie set. In it sat a giant toy gorilla that Ryan had spotted in New Orleans and that the National Education Association sent him. On the walls were Alyssa Milano's friendship bracelet, *Max Headroom* posters, and the hearts needlepointed by Kris, Ryan's old girlfriend in Kokomo. Hanging from the ceiling was a real parachute, a present from Aunt Janet, and a thousand paper cranes—Japanese symbols of long life that an Indiana school had folded for Ryan from colored papers. In the closet was the heavy new leather jacket Michael had wanted him to wear.

Michael, a fellow G. I. Joe collector, sat quietly looking at everything for a long time. He told Jeanne he felt close to Ryan in his room. Jeanne offered him anything he liked there as a keepsake, but he asked her to leave Ryan's room just as it was.

In the Whites' front yard sat the red Mustang

Michael had given Ryan. Now it was covered with flowers and Easter eggs, gifts from children. Andrea took Michael out to show him the car and they sat in it together. When Michael turned on the CD player, Ryan's favorite song, Michael's "Man in the Mirror," began to play. Michael smiled proudly. He knew it must have been the last song Ryan had played.

Jeanne told Michael she had recorded a phone conversation he'd had with Ryan. She was afraid Michael might be offended, but he said he wished she'd recorded all their talks.

For that night, and the next few, Heather, Steffonie, John Huffman, and another friend stayed over with Andrea so she would not be alone when she woke up. The friends camped out in Jeanne's spare bedroom and on the floor. John stayed on for about a week, washing dishes, walking the dogs, and running errands for Jeanne. He told her about the times the police had stopped Ryan for speeding. They had never given him a ticket, only warnings. "*Now* you tell me!" Jeanne said. "Now that I can't ground him!"

Elton picked out music and helped Jeanne plan the funeral. Together they went to choose a casket. Ryan had wanted a very plain dark wood casket. But there were so many different kinds that Elton and Jeanne found themselves looking at each other and feeling overwhelmed. Eventually they settled on a walnut one with a cream interior. As Ryan had asked, he was dressed in his jeans and jean jacket, a surf shirt, sneakers, his favorite reflecting sunglasses, and the watch Michael had given him.

The morning of the funeral, April 11, was cold, windy, and drizzly. Outside the largest church in Indianapolis, long lines of people in their best clothes waited to view Ryan's body. Since Ryan never took his fame seriously, Jeanne thought he'd be astonished. She said, "I bet he was looking down and laughing. He must have been saying, 'I can't believe all you silly people are getting wet to see *me*.'"

Fifteen hundred squeezed inside the church for the funeral service. Elton played the piano, led the congregation in a hymn, and sang "Skyline Pigeon," his song about a bird soaring toward freedom. The First Lady Barbara Bush, Michael Jackson, Howie Long, and Phil Donahue—who with his wife Marlo Thomas became close friends with the Whites after Ryan answered kids' questions about AIDS on his talk show—sat up front with Andrea, Jeanne, her parents, her brother and sister, Steve Ford, Ryan's cousins, and Wayne White. Sitting behind them were some of Ryan's many friends, including Judith Light, Lukas Haas, and Linda Otto, who had worked with him on *The Ryan White Story*, Dr. Kleiman, Laura Kreich Block, Dr. Woodrow Myers, who had supported Ryan when he was Indiana state health commissioner, and Charles Vaughan, Ryan's lawyer who had represented him in his fight with Western School Corporation.

But most of the crowd of mourners were

ordinary people and children. There were soldiers in dress uniform, elderly men and women, and many, many teenaged friends and students from Hamilton Heights High School. Jeanne was happy that so many black people had come to say good-bye to Ryan. In dealing with his illness, she said, her family had learned a lot about prejudice. "I think I understand what many blacks have gone through," Jeanne said.

Ryan's casket stood in front of the church beside Elton's piano. On the piano was his yearbook picture that had sat by his bed in the hospital. Around the casket were many flowers, including a giant heart from Elton made entirely of red roses. One of Ryan's friends counted up to 250 of them. Across the heart ran a red ribbon that read, "Dear Ryan, you will always be with me. You have touched many people. Thank you. I love you, Elton." There were souvenirs of Ryan's TV movie and his public appearances, and the Hamilton Heights High School banner.

Before the funeral service began, some of Andrea's roller skating friends walked up to her in the front pew. Each presented her with a long-stemmed white rose. In addition to the church choir, who had taken time off work to come, Jeanne had asked the Hamilton Heights choir to sing. The dozen girls had been rehearsing only three songs. One of them was "That's What Friends Are For," which had been written to raise money for AIDS research.

So they joined hands around Ryan and sang. As they sang, the congregation saw the sun break briefly through the clouds overhead and shine through the church windows.

Reverend Probasco gave the eulogy. He told how Ryan and his family had hoped for a miracle—that Ryan would be cured. That hadn't happened. But the minister went on, "I believe God gave us that miracle in Ryan. He healed a wounded spirit and made it whole.

"Many of you who are here are very successful," he continued. "Your lives are filled with glamour and fame. Yet you brought Ryan and his cause into your lives and aided him in his mission and showed us how to do the same.

"Now I challenge all of us to accept his faith. For you see, Ryan was successful too, in getting all of us involved. He helped us to care and to believe that with God's help, nothing is impossible—even for a kid."

Borrowing a phrase from Ryan, the minister urged everyone to go on working for a cure and to "make AIDS a disease—not a dirty word."

Ryan's funeral was the largest Indiana had ever seen. Six pallbearers carried his casket from the church to the hearse: Elton, Phil Donahue, Howie Long, Ryan's uncle Tommy Hale, his aunt Janet's husband Leo Joseph, and his best friend John Huffman. The funeral procession had to travel an hour from Indianapolis to the Cicero cemetery, where

Ryan was going to be buried. Two hundred and fifty cars followed his hearse.

Aunt Janet was struck by the number of people, some with their children, who stood alongside the road to watch the procession. Some stood with their hands over their hearts. A few held up handmade signs, saying "God bless Ryan" or "Ryan's hope is alive." Janet said, "Most of us don't know our purpose in life. Ryan knew his."

Along the highway north toward Cicero, truckers pulled over and kept their lights on as the funeral procession passed. Indiana's governor had ordered flags at the statehouse flown half-staff in Ryan's honor. Along the funeral route, towns and office buildings did the same. People stood at their office windows as the funeral procession went by. When it turned off the highway onto the country road toward Cicero, farmers and their families watched in front of their homes and fields of pigs and cows. Seeing them, Howie Long said, "Every time Ryan heard the bell, he got up and went back into the ring. The only other person I've known like that is Muhammed Ali."

At the graveside, Judith Light remembered Ryan working as a second AD on the movie set. Just advising the actors hadn't been enough for him, she said. "He needed to be doing something *he* came up with. That tells the story of Ryan's life. He was not able to choose whether he got AIDS, or other hardships which fell in his path. But he *could* choose to turn whatever happened to him into a contribution to others." The day of Ryan's funeral, a new study found that having purpose in life helps people live longer.

Some of Ryan's friends took red roses from Elton's heart home with them. Jeanne used them to spell out "RYAN" on the ground, marking the grave.

During the next week Greg Louganis and Matt Frewer came to see Jeanne and to visit Ryan's grave. Matt promised her that Ryan would have a headstone. It was set in place on Memorial Day. The black granite marker was six feet high. "Ryan would be happy," Jeanne said. "He always wanted to be tall."

Today the dirt road through the cemetery has been widened by the many cars and people who have come to see Ryan. Children frequently leave letters, poems, toys, and friendship bracelets. One boy left a He-Man toy in a plastic bag, with a note saying, "You're my hero so I'm leaving you my He-Man." Someone left the earring Ryan had wanted, and another child left a cassette of "Man in the Mirror."

Since Ryan's death, Jeanne and Andrea have gotten over 50,000 letters, cards, and poems, many from children. Dr. Kleiman also gets mail from children. They write, "What was Ryan really like?" or "You must be sad not to have Ryan any more."

One card came to the Whites from Julie's mother, whom Jeanne had met at Riley in 1984 when Ryan was diagnosed with AIDS. The two women had wept together every day in the waiting room between visits to their children in intensive care. Jeanne finally learned that Julie had died of a brain tumor in 1985. "It's still very hard," her mother wrote. "I still have the doll your mother made for Julie."

On April 28, John Huffman took Andrea to the Hamilton Heights High School prom. Heather, who had been looking forward to going with Ryan, dropped by to help Andrea put on her dress, a white strapless with a full skirt, and to see her off to the dance.

Heather did get to go to another school's prom: A neighbor invited her to his. But she borrowed a friend's dress for it; she didn't want to wear the glittery green and black tulle gown she had bought for the Hamilton Heights dance. "That dress is kind of far out, but I thought Ryan would like it," she said wistfully. She visits his grave frequently and stays in close touch with Jeanne and Andrea.

In July Andrea won second place in the regionals. As one of the top three to place, she went in August to the National Roller Skating Championships in Florida. There she cut her foot, missed three days of practice, and had to compete with seven stitches. Even though she simply could not perform some moves, she still managed to place eighth. Now eighteen, she has just graduated from Hamilton Heights High School. John Huffman has moved to California, but he and Andrea talk and correspond. Jill Stewart is at Indiana University, where she is studying biology and is still active in student government. Dee Louks is a secretary in Indianapolis and lives in Noblesville. Steffonie Garland has just finished Hamilton Heights High School and Wendy Baker, who also has graduated, lives in Cicero. Like other townspeople, she says she still looks for the familiar sight of Ryan's red Mustang at the main intersection.

During the filming of *The Ryan White Story* in Statesville, North Carolina, both Linda Otto, the producer, and John Herzfeld, the director, were worried about their own health. They say that Ryan's attitude toward his helped them keep their own problems in perspective. Lukas Haas's little brother, Nikolai, who was only five when Ryan died, still likes to mousse his hair in Ryan's style.

Jeanne has accepted many awards on Ryan's behalf, including honors from the National Association for the Advancment of Colored People (NAACP) and the American Civil Liberties Union (ACLU). She has spoken at the United Nations at ceremonies honoring the world's children. Participants honored Ryan with a minute of silence. She has worked with Senators Kennedy and Hatch lobbying Congress for a bill they co-sponsored, known as "The Ryan White Care Bill," to provide comprehensive care for AIDS patients and their families. While lobbying, she described trying to get medical help for Ryan from overcrowded clinics during his last trip to Los Angeles. "

Ryan couldn't get help—and he was one of the best-known AIDS patients in the United States—can you imagine what it's like for the others?" The bill was eventually passed.

Jeanne says, "The worst thing Ryan did when he died was leave me all his animals to take care of." Jeanne is thinking about adopting a child—the brother or sister Ryan and Andrea always wanted. But she adds, "If people refer to me for the rest of my life as 'Ryan White's mother,' I'll be proud."

Meanwhile, Jeanne would like to go on working in AIDS education. She spends hours on the phone with other children who have AIDS and their parents—as she and Ryan both did when he was alive. Last September she spoke to the mother of an eleven-year-old boy in Brooklyn, New York. He was infected with AIDS from a blood transfusion in 1984. When he told his junior high school that he had AIDS, parents of about a dozen classmates threatened to keep their children out of school.

This boy's predicament is the kind of injustice that Ryan always wanted to fight—or, as he put it, "die trying."

AFTERWORD

RYAN'S BEEN gone more than two years now, and I still can't quite believe it. Andrea and I certainly feel he's always with us; it's just that his physical presence is missing. One reason I feel that way is because I haven't collapsed. Ryan has given me strength. You wouldn't believe what a weakling I used to be—I'd cry so easily. But little things *will* get to me. I don't watch television much anymore because that was something Ryan and I liked to do together in the evening. When I have to travel and speak in public, I hate staying in hotel rooms by myself, because I'm so used to having him there with me.

I still get letters about Ryan every day. I often hear from other sick kids—he was such an inspiration to them. He helped them to set high goals for themselves, to think, "I could live longer, too."

Ryan always said he thought his life was pretty normal. That tickled me. *How* could anyone say the things he went through were normal? Take the first time we got Factor VIII to control his hemophilia. One time I stuck him twenty-one times straight, just trying to find a vein.

Whenever I talk about Ryan, I remember things I want to add to this book. When the Gulf War came, all I could think was how interested Ryan would have been. He turned eighteen just four months before he died; the very first thing he did was register for the draft. He always wanted to do everything he could, and he was sure one of the armed services would have found a job for him.

Some of my memories make me laugh out loud. Like the way Ryan always insisted on taking his T-shirts out of the dryer while they were still damp, spread them flat on a towel, and patted the collars down as carefully as he could, so the ribbing wouldn't stretch and bag. He wanted them to fit snugly so his neck wouldn't look so skinny—he was always so particular about the way he looked. I remember one time we had to go see Dr. Kleiman because Ryan had a red rash all along the outside of his legs. We couldn't figure out if it was flea bites or allergies or what. It turned out that Ryan had been turning up the cuffs of his jeans so tight they were irritating him!

I've left Ryan's room just as he kept it. Right after he died, people started driving by the house, just to see it. So in his bedroom window I put four big red wooden letters spelling out R-Y-A-N, to show visitors which room was his. We have a sign on the front lawn, too: "The White House . . . Home of Ryan White . . . Established 1987"—the year we moved to Cicero from Kokomo. Ryan's guardian angel nightlight sits on the mantelpiece in our living room now, and I always light it on holidays.

You may have heard that since we buried Ryan in the Cicero cemetery, his grave has been vandalized three times. The first couple of times, the vandals tore up the flowers I had planted and stole some things we had left on the grave. One was a statue of a dog who looked like Barney. That was bad enough. But the third time, in June 1991, they knocked over the big headstone Matt Frewer gave us and broke it. Someone saw two boys do it, and the police arrested them. What really upset me was that these boys weren't from Kokomo; they had gone to Hamilton Heights High School with Ryan. They actually knew him!

After that, our friend Phil Donahue suggested moving Ryan, perhaps to the grounds of Riley Hospital in Indianapolis. But that's about an hour away, and I really love having Ryan close enough so I can always pay him a quick visit. It was difficult and expensive to repair the headstone, but it's back up now.

Other people come visit Ryan's grave all the time. The cemetery has to keep putting extra gravel on its driveway—there are so many visitors that they wear muddy holes into it! They still leave flowers, notes, and little presents behind for Ryan. Last Christmas, someone left a little Christmas tree, all decorated, and a seventeen-year-old girl left a laminated copy of a long poem she had written about Ryan.

Even when you think nothing worse can happen in life, it can happen. My brother Tommy had had cancer once, not long before Ryan died. In the last year, Tommy has been real sick again. My parents are still very upset over losing Ryan, their first grandchild, and the thought of losing Tommy as well is almost too much for them. But he has had some experimental treatment—very high doses of chemotherapy—and right now, he's okay. He's sure the cancer is not going to come back, so my family is trying to think that way, too. We've always believed that you keep going. You can't wallow in self-pity.

My parents always go to Florida in the winter, and my mother has been doing volunteer work at a hospital down there. She also wanted to do something for people with AIDS, so she visited a hospice she had heard was doing a lot for them. She met one young man there who had come for a support group meeting. He had looked after a close friend who had had AIDS, and his friend had just died. This man told my mom, "I always looked up to Ryan. I really admired his strength and courage. Your grandson gave hope to everyone." My mom was so proud!

As for the rest of us, my sister Janet, Ryan's aunt, is busy helping a home for babies with AIDS in Birmingham, Alabama. This home takes babies whose mothers can't care for them. Dr. Kleiman is now in charge of caring for patients at Riley Hospital's new Ryan White Center for Infectious Disease, set up with contributions made in memory of Ryan.

And I'm really just so proud of Andrea. After she placed eighth at the National Roller Skating Championships the summer after Ryan died, she decided to give up skating. I think she was just ready for a change. She really concentrated on her schoolwork, and this fall, she'll start Indiana University as a pre-med student. Elton John has set up an education fund to help Andrea with her college tuition. When she goes to medical school, all those hours she spent hanging around in hospitals with Ryan and me will turn out to be good for something, after all. I'm sure Andrea will be a great doctor and help lots of people.

Andrea and I still have Ryan's dog, Wally, and our cat, Chi Chi. Herbie, Ryan's hamster, the one Andrea brought to him in Riley Hospital, died exactly a year after Ryan—on April 8, 1991. We buried him in the Cicero cemetery, right next to Ryan.

Our friends here and in California stay in touch. Lukas Haas and Greg Louganis helped us by recording the audiocassette version of this book. Whenever I go to Los Angeles, I talk to Matt Frewer, or I have lunch with Judith

Light or Alyssa Milano between tapings of *Who's the Boss*? In March 1991, I visited Michael Jackson at the recording studio where he was working on his new album, *Dangerous*. One of the songs on that album is called "Gone Too Soon," and Michael said Ryan was his inspiration. You can see Ryan in the video for that song. It's a very moving tribute to my son.

There have been so many wonderful tributes—I'm just thankful that so many different people have not forgotten Ryan and his fight. Ryan has been given the Norman Vincent Peale Award for Postitive Thinking, and the first annual Elmo Zumwalt III Award of Courage. On December 6, 1990, to honor what would have been Ryan's nineteenth birthday, the Indianapolis Colts, our professional football team, put together a song and a music video about Ryan, called "Colors." They used a lot of my old photos of him in the music video. They gave cassettes of the song to everyone who came to "Ryan White Night", when the Colts played the Washington Redskins.

I'm especially glad that I've been able to carry on the work that Ryan started, educating people about AIDS. Congress did pass the Ryan White Care Bill, and now Indiana has gotten a lot more money to look after people with AIDS. I've gone to several events for Athletes and Entertainers for Kids, the American Foundation for AIDS Research (AmFAR), and the AIDS quilt. I couldn't believe how many panels people have made for Ryan—there are about twenty now. In October, when the whole quilt is displayed in front of the White House in Washington, I'm going to present my own panel.

Besides being active with other AIDS education groups, I've started my own, the Ryan White Foundation. Phil Donahue and Dr. Kleiman are members of the board, and I'm executive director. Among other activities, we want to provide support all over the country for adults and children with AIDS, and for their relatives and friends as well. It's my ultimate hope to form a national network so that parents dealing with the AIDS crisis can talk to each other. I remember how all alone I felt back in Kokomo, and I don't want any parent who has a child with AIDS to feel that way ever again.

I'm glad to be so busy—it's the perfect way to remember Ryan. But sometimes, even now, I slip and say, "Ryan is . . . Ryan says . . ." instead of "Ryan was . . . Ryan said. . . ." When I realize what I've done, I feel upset. I loved my son more than anything, but the Lord wanted him more. I know that he's better off now, and that helps me to get through things.

I never really believed that Ryan would die of AIDS. Our whole family thought that God would send us a miracle. I believe now that He did send us a miracle in Ryan. Sometimes a miracle isn't long life; it's what a person is able to do with life.

—*Jeanne White*

If you'd like to know more about the Ryan White Foundation or to make a donation, you can write or call:

> The Ryan White Foundation
> P.O. Box 3218
> Carmel IN 46032
> 1-800-444-RYAN

RYAN WHITE

by *Michael Jackson*

Ryan White, symbol of justice.
Or child of innocence,
Messenger of love.
Where are you now,
Where have you gone?

Ryan White, I miss your sunny days.
We carelessly frolicked in extended play.

I miss you Ryan White.
I miss your smile,
Innocent and bright
I miss your glory,
I miss your light.

Ryan White, symbol of contradiction.
Child of irony, or
Child of fiction?

I think of your shattered life
Of your struggle,
Of your strife.

While ladies dance in the moonlit night.
Champagne parties on chartered cruises.
I see your wasted form
Your ghostly sight.
I feel your festering wounds,
Your battered bruises.

Ryan White, symbol of agony and pain.
Of ignorant fear gone insane.
In a hysterical society,
With free floating anxiety
And feigned piety.

I miss you Ryan White,
You showed us how to stand and fight.
In the rain,
You were a cloud burst of joy.
The sparkle of hope
In every girl and every boy.

In the depths of your anguished sorrow
Was the dream of another tomorrow.

A TRIBUTE TO RYAN WHITE

by Elton John

I have met a lot of people in my life who were brave and courageous. But when I met Ryan, he gave new meaning to these words. Having the AIDS virus is a scary horrible thing to cope with. But Ryan coped silently and with great pain. He had the dignity to bring the message of hope to all those who have this terrible disease. Although young, he had wisdom beyond his years. It is as if God had chosen him to ease the prejudice that people have towards AIDS victims. I firmly believe that during his short life on earth, Ryan touched millions of people, and I believe that in his new life he is doing the same. Ryan White was a miracle of humanity.

Ryan's Testimony Before The President's Commission on AIDS

Thank You, Commissioners:

My name is Ryan White. I am sixteen years old. I have hemophilia, and I have AIDS.

When I was three days old, the doctors told my parents I was a severe hemophiliac, meaning my blood does not clot. Lucky for me, there was a product just approved by the Food and Drug Administration. It was called Factor VIII, which contains the clotting agent found in blood.

While I was growing up, I had many bleeds or hemorrhages in my joints which made it very painful. Twice a week I would receive injections or IVs of Factor VIII which clotted the blood and then broke it down. A bleed occurs from a broken blood vessel or vein. The blood then had nowhere to go so it would swell up in a joint. You could compare it to trying to pour a quart of milk into a pint-sized container of milk.

The first five to six years of my life were spent in and out of the hospital. All in all I led a pretty normal life.

Most recently my battle has been against AIDS and the discrimination surrounding it. On December 17, 1984, I had surgery to remove two inches of my left lung due to pneumonia. After two hours of surgery the doctors told my mother I had AIDS. I contracted AIDS through my Factor VIII which is made from blood. When I came out of surgery, I was on a respirator and had a tube in my left lung. I spent Christmas and the next thirty days in the hospital. A lot of my time was spent searching, thinking, and planning my life.

I came face to face with death at thirteen years old. I was diagnosed with AIDS: a killer. Doctors told me I'm not contagious. Given six months to live and being the fighter that I am, I set high goals for myself. It was my decision to live a normal life, go to school, be with my friends, and enjoying day to day activities. It was not going to be easy.

The school I was going to said they had no guidelines for a person with AIDS. The

school board, my teachers, and my principal
voted to keep me out of the classroom
even after the guidelines were set by the
I.S.B.H., for fear of someone getting AIDS
from me by casual contact. Rumors of
sneezing, kissing, tears, sweat, and saliva
spreading AIDS, caused people to panic.

We began a series of court battles for nine
months, while I was attending classes by
telephone. Eventually, I won the right to
attend school, but the prejudice was still
there. Listening to medical facts was not
enough. People wanted one hundred
percent guarantees. There are no one
hundred percent guarantees in life, but
concessions were made by Mom and me to
help ease the fear. We decided to meet
everyone halfway.

(1) Separate restrooms
(2) No gym
(3) Separate drinking fountain
(4) Disposable eating utensils and trays

Even though we knew that AIDS was not
spread through casual contact.
Nevertheless, parents of twenty students
started their own school. They were still
not convinced.

Because of the lack of education on AIDS,
discrimination, fear, panic, and lies
surrounded me.

(1) I became the target of Ryan White jokes
(2) Lies about me biting people
(3) Spitting on vegetables and cookies
(4) Urinating on bathroom walls
(5) Some restaurants threw away my dishes
(6) My school locker was vandalized inside and folders were marked FAG and other obscenities

I was labeled a troublemaker, my mom an unfit mother, and I was not welcome anywhere. People would get up and leave, so they would not have to sit anywhere near me. Even at church, people would not shake my hand.

This brought on the news media, TV crews, interviews, and numerous public appearances. I became known as the AIDS boy. I received thousands of letters of support from all around the world, all because I wanted to go to school. Mayor Koch, of New York, was the first public figure to give me support. Entertainers, athletes, and stars started giving me support. I met some of the greatest, like Elton John, Greg Louganis, Max Headroom, Alyssa Milano (my teen idol), Lyndon King (Los Angeles Raiders), and Charlie Sheen. All of these plus many more became my friends, but I had very few friends at school. How could these people in the public eye not be afraid of me, but my whole town was?

It was difficult, at times, to handle; but I tried to ignore the injustice, because I knew the people were wrong. My family and I held no hatred for those people because we realized they were victims of their own ignorance. We had great faith that, with patience, understanding, and education, that my family and I could be helpful in changing their minds and attitudes around.

Financial hardships were rough on us, even though Mom had a good job at G.M. The more I was sick, the more work she had to miss. Bills became impossible to pay. My sister, Andrea, was a championship roller skater who had to sacrifice too. There was no money for her lessons and travel. AIDS can destroy a family if you let it, but luckily for my sister and me, Mom taught us to keep going. Don't give up, be proud of who you are, and never feel sorry for yourself.

After two and a half years of declining health, two attacks of pneumocystis, shingles, a rare form of whooping cough, and liver problems, I faced fighting chills, fevers, coughing, tiredness, and vomiting. I was very ill and being tutored at home. The desire to move into a bigger house, to avoid living AIDS daily, and a dream to be accepted by a community and school, became possible and a reality with a movie about my life, *The Ryan White Story*.

My life is better now. At the end of the school year (1986–87), my family and I decided to move to Cicero, Indiana. We did a lot of hoping and praying that the community would welcome us, and they did. For the first time in three years, we feel we have a home, a supportive school, and lots of friends. The communities of Cicero, Atlanta, Arcadia, and Noblesville, Indiana, are now what we call "home." I'm feeling great.

I'm a normal happy teenager again. I have a learner's permit. I attend sports functions and dances. My studies are important to me. I made the honor role just recently, with two A's and two B's. I'm just one of the kids, and all because the students at Hamilton Heights High School listened to the facts, educated their parents and themselves, and believed in me.

I believe in myself as I look forward to graduating from Hamilton Heights High School in 1991.

Hamilton Heights High School is proof that AIDS education in schools works.

"Does AIDS Hurt?"
Answers to Questions People Ask

RYAN FREQUENTLY appeared on television and in public to answer questions from people of all ages about AIDS. He made a special point of talking to children and teenagers because they responded so well to him. He also was particularly concerned about teenagers because they are at such high risk—they are more likely to experiment with sex and drugs. More than twenty percent of people who have AIDS are diagnosed in their twenties. That means that they may have been infected during their teens. And AIDS is spreading faster and faster among teenagers.

Today it's extremely unlikely that you could get AIDS the way Ryan did. Blood transfusions and blood products like Factor VIII are treated so that they no longer harbor the virus. AIDS is a disease that is hard to catch. You usually have to behave in certain ways to get it, so there are ways to make sure you don't.

Ryan believed that both AIDS and prejudice against people with the illness are spread by ignorance. He was convinced that education would cut down the number of AIDS cases— and quell the prejudice that he and other patients have suffered.

Ever since 1981, when AIDS was discovered, it has been an epidemic. Across the United States, about sixty-five people die of it every day, and over 130 more learn they are infected. People infected with the AIDS virus live in every state, and in most other countries around the world. To continue Ryan's campaign, here are answers to questions people asked him most frequently about the illness.

What is AIDS?

AIDS stands for Acquired Immune Deficiency Syndrome. "Acquired" means it's a disease that you can be infected with; it's not an illness you are born with, like hemophilia.

"Immune deficiency" means a breakdown in your body's defense system against disease. AIDS is caused by a virus, a tiny germ that has to live inside a living cell. The AIDS virus is also called HIV, which stands for human immunodeficiency virus. When the virus enters your body, it invades a cell that's part of your immune system, and turns the injected cell into a virus factory, churning out copies of its invader. Those many copies of the original virus attack other cells that are key parts of your immune system. You then can get rare diseases that would not affect you if you were in normal health.

"Syndrome" means a group of signs or symptoms that occur in a particular illness. If you have either of two unusual diseases, that's almost always a sure sign that you have AIDS. Those diseases are *Kaposi's sarcoma*, an uncommon cancer, and *pneumocystis carinii pneumonia* (also known as pneumocystis pneumonia or PCP), the rare kind of severe pneumonia Ryan had when he was first diagnosed in 1984.

When you're in normal health, your immune system can withstand many kinds of viruses, including those that cause flu. But when you have AIDS, your body can't fight off infections. Over time you become less and less able to fight off diseases. Eventually the illnesses you're susceptible to lead to your death.

How does it feel to have AIDS? Does AIDS hurt?

Many people with AIDS are like Ryan: They feel fine for long periods of time. People with AIDS can take medicines to help strengthen their immune systems and ward off dangerous illnesses that don't threaten healthy people. But AIDS can be very uncomfortable, and some of the drugs you may be given have unpleasant side effects.

Many of the symptoms of AIDS feel rather like having the flu. Like Ryan, you may have night sweats, fevers, a cough, and shortness of breath. You may have swollen lymph glands that last a long time—six weeks or so—in your neck, under your arms, or in your groin. You may lose your appetite and have diarrhea constantly. You may feel very tired and run-down. Some people with AIDS say they often feel as though they've aged prematurely. You may have persisting skin rashes, or white patches or sores in your mouth that last a long time. If you have Kaposi's sarcoma, you may find patches or bumps the color of bruises on any part of your body.

But many other diseases besides AIDS have these symptoms too. To be absolutely sure you have AIDS, you must take a test. A sample of your blood is checked to see if it contains antibodies to the HIV virus, which causes AIDS. If it does, then at some point in the past, the virus has entered your body and you have been infected. This is known as being HIV positive.

If you are HIV positive, you are capable of infecting someone else, whether or not you are actually sick. In fact, you may look and feel perfectly fine. You should be very careful to avoid other infectious illnesses, like hepatitis or sexually transmitted diseases besides AIDS. Extra infections could trigger the AIDS virus, or make full-blown AIDS worse.

Today there are many people who are HIV positive but who have never had symptoms of AIDS. Actually, in this country there are more people who are HIV positive than there are patients who are sick with AIDS. Because scientists have been studying this disease such a short time, they don't know whether everyone who is now HIV positive will eventually come down with AIDS.

Will everyone who has AIDS die?

As far as we know right now, AIDS is fatal. Most AIDS patients die within two years of their diagnosis. But infected people react differently to the virus. Some people test positive for HIV but go for years without symptoms. Some people who are infected get very sick right away and die within a short time. Others go back and forth between sickness and health. Still others can live longer and stay quite healthy, the way Ryan did.

Ryan may have stayed well for so long partly because he was young and strong when he was infected. A new drug, AZT, helped him too. Today doctors know more about how to use drugs to treat people with AIDS, so that many do live longer. Some adults who have AIDS are still living after ten years or more, and a few children who were born with AIDS have lived up to age twelve or thirteen.

Can you tell if someone has AIDS by how he or she looks?

No, not at all. Some people who have AIDS look like anyone with a deadly disease. They're pale and thin. They move slowly and seem very tired. If they have Kaposi's sarcoma, they may have purplish marks on their faces or bodies. But many people who have AIDS are like Ryan: They don't seem sick at all. They look like everyone else. You can't tell if someone has AIDS just by looking at him or her.

How come no one knew that the Factor VIII Ryan got had the AIDS virus in it?

No one knows exactly when Ryan got the transfusion that infected him. Whenever it happened, it's certain that no one knew much about AIDS then. Doctors found what they think was the first case in the United States in 1978. When Ryan got contaminated Factor, no one realized that the AIDS virus could be passed from one person to another by accident in transfusions of blood or blood products.

If I need a blood transfusion, could I catch AIDS?

Today that's very very unlikely. When people give blood now, it's tested carefully several times to make sure that it's not contaminated with the AIDS virus. Nowadays, hemophiliacs don't have to worry about their Factor. Nonhemophiliacs who know they are having an operation and are going to need a transfusion can even donate their own blood so that it's there when needed.

What if I give blood?

That has never been dangerous. When you give blood, the blood bank uses a brand-new needle for each donor. There is no possible way you could pick up the AIDS virus by giving blood.

What if I get a vaccination?

In the United States there's no evidence that getting a shot to immunize you against small-pox, polio, measles, mumps, whooping cough, or any other disease will transmit the AIDS virus. Doctors use a new needle and a new syringe for each patient, for each separate innoculation.

How could I catch AIDS?

Now that the blood supply is safe, there are just a few ways. The AIDS virus lives in human blood, semen, or vaginal secretions. Outside the human body, it can survive in small amounts of blood in hypodermic needles or syringes.

You can catch AIDS by doing certain things that let an infected person's blood or other bodily fluids into your own bloodstream. This could happen if you have sex with an infected partner without using a condom (latex, prefera-bly with spermicide containing nonoxynol-9) or if you use a hypodermic needle without steriliz-ing the needle first. You risk using a contami-nated needle if you shoot drugs, or if you get tattooed, have steroid injections for body building, have acupuncture treatments, or have your ears pierced *by anyone who isn't a professional*.

Having unprotected sexual intercourse with a stranger whose sexual history you don't know or with several partners is also very dangerous. Even if only one partner is infected, he or she could pass the virus onto you and then you could infect other people. Remember that you can't tell if someone is healthy by the way he or she looks. It's also risky to combine drinking or drug use with sex. Even if you meant to play safe, you may lose your head and forget.

By having sex without using a condom, an infected man can transmit the AIDS virus to other men or to women. Through unsafe sex, a woman can also infect men and perhaps other women. If a woman is infected with AIDS and becomes pregnant, there's about a thirty percent chance that she could pass the virus along to her newborn baby. Today thousands of babies are born with HIV infection and will later develop AIDS. They could be infected before, during, or soon after birth. A mother who has AIDS and breast feeds could pass the HIV virus to her baby in her milk.

So even if people who are HIV positive or who have AIDS are feeling quite well, they have to make sure they don't infect other people. They cannot give blood, share needles, or have unprotected sex. Women with AIDS should not become pregnant or try to nurse.

What's safe sex?

Of course, not having sex is absolutely safe. So is sex with one faithful, long-term partner who is not HIV positive. Hugging, stroking, dry kissing, massage, and masturbation are all safer sex. If you're having sex with more than one person, if your partner is infected, or if you don't know what the state of his or her health is, you *must* use condoms during sex—anal, oral, or vaginal.

You can buy condoms in most drugstores. You don't need a doctor's prescription, and you don't have to be any particular age. Large drugstores and discount chains display them in sections marked "Family Planning" or "Prophylactics," so you don't have to ask for them. In New York City, where there are over 40,000 people with AIDS—twenty percent of all cases reported in the nation—condoms are distributed in public high school clinics.

Condoms are inexpensive. Use latex condoms—not ones made of animal skin, which the AIDS virus can penetrate. Condoms have no side effects. If you use condoms properly, they will prevent pregnancy and will protect you.

For more on safe sex and using condoms properly, see the RESOURCES section, especially the video *AIDS: Changing the Rules.*

Don't condoms break or leak?

Sometimes, but not if you use them properly. Practice on an unpeeled banana. Most condoms come sealed in flat foil packages. Unwrap the flat disc and place it over the tip of the banana, with the raised rim facing up. If this ring faces down, you'll be putting the condom on backward. Push down on the ring, and the condom will slide snugly down around the banana. Some condoms have a space at the tip to hold semen. If a condom doesn't have this reservoir, make your own by pinching its tip as you roll it on.

Condoms will break or leak if they are too old or if they have been exposed to heat. All condom packages have an expiration date. Keep them at room temperature, not in a wallet or glove compartment. Never buy or use an unsealed condom, and don't reuse them. Never use a condom along with petroleum jelly or any other lubricant with oil in it; the condom may break. Always use K-Y jelly, a water-based lubricant.

Can you catch AIDS from having sex only once?

If your partner has the virus and you don't use protection, yes—just as you can get pregnant from having sex just once. Alison Gertz, who's twenty-five now, said she was infected at sixteen after having sex only once with a bisexual man who later died of AIDS. Now she speaks to other teenagers about avoiding AIDS.

How can I tell if I'm at risk of getting AIDS?

You're not at risk unless you're behaving in a risky way. That means taking drugs intravenously, or having unprotected sex.

Can kissing spread AIDS?

As far as we know, the AIDS virus has never been transmitted during any kind of kissing. But tiny amounts of the virus are found in an infected person's saliva, so unless you are sure your partner is free of the virus, kiss him or her on the cheek.

Can I touch someone who has AIDS?

Certainly. People with AIDS need affection as much as everyone else—if not more. If you touch or hug or kiss someone with AIDS on the cheek or shake hands with him or her, you are not in danger.

What if you are splashed with the blood of a person with AIDS and have a small cut?

The AIDS virus could enter your bloodstream, but that's not very likely. For the infection to be passed from one person to another, there usually has to be *direct blood contact:* The person's blood has to enter your bloodstream. That's because the AIDS virus cannot survive very well outside of the human body. It can't live in water, and you can wash it off with soap.

Sometimes hospital workers or family members looking after people with AIDS do get stuck with a needle that's been used on an AIDS patient. If they actually have been infected, they will test positive for HIV within three months, but most will not be infected; the chances are about one in two hundred.

Is it safe to be "blood brothers" or "blood sisters"?

Not with a child who has AIDS. In this playground ritual, children prick each other's fingers and press them together to mix their blood. If one child has AIDS, it would be possible to infect the other because there is direct blood contact. But right now, we know of no cases of children being infected this way.

Can you catch AIDS at the dentist's?

It's technically possible, if the dentist had a cut on his or her hand, and wasn't wearing gloves, and some blood fell onto your bleeding gums. However, this would be extremely unlikely. As far as we know, there have been only five cases of patients thought to have been infected by a dentist. At the moment, these cases are something of a mystery: Investigators have not been able to figure out exactly how the dentist's infection was passed to the patients.

Nowadays, dentists are supposed to wear masks and latex gloves during dental procedures to protect their patients—as well as themselves. A patient with AIDS could infect a dentist. Many people with AIDS have trouble finding dentists who are willing to treat them. Luckily, this was not a problem for Ryan. He was able to get dental care at Riley Hospital.

How can't I catch AIDS?

You can't catch it from normal, everyday contact with someone who has it. The AIDS virus is not airborne, so it is not dangerous to live in the same house or be in the same classroom or day care center or office with someone who has the disease. In the United States no family members living with someone who has AIDS, no children in school with someone who has AIDS, and no coworkers working with someone who has AIDS have been infected through casual contact.

You cannot pick up AIDS from a doorknob, a telephone receiver, or a toilet seat. If someone with AIDS sits next to you or coughs or sneezes on you, you are not at risk. If you bump into someone with AIDS in a locker room or gym, you will not be infected. You cannot catch AIDS from someone's perspiration, urine, saliva, or tears. Small amounts of the virus have been found in tears and saliva, but there are no known cases of the virus being transmitted this way. It's probably a bad idea to share razors or toothbrushes, which might have tiny specks of blood on them. Wear rubber gloves to clean up feces or vomit, which may contain small amounts of blood.

AIDS is not spread in food or drink, so it is safe to share a meal and utensils with a friend who has AIDS. You can eat off the same plate, or even drink from the same glass or pass a can of soda back and forth. Using the same water fountain, comb, hairbrush, toothpaste, money, books, computer, or any school or office equipment is quite safe. So is swimming in a public pool, sitting in a hot tub or steam room, or sharing a shower. You can share a towel or sheets or a sleeping bag. You can play games or sports with someone who has AIDS just as you can with any other friends.

You can't catch AIDS from pets or farm animals, and they cannot catch AIDS from people. Rats, mice, or mosquitos don't spread AIDS. Neither do fleas, lice, bed bugs, or any other insects.

Where did AIDS come from? How did it start?

No one knows. Scientists have had several theories, but there isn't enough evidence to say for certain. They do think that AIDS probably has been around for a long time, and wasn't noticed until it became an epidemic among certain groups of people who were at high risk. For example, by analyzing tissue samples that had been stored, doctors in England recently discovered that a twenty-five-year-old sailor who died in 1959 actually had AIDS. At the time of his death, no one could figure out what was really wrong with him. So far, this is the oldest documented case of AIDS, but others may turn up.

Today about one million people in the United States are probably HIV positive. By the end of 1993 up to 480,000 will have AIDS, and about

320,000 will have died. Around the world as many as 10 million people may be infected.

Do people with AIDS take medicine every day?

Usually. Most take several different medicines for various reasons. As for medicine for AIDS itself, you don't have much choice. There are only a few drugs for AIDS, and none can cure it.

Right now many doctors think that the earlier you start taking medicine, the better your chances of living longer are. So if you think you may be infected, it's important to take the AIDS test right away, find out for sure, and start treatment promptly.

AZT, which Ryan took for the last two years of his life, is one of the very few drugs for AIDS patients. AZT is not new; it was developed as a cancer drug but did not work well. However, it *does* effectively slow reproduction of the AIDS virus in the body, so AZT helps patients live longer. If you test positive for the virus and have no symptoms, yet tests show that your immune system is being weakened, your doctor may have you take AZT as preventive medicine.

Unfortunately, AZT has some unwanted side effects: It can damage bone marrow, leading to anemia, and also irritate muscles. AZT's side effects are sometimes bad enough that half the people who need this drug cannot take it because it makes them so ill. ddI is a new drug that could be used instead of AZT. It works the same way AZT does, and also blocks viruses that resist that drug. At first, doctors thought ddI's side effects weren't as bad as AZT's. But then they found that it too can cause serious problems.

Pentamidine is another drug Ryan took to treat and later to prevent pneumocystis pneumonia, or PCP. Pentamidine destroys the germ that causes PCP. Doctors found that pentamidine, given in aerosol spray that patients breathe in, prevents recurrences of PCP in AIDS patients. Like AZT, it has helped many of them live longer.

Many people believe that there is already a cure for AIDS. *Unhappily, none of these current treatments cures AIDS.*

When will there be a cure?

Not in the near future. In the meantime we have to rely on education to prevent more AIDS cases.

Doctors have made some progress treating the diseases that often kill people with AIDS. But that's not enough: They have to treat a patient's weakened immune system. Otherwise, sooner or later the patient comes down with another illness.

Researchers are having trouble coming up with a drug that kills the virus itself. One problem is that the AIDS virus is constantly changing and adapting itself to new conditions, including drugs.

Scientists also are working on developing an AIDS vaccine, like the vaccines against smallpox or polio. A vaccine is a weakened or killed form of a virus that causes a particular disease. When healthy people receive a vaccine, their immune systems develop antibodies that protect them from the weakened virus. Later, if they are exposed to the real thing, their new antibodies will protect them, and they won't come down with that disease.

One problem with developing a vaccine against AIDS is that new vaccines usually are tested on animals first. This is to make sure they are safe, and do not accidentally infect people. But in animals, the AIDS virus does not cause illness. So scientists have no way of knowing whether a vaccine tested on animals will protect people. It's possible that they may never come up with a vaccine. Even if we do have one eventually, it won't cure anyone who is already infected with AIDS.

If the AIDS virus is in blood, couldn't you cure patients by changing all the blood in their bodies?

No. It's possible to change *most* of the blood in a person's body, but not absolutely *all* of it. The HIV virus also hides in many other areas such as the brain. Unless you changed all of a patient's blood, you could not completely rid his or her body of the AIDS virus.

If you pass the virus to someone else, does that mean you won't have it any more?

No. You'd still have it, and someone else would too. You can't get rid of the AIDS virus by giving it to other people. Once you have it in your bloodstream, you'll always have it.

What if I think I have AIDS?

Don't panic. Many other illnesses have the same symptoms. But do take a test right away. That way, you can start treatment early and avoid infecting anyone else if you do have it. Call your local city, county, or state health department to find out where to take the test, which is confidential and usually free.

What if I have other questions about AIDS?

The National AIDS Hotline (1-800-342-AIDS) is a toll-free number where you can get any question answered. You don't have to give your name or address.

RESOURCES

RYAN WHITE ON VIDEOCASSETTE

Ryan answered questions from children and teenagers on several television programs. Three of them are available on videotape:

"I Have AIDS"—A Teenager's Story, a 3-2-1 CONTACT Extra produced by Children's Television Workshop. This award-winning half-hour program for eight- to twelve-year-olds combines Ryan's story and feelings about his illness with basic information about the workings of the AIDS virus. Available for $12.00, including a free teacher's guide, from:

The National AIDS Information Clearinghouse
P. O. Box 6003, Department G
Rockville, MD 20850
1-800-458-5231

Ryan White on Prime Time Live, April 5, 1990. This is the ABC news program Jeanne saw in the hospital during Ryan's final illness. Ryan answers teenagers' questions about AIDS and his experiences in Kokomo. To request a copy, write:

> Pamela Schaub, Video Sales
> ABC Distribution Company
> 825 Seventh Avenue
> New York, NY 10019

Ryan White's Appearance on The Phil Donahue Show. Ryan answers questions from youngsters in Donahue's audience. School systems may obtain copies at no cost by writing on their letterhead to:

> Multimedia Entertainment
> 75 Rockefeller Plaza
> New York, NY 10019
> Attention: Dick Thrall

The Ryan White Story, the television movie about Ryan, in which he appears as Chad, will be available in home video. For rental or purchase information, contact:

> The Landsburg Company
> 11811 West Olympic Boulevard
> Los Angeles, CA 90064
> 213-478-7878

A study guide to *The Ryan White Story* is available from:

KIDSNET
6856 Eastern Avenue, N. W.
Suite 208
Washington, DC 20012
202-291-1400

NATIONAL ORGANIZATIONS

The National AIDS Hotline (1-800-342-AIDS) can answer any questions you have in English or Spanish. You can also request brochures and information for children, parents, and teachers.

The National AIDS Information Clearinghouse supplies posters, brochures, the Surgeon General's report on AIDS that was mailed to households all over the United States, and all kinds of other useful information in both English and Spanish. Contact:

The National AIDS Information Clearinghouse
P. O. Box 6003, Dept. G
Rockville, MD 20850
1-800-458-5231

American Foundation for AIDS Research (AmFAR): This private, national, non-profit group provides funding for research into the cure, prevention, and treatment of AIDS. It also produces educational materials for the public, medical and scientific workers, and people with

AIDS. AmFAR has offices in New York and Los Angeles:

AmFAR
1515 Broadway,
Suite 3601
New York, NY
10036
212-719-0033

AmFAR
5900 Wilshire
Boulevard
Second Floor—
East Satellite
Los Angeles, CA
90036

Gay Men's Health Crisis (GMHC) describes itself as "the oldest and largest AIDS organization in the United States providing direct services, education and advocacy for men, women and children with AIDS." The group answers questions over their hotline, and volunteers act as "buddies" to look after people with AIDS.

Gay Men's Health Crisis
129 West 20 Street
New York, NY 10011
212-807-6664
Hotline: 212-807-6655

OTHER MATERIALS

The National Education Association's Health Information Network, which prepared the study guide for *The Ryan White Story*, has prepared a range of other materials to help teachers and parents answer kids' questions about AIDS. Contact:

NEA Health Information Network
1590 Adamson Parkway, Suite 260
Morrow, GA 30260
404-960-1325

Ryan White "For Teens Only" AIDS Poster. This poster is one of the last photographs taken of Ryan before he died. Single posters are $3.50. If you'd like to place a bulk order or add your own hotline number or logo to the poster, contact Carrie Jackson Van Dyke, 317-633-0600. Make your check or money order out to the Indiana State Board of Health and mail it to:

Indiana State Board of Health
Cashier's Office
1330 West Michigan Street
Indianapolis, IN 46206-1964

Other Videos on AIDS for Teenagers

AIDS: Changing the Rules. Host Ron Reagan, son of former President Reagan, model Beverly Johnson, and salsa star Ruben Blades teach viewers how to protect themselves. The language is sexually explicit. In one sequence, Ruben Blades uses a banana to demonstrate the proper technique for using a condom. The Hispanic version of the film features actor Esai Morales and actress Maria Conchita Alonso. Both versions produced by AIDSFILMS and available from:

PBS Video
1320 Braddock Place
Alexandria, VA 22314-1698
1-800-424-7963

AIDS: Everything You and Your Family Need to Know But Were Afraid to Ask. Former U. S. Surgeon General C. Everett Koop, M.D., answers questions about AIDS from people of all ages. For a free three-day preview and sales information, contact:

Ambrose Video Publishing Company
1290 Avenue of the Americas
New York, NY 10104
1-800-526-4663

AIDSFILM has produced three short films for young African American and Latino audiences. *Are You With Me?* is for African American women; *Vida* is for Latina women; and *Seriously Fresh* features a group of young African American men. All three films explore ways of insisting on safe sex and condom use. Distributed by:

Select Media, Inc.
74 Varick Street, Suite 305
New York, NY 10013
212-431-8923

A Book for Younger Children

AIDS: You Can't Catch It Holding Hands, by Niki de Saint Phalle. (San Francisco: The Lapis Press, 1987). An introduction for children and parents to AIDS.

ACKNOWLEDGMENTS

THIS BOOK could not have been written without the help of many generous people. Ann Marie Cunningham and I would like to thank especially my mother, Jeanne White; my sister, Andrea White; my grandparents, Gloria and Tom Hale; my uncle and aunt, Tom and Deb Hale; their children Monica, Josh, Matt, and Brian; my aunt and uncle, Janet and Leo Joseph; and their daughters Misty, Sara, and Lisa. We are also deeply grateful to my friends Steve Ford; Mary and Steve Baker; Gary Collins; Phil Donahue and Marlo Thomas; Senator Orrin G. Hatch; Michael Jackson; Elton John; Senator Edward M. Kennedy; David Kirby; Ted Koppel; John Cougar Mellencamp; Woodrow A. Myers Jr., M.D.; Paul Newman; Tony O'Dell; David Quinn; Charlie Sheen; Bruce Springsteen; Betsy and Jim Stewart; and Elizabeth Taylor. We thank the following people for their invaluable support: Shelley Henson, Connie Hillman, Michael Iskowitz, Elise Kim, Karin Lippert, Sharon Nixon, Barbara J. Peterson, Paul Smith, Norma Staikos, and William D. Maddux, Esq.

We owe special thanks to the photographers and agencies who contributed their work to this book: Athletes and Entertainers for Kids, Associated Press/World Wide Photos, American Foundation for AIDS Research (AmFAR), Jeff Atteberry, Bud Berry, Boys Town, Mary Ann Carter, Contact Press Images, Frank Espich, Diana Frysinger, Chris Gulker, Gloria Hale, Indiana State Board of Health, *Indianapolis Star*, Dilip Mehta, National Roller Skating Championships, *People Weekly*, Chuck Robinson, Seth Rossman, *SIPA Press*, and Taro Yamasaki. Unless otherwise indicated, the wonderful photographs in this book of my family, friends, and public appearances were taken by Jeanne White.

Around the country, many of my friends helped us. In Cicero, Indiana: Wendy Baker, Steffonie Garland, John Huffman, Sandy Huffman, Dee Louks, Heather McNew, Sue McNew, Rev. Ray E. Probasco, Jr., and Jill Stewart. At Hamilton Heights High School in Arcadia, Indiana: Tony Cook, Barbara Cook, Steve Dillon, J. Stanton Renner, Mary Schwartz, and Fred Woodruff. In Los Angeles: Kareem Abdul-Jabbar, Matt Frewer, Howie Long, Greg Louganis, and Alyssa Milano. Among my colleagues from the making of *The Ryan White Story:* Kurek Ashley, Stephanie Cicero, Lukas Haas, Emily Haas,

John Herzfeld, Judith Light, Linda Otto, Annette Sutera, and Doug Whitley. Other helpful friends of the White family include Jane Brittain, Diana Frysinger, John Riser of Maui Surf and Sport, and James H. Williams of the Health Information Network of the National Education Association.

The following people contributed their expertise on my illnesses, treatments, and hospital stays: Martin B. Kleiman, M. D.; Laura Kreich Block, R.N.; Barbara Godshall, R. D. M. S.; and Linda Dye and the public relations staff of James Whitcomb Riley Hospital in Indianapolis. Peggy Anderson; Darene Cahill, R.N.; and Mary Spencer also gave us the benefit of their knowledge of chronically ill children.

For an understanding of the workings of the AIDS virus, we are most grateful to Edward G. Atkins, Ph.D.; Jeffrey A. Cohen, M.D.; Martin B. Kleiman, M.D.; the Center for Study of Gene Structure and Function at Hunter College of the City University of New York; the Centers for Disease Control; and Sara Nelson. Alvaro J. Simmons, M. S. W.; Richard Wortman, M.D.; and Frances Yancovitz, M. S. W. of the Adolescent Health Center of Mount Sinai Medical Center; and Margaret Hilgartner, M. D., shared their knowledge and observations of teenage hemophiliacs with AIDS.

Several journalists who have covered my family and AIDS also helped us: Jude Dratt, Lisa Hsia, Carrie Jackson Van Dyke, Christopher MacNeil, and Brian Reynolds. For technical assistance at the ballpark, we thank Christopher P. Cunningham, Dan Humphrey, Mary and Robert Ihle, and David M. Rubin.

Our deep appreciation to Children's Television Workshop, where our work on the science series *3-2-1 CONTACT* introduced us, and where producer Susan Schwartz Lynn suggested our collaboration. Mary Baker, Sarah Butterfield, Christopher T. Cory, Judy Katz, Elizabeth Leckie, Kate Manning, Elizabeth Mehren, Kate Rousmaniere, and Anna Cory Watson read early drafts and provided incisive criticism and best of all, encouragement. A special thanks to Nissan Motor Corporation and Marriott of Torrance, California.

—*Ryan White*

My thanks to William Smart, Craig and Sheila Pleasants and the staff of the Virginia Center for the Creative Arts, and John Martini of Key West's Lucky Street Gallery, who provided space, quiet, and freedom to write. Kate Rousmaniere, Betty Engel, Garrett Brown, Sue Grand, Ruth and Sandy Levy, Michael Meltsner, Joel Schneider, and Harriet Wald got me started and kept me going.

For special assistance, I heartily thank Marjorie Benton; Arnold J. Civins, C. P. A.; Ria Eagan, D. C.; Adrianne Benton Furniss; Gene Messinger; Ralph Novak; Kip Niven; Carol E. Rinzler, Esq.; Faith Sale; and Paula Wiseman.

Finally, I cannot thank my publisher, Dial

Books, and my agent, Anne Borchardt, enough for their endless patience and unfailing support. At Dial, Phyllis Fogelman, editor in chief, gave this book commitment that is unparalleled in my experience of publishing. Toby Sherry, my editor, who believed in the project from the beginning, followed suit with enthusiasm and energy. At key moments, I've been especially grateful for her cheerful phone calls and her laugh. I admired and benefited from production editor Michele Foley's keen eye and gentle manner. I greatly appreciate art director Atha Tehon's efforts that have resulted in such an attractive book. I am very happy to have the backing of a committed sales manager like Maureen Gordon, and an enthusiastic director of marketing like Mimi Kayden. This book would not exist without the energy and dedication of production director Shari Lichtner. Suzanne Patterson provided able and conscientious assistance.

At New American Library, my heartfelt thanks to the following people whose hard work produced this paperback edition: my editor, Alexia Dorszynski, associate editor Kristin Olson, copy editor Maggie Sutherland, and designer Eve Kirch.

And most of all I want to thank Ryan White, whose courage inspired this book.

—*Ann Marie Cunningham*